THE CONCEPT OF THE KNOWLEGE OF GOD

The Concept of the Knowledge of God

Brian Haymes
Principal
Northern Baptist College, Manchester

St. Martins Press   *New York*

First published in the United States of America 1988

Printed in Hong Kong

Library of Congress Cataloging-in-Publication Data
Haymes, Brian
The concept of the knowledge of God.
Bibliography: p.
Includes index.
1. God—Knowableness. 2. God—Knowableness—Biblical
teaching. 3. Experience (Religion) I. Title.
BT102.H369 1987   231'.042   87–3500
ISBN 0–312–01185–7

To Jenny with Debby and Vicky

Contents

Preface

This book has its origin in a thesis submitted to the University of Exeter and in a pastoral concern to explore the nature of religious knowledge.

I want to thank my supervisors, Professor J. R. Porter and Dr W. D. Hudson, for their encouragement, criticism and friendship.

Much of the work relating to this book was undertaken while I was the Minister of South Street Baptist Church, Exeter. The kindness of the officers and members knew no limit towards the family of the manse. By their questions and support they made such a study possible. In particular I record my gratitude to Revd. J. M. Tosh and Revd. N. Jenkins both of whom came out of 'retirement' to assist the church during my study leave.

A small part of Chapter 12 appeared as 'A Note on God acting in History' in *The Baptist Quarterly*, vol.XXX, No 8' October 1984. I am grateful to the Editor for permission to use the material here.

Finally, my deepest gratitude is to my wife who typed this work in all its many forms. To her, with our daughters, this book is dedicated.

BRIAN HAYMES

Acknowledgements

The Author and Publisher wish to thank Basil Blackwell, for permission to use copyright material from *Philosophical Investigations, On Certainty* and *Lectures and Conversations on Aesthetics, Psychology and Religious Belief* by Ludwig Wittgenstein; and to the Oxford and Cambridge University Presses, for permission to quote from The New English Bible.

List of Abbreviations

Anchor	The Anchor Bible, Doubleday
Black	Black's new Testament Commentaries, A. and C. Black
CBC	The Cambridge Bible Commentary (NEB) (Cambridge University Press.)
Hermeneia	Fortress Press
ICC	The International Critical Commentary (T. and T. Clark)
Investigations	*Philosophical Investigations* by L. Wittgenstein
Lectures	*Lectures and Conversations on Aesthetics, Psychology and Religious Belief,* by L. Wittgenstein
Moffatt	The Moffatt New Testament Commentary, (Hodder & Stoughton)
NCB	The Century Bible (New Series), (Nelson)
NEB	New English Bible
NT	New Testament
OC	*On Certainty* by L. Wittgenstein
OT	Old Testament
OTL	Old Testament Library, SCM Press
PAS	*Proceedings of the Aristotelian Society*
Pelican	Pelican New Testament Commentaries (Penguin)
Torch	Torch Bible Commentaries (SCM Press)
Tractatus	*Tractatus Logico-Philosophicus* by L. Wittgenstein

1

Purpose and Method

My purpose in this book is to examine, with special reference to the Bible, the concept of the knowledge of God. This task will involve me in both philosophical analysis and biblical exegesis. Philosophically, I shall have to examine whether or not the expression 'the knowledge of God', as used in the Bible, makes sense. This will involve me in a consideration of what anything has to be in order to be knowledge, and what God has to be in order to known. Exegetically, my task will be to examine a selection of claims to know God which occur in the Bible in order to discover precisely what they purport to claim.

My approach will be analytical but I hope that it will contribute something positive to our understanding of the doctrine of God in Christian theology. However, I want to differentiate my work clearly from that of other authors who, to quote one, have attempted 'to investigate the nature of the knowledge which Christians have of God'.[1] In contrast, I shall not contend that Christians *do* know anything of God. I shall simply consider the nature and meaning of their claims to do so.

I realize that my work may attract two sorts of criticism. On the one hand, some may well object that I have limited my investigation too narrowly in confining my attention to Biblical claims to know God. On the other hand, I may be criticized by theologians for using methods inappropriate to their subject matter. I think one can reply quite shortly to the former criticism. In a study of this kind it is far more worthwhile to devote one's attention to a limited field and to examine it in depth than to take any other alternative course. I have chosen to concentrate on the Bible because it is the religious classic with which I, like most of those within my society, am most aware. I would not wish to conceal the fact that I am myself a Christian believer but, as I have indicated above, this book does not purport to make any special claims for Christianity. In the light of my analysis of what it is to know anything and of what would have to be the case for God to be known, it would be possible to subject other forms of religious belief to critical examination of their knowledge claims. As for the latter criticism, I think that I should attempt at some length to describe my method carefully and justify its use.

1   *I shall take it for granted that the way to discover a word's meaning is to ask how it is ordinarily used.* In asking what 'knowledge' means, I shall seek an answer by analysing the everyday use of the word 'know' and its cognates. This is a method I have learned from Ludwig Wittgenstein.

Wittgenstein was concerned all his philosophical life with the problem of the meaning of language. He believed at one time that he had answered all the main questions in his first work *Tractatus Logico-Philosophicus*.[2] The theory of language he propounded is sometimes called the 'picture' theory. His basic assertion was that the meaning of language is that to which it refers, i.e. its referent.[3] It is said that Wittgenstein came to this picture theory on reading an account of a court case in Paris concerning a motor accident. In the court room a model was assembled with figures to indicate the position of the characters and vehicles involved. Wittgenstein saw that for the making of any such model three things were necessary:

(a)   There had to be objects such as dolls, cars, etc. which symbolized the persons or vehicles concerned.
(b)   There had to be a certain configuration or arrangement of these objects which represented their position appropriate in the modelled situation.
(c)   There also had to be a convention, understood and accepted by all who would use the model.

Wittgenstein claimed that language modelled, or mirrored, or pictured reality as the model in the law court represented the accident. The model *refers* to the world in a similar way. Wittgenstein thus believed that a proposition represents a logical picture of the situation.

Two things in particular are taken by Wittgenstein to follow from this theory of the meaning of language:

1   He held that all meaningful language is analysable into 'elementary propositions'.[4] An elementary proposition is a 'concatenation of names'.[5] By 'names' he meant signs which do not describe but denote or designate. Such names are the elements of language, each name referring to one element in reality. Wittgenstein believed

that 'a proposition has one and only one complete analysis'.[6] The signs are one to one with the elements of reality and to know the meaning of a proposition is to know this correspondence. Language consists of elementary propositions, in the last analysis, which in turn consist of simple signs or names.

2   Wittgenstein also held that the world divides into objects. Language, on this theory, consists of signs. The world must therefore consist of objects we can refer to by naming them. Wittgenstein spoke of 'objects' which 'make up the substance of the world'.[7] Reality consists of elements to which determinate reference can be made. Wittgenstein argued that, although he refused to give examples of 'names' or 'objects', they none the less existed for if they did not then language would have no precise meaning. It is not just that if in reality there is no object X then the name X is meaningless. It is that for any proposition to have sense and meaning there must be correspondence between the elements of language in the proposition and the configuration of objects in reality.

There is of course much more to the theory than what I have briefly indicated above. The *Tractatus* is a monumental work of logic. But Wittgenstein himself came to be dissatisfied with it.[8] He came to believe that he had *imposed* a theory of meaning on language rather than simply looked at language to see how it gets its meaning. If we take this latter course we see that observation of the use of language soon reveals that 'naming' is only one use to which language is put. In fact language has many uses. Thus Wittgenstein came to argue in his *Philosophical Investigations* that the meaning of language is the use to which it is put.[9] 'Look at the sentence as an instrument and at its sense as its employment.'[10] The employment of language is multifarious.

'But how many kinds of sentence are there? Say assertion, question, and command? – there are countless kinds: countless different kinds of use of what we call "symbols", "words", "sentences". And this multiplicity is not something fixed, given once for all; but new types of language, new language games, as we may say, come into existence, and others become obsolete and get forgotten. (We can get a *rough picture* of this from the changes in mathematics).

Here the term "language-game" is meant to bring into prominence the fact that the *speaking* of language is part of an activity, or of a form of life.

Review the multiplicity of language-games in the following examples, and in others:

Giving orders and obeying them –
Describing the appearance of an object, or giving its measurements –
Constructing an object from a description (a drawing) –
Reporting an event –
Speculating about an event –
Forming and testing a hypothesis –
Presenting the results of an experiment in tables and diagrams –
Making up a story; and reading it –
Play-acting –
Singing catches –
Guessing riddles –
Making a joke; telling it –
Solving a problem in practical arithmetic –
Translating from one language into another –
Asking, thanking, cursing, greeting, praying.
– It is interesting to compare the multiplicity of the tools in language and of the ways they are used, the multiplicity of kinds of word and sentence, with what logicians have said about the structure of language. (Including the author of the *Tractatus Logico-Philosophicus*)'[11].

This theory of the meaning of language is different from that propounded in the *Tractatus*. In the *Investigations* Wittgenstein is arguing that to get to the meaning of any form of language we must ask 'what is this language being used for?' The meaning of a word will depend on how it is being used and this in turn will relate to its context or 'language-game'.

Wittgenstein was not the only philosopher who pursued the study of language in this direction. J. L. Austin is, among others, another important figure in this development in philosophy.[12] But is Wittgenstein right? With regard to the argument that the meaning of language is the use to which it is put, I believe he is. Language is not static. It is a matter of fact that words do change their meaning in use both historically and in present contexts. Thus historically the word 'prevent' does not mean in contemporary use what it normally meant in the seventeenth century. This is not to say that its seventeenth century use is improper now. It would be quite proper so long as we were aware that when the Psalmist prays 'let thy tender mercies speedily prevent us' (Psalm 78:8 in the Authorized Version 1611) he is not asking God to stop him doing anything. 'Prevent' may mean 'hinder' or 'stop' in today's use. But in its older usage it normally meant 'go before'. The word has changed its use over the years and with it, its meaning.

An example of change of meaning in straightforward contemporary use appears if we contrast what the word 'ball' means to a cricketer and a debutante. The 'ball' to a cricketer is the hard round object with which he plays the game of cricket. Debutantes go to 'balls' which have nothing to do with cricket. 'Hit the ball' is a meaningful phrase in cricket but the 'balls' to which debutantes go are impossible to hit. One use describes a solid object, the other a social function. The meaning of 'ball' will therefore relate to its use.

I shall have more to say about words and definitions in Chapter 2 but as a principle of philosophical method I believe Wittgenstein is right to charge us to consider a word's use. For this reason I shall later examine the uses of the word 'know' in order to discover what it means.

3 *I shall take it for granted that in speaking of 'language-games' we are describing not separate languages but language used in various forms of discourse.* Wittgenstein's concept of language-games is useful and clearly relates to the various forms of discourse in every day life. However, it is erroneous to suppose that the concept of a language-game means that we can use language in any way we wish and apply our own meaning to it.

A language-game is *both continuous and discontinuous* with other language-games. Let us use the language of religion as an illustration. Religious language is discontinuous with, say, the language of physical science. The physicist and religious believer *qua* physicist and religious believer participate in different language-games (with correspondingly different forms of life). A failure to appreciate this might lead to someone trying to measure the speed of prayer or the density of grace. But both disciplines use the same words, the same language. There is continuity. In this sense no language-game is autonomous. Because all participate in language it is therefore always appropriate, say, for the non-believer to ask the religious believer what he means by the word 'world' when he speaks of God loving the world. How like or unlike is this use, and consequently the meaning, with that employed by the physicist when he talks about the world? Saying how like and unlike any particular word's use is in any particular language game is what W. D. Hudson calls 'mapping logical frontiers'.[13]

This is a necessary task for the theologian or religious believer if he is prepared to say what he means when he uses ordinary words in religious discourse. What seems to me to be highly inappropriate is for the theologian to attempt some special pleading such as is attempted by Ian Ramsey when he calls religious language 'logically odd'.[14] In speaking of the 'goodness' of God Ramsey begins with a 'scale' of goodness with unattractive characters at the bottom rising steadily to good and very good men.[15] There then comes a gap before coming to God who is *infinitely* good. This is 'something outside "good" language altogether'.[16] But here is the problem. Ramsey wants to say that God is good but that his goodness is beyond our meaning of good when we use it in everyday language. But how then is this use of the word intelligible to us?[17] This same special pleading for religious discourse comes from Professor John Macquarrie when he says, 'We have no understanding of what the word "good" could literally mean when applied to God, for it must transcend any notions of goodness that we may have. Yet we are entitled to use it because it is more appropriate to say that God is good than that he is not good, for he is the prior enabling condition of all goodness whatsoever.'[18] It may be more appropriate to say that God is good, but what sense is there in that assertion if, although we know what goodness normally means, we do not know what it means when applied to God? This is but to say that 'the goodness of God' is unintelligible to us.

Therefore, although I am convinced by the appropriateness of Wittgenstein's concept of language-games, and that religious belief may be regarded as one such 'game', it seems a proper method philosophically to analyse the ordinary use of language about knowledge for although religious language may have a certain distinctiveness, as have all language-games, knowledge claims both in and out of religious discourse must relate to intelligible uses of the word 'know'. 'Knowing God', 'knowing London', 'knowing what to do' and 'knowing scientific theory' may all have different logical features. But none of these claims can appeal to a special way of knowing in such wise that the use of the word 'know' is unintelligible when considered alongside other acceptable uses.

4 *Now, having described my method I go on to ask whether it is justified (a) philosophically and (b) theologically.*

(a) There are sound philosophical reasons for carefully scrutinizing the Bibical material in elucidating the concept of 'knowing God' in Christian belief. If it is objected that the philosopher's appeal should be to ordinary language, my reply is that biblical language *is* ordinary language for the Christian believer. For the Christian the most important context for all talk about God, and knowing God, is the Bible. This is not to be committed to any particular understanding of biblical authority. Christian believers have different understandings of the nature of biblical authority. However, all Christians in some way or another make recourse to the Bible, Old and New Testaments, and in this sense it is their ordinary language.[19] Theologians and religious believers may say other things about their faith which are not specifically mentioned in the biblical literature, e.g. the nature of the Trinity. But all Christians *qua* Christians look to the Bible as a unique resource. Thus I claim the philosophical position is secure. I do not intend 'reading in' any preconceived philosophical notions save that the meaning of a word is its use. It is an appropriate study philosophically to ask how a word is used in any particular tradition. It is further justifiable to examine how like and unlike the use of that word is with regard to other commonly accepted uses. Does the religious believer mean the same thing as other people when he says he 'knows' God? In what sense is this use of the word proper or improper? And what would God have to be like to be 'known' according to the ordinary uses of the word 'know'? And how like and unlike everyday use is the ordinary Christian use in the Bible? These are questions I shall pursue philosophically.

(b) But is this method of study appropriate theologically? After my analysis of the use of the word 'know', revealing the conditions necessary and sufficient for the various knowledge claims, I shall take that analysis to the Bible. Is this an appropriate method with regard to the Bible and one that can do justice to its teaching? It might be argued, for example, that it would be preferable to go directly to the biblical literature and from a careful examination then describe the biblical concept of knowing God that presumably would be normative within Christian theology.

This would be an approach much in keeping with the attitude described as 'Biblical Theology'. 'Biblical Theology' refers not so much to a 'school' or even a distinct group of theologians. Rather it relates to an attitude of mind that is cautious concerning the relationship of philosophy and theology and concentrates more on the authority of the Bible, although various understandings of biblical authority are involved.[20] From the Biblical Theologians came Old and New Testament theologies constructed around what was taken to be a central and illuminating biblical concept.[21] They also produced many detailed 'word studies', the fullest expression of such work being Kittel's *Theologisches Worterbuch zum Testament* (Stuttgart, from 1933).[22]

The assumptions and expectations of the biblical theologians have been vigorously attacked in more recent years. Professor James Barr, in particular, has revealed a number of weaknesses in the methods and suppositions of their work. [23] It is in the light of his criticisms that I will attempt to justify my analytic approach to the Bible.

Thus, for example, I suggested above that it might be argued that the appropriate method would be to seek out 'the biblical concept of "knowing God"' from within the Bible. But what is there to lead us to assume that there is 'a' Biblical concept? One of the assumptions of the biblical theologians was the unity of the Bible. In one sense this stress was a reaction against the fragmenting effect of earlier studies, for example those of the 'historical–critical' approach.[24] The biblical theologians assumed there was an essential unity in biblical thought. This found its expression in the contrast they often drew between Greek and Hebrew ways of thinking and their insistence upon the importance of biblical, which often meant Hebrew as opposed to Greek, thought forms.[25] The unity of the Bible meant for the biblical theologians that 'the differences disclosed by historical criticisms were admitted but it was believed that the centre or core, whether of the Old Testament or of the New or of the entire Bible, could be seen and expressed as a whole'.[26]

It may be that there is a centre or core in the concept of knowing God in the Bible. But it is not necessarily the case. It seems therefore more appropriate to use my method of analysis without making this assumption. If there is an essential element this will then come to light. But it may also be the case that, far from the knowledge of God being a simple unitary conception in the Bible, [27] it is in fact complex and varied. My method will allow for this to be shown if it is the case. It also has the advantage of not committing me to any particular theological position with regard to the authority of the Bible.

A further advantage of my position over that of the Biblical theologians is that I shall not assume that the language and thought of the Bible is 'distinctive' save in regard to its content. The biblical theologians readily drew contrasts between biblical and non-biblical thought. But as Barr has indicated the assumed distinctiveness of the Bible was a necessary part of their method, yet it was also a principal purpose of that method to demonstrate the distinctiveness.[28] The putative distinctiveness has often been claimed in the 'word studies'. These words are claimed to be semantically distinctive and this leads to claims for a distinctiveness of the faith and theology of the Bible. My method is to analyse words in their use, to examine the form of knowledge claims. Thus, rather than attempting any special pleading for biblical words and their meaning, I agree with Barr when he asserts that 'the distinctiveness of biblical thought and language has to be settled at sentence level, that is, by the things the writers say, and not by the words they say them with'.[29]

The distinctiveness, if any, of biblical claims to know God will be better brought to light by the analytic method. My method of examining the various claims to know God in the Bible will involve careful linguistic, textual and historic studies. And the problems of hermeneutics will always be with us. My method does not therefore rest on the assumption that the Bible will necessarily have one 'biblical' concept of knowing God nor on the more questionable assertion that such knowledge claims are distinctive because they are biblical. If the 'knowing-God-claims' in the Bible are quite unlike anything we count as knowledge then we must say that the Bible does not use the word 'know' as we do and therefore means something different from what we mean by 'knowledge'. But it would be foolish to assume either that this will, or will not be the case, based on any prior expectations about biblical literature.

In conclusion, it is my aim to uncover the nature of the claims to know God in the Bible. I shall not therefore be making in the first instance any creative theological statements. I am only attempting to evaluate the knowledge claims of the Bible in the same way as the knowledge claims of the Koran or the Book of Mormon might be assessed. I shall not be reading the Bible through the eyes of Idealism, Existentialism, Thomism or any other conscious philosophical position. In so far as it is possible I shall attempt a neutral attitude to the Bible taking the text at its face value, assessing the claims to know as they arise. My aim will be to show, by means of analysis, what knowing God means in the Bible. Whether such claims are in fact the case is, of course, quite another matter.

2

Towards a Definition of Knowledge

I begin then to examine the meaning of the word 'knowledge'. Although this book is concerned specifically with the knowledge of God, I wish in the coming chapters only to examine what it is to know anything, what 'knowledge' means. Then, perhaps, given this meaning it will be correct to ask whether it is logically possible to know God.

Some may feel that it would have been more sensible to establish first that there is a God to know. After all, there is doubt as to the existence of God as there is not doubt as to the existence of knowledge. I agree, of course, that any questions concerning the knowledge of God relate to his existence and that that is therefore an important question. I concede that if the concept of God is such that his existence is a logical impossibility, then God does not exist; and if he does not exist, he cannot be known. But this is a question about the logic of the word 'God' and I do not wish to make this my present concern. I am concerned to discover whether it follows from what 'knowledge' means that God cannot be known. I shall argue that it does not. I shall not be arguing that any particular truth claims concerning God are veridical, but simply that it makes sense to say that God could conceivably be the object of knowledge, given the ordinary meaning of 'know' and its cognates.

If God is in fact known then it must be true that he exists. It must also be true that there is some way of showing that God exists because, if I know X then it must be true that X and I must have some answer to the question 'how do you know that X'. Whether it can be shown to be true that God exists and whether there is some satisfactory way of answering the question, 'how do we know that he exists?' are matters which will come up for consideration in due course. But they arise if and only if it is conceivable that God should be known to exist. For this to be conceivable the meaning of the word 'God' should be such that it is logically possible for him to be known and the meaning of the word 'knowledge' such that it is logically possible for God to be known. Thus, in this part of the book, I shall be concerned to give an account of the meaning of the word 'knowledge' which shows that God could conceivably be its object.

What then does the word 'knowledge' mean? The question seems to require an answer in the form of a definition. But is it reasonable to imagine that there will be forthcoming a definition inclusive of all that the word means? A question of this form was posed by Wittgenstein and we can begin to answer it here. Wittgenstein challenged the assumption that it was the task of the philosopher to formulate definitions and thereby declare what the essential meaning of a word is. He argued that the meaning of a word was its use in its own language-game. 'One cannot guess how a word functions. One has to *look at* its use and learn from that.'[1] As I indicated in the previous chapter, he had come to see the inadequacy of the theory of meaning he had propounded in the *Tractatus* where he argued that the meaning of a word was its referent. There he asserted 'A proposition has one and only one complete analysis.'[2] He came to believe this theory wrong because it imposed on language a preconceived idea of what its meaning is.

In his later thought he stressed the need to look at language to see how it functions. When we do this we find that sentences are not all of the same kind. There are in fact countless kinds, ' countless different kinds of what we call "symbols", "words", "sentences"'.[3] The function of words is as varied as the many different uses of tools in a tool box or the handles, albeit of similar appearance, in a locomotive's cabin.[4] It is important for the philosopher to notice these different uses in ordinary language. Here, in their use, is their meaning to be found. Thus Wittgenstein saw the philosopher's task as descriptive rather than definitive. He challenged the 'craving for generality' and 'the contemptuous attitude towards the particular case'.[5] Philosophy, according to Wittgenstein, proceeds by seeking and providing detailed descriptions of concrete particular instances.

Our temptation is to look for the 'essence' of knowledge. Wittgenstein urges us to resist the temptation and argues, with references to the meaning of language-games, 'these phenomena have no one thing in common which makes us use the same word for all – but that they are related to one another in many different ways'.[6] He uses the illustration of 'games', indicating the many different kinds of games people play. But he urges 'Don't say: "There *must* be something common, or they would not be called 'games'"

– but *look and see* whether there is anything common to all.'[7] If we look, Wittgenstein suggests, we shall find many resemblances, many features and similarities. These similarities he characterizes as 'family resemblances'.[8]

What did Wittgenstein mean by this? He is saying that it is mis-leading to assume that because certain things have a quality or set of qualities common to them all, they are therefore called by the same name or word. What we see if we examine the use of a word is not a common quality but a complex pattern of resemblances in the different cases. These resemblances are 'determinate characteristics'. In the case of a human family, what Wittgenstein seems to have in mind 'is a "family" in which some members have either (1) one or more determinate characteristics in common (say hazel eyes), or (2) relatively determinate characteristics in common (say brown eyes of different shades), and each of these members has one or more different, or relatively determinate characteristics in common with some (at least one) or all of the other members'.[9] Wittgenstein is not suggesting that all we have is a free collection of things that just happen to be called by the same name. But he is making an 'attack on essentialism'.[10] The use of the word will not yield its 'essential meaning', but the family resemblances in use will be apparent to the philosopher who cares to look. 'So there is a good reason for applying a single general term to a range of different things, only it is not what believers in essence have thought it was.'[11] For Wittgenstein, the fact that a word had several meanings meant that it had several modes of uses or came under several sets of rules for its use.[12] However, he noted that many words do not seem to have sharply defined sets of rules for their use, and therefore do not have definite meanings. They are members of a family.[13] Whether anyone knows the rules for the use of the word – that is whether he understands its meaning – will be revealed in his use of it, not in his ability or inability to give a definition of it. As G.Pitcher remarks, Wittgenstien was interested in ordinary lan-guage and 'ordinary language was not designed with the philosopher's special interests in mind, its purpose is to allow human beings to communicate with one another so that work can be accomplished, transactions can be carried out, wishes can be expressed, and so on'.[14] In this ordinary language one word may have different uses and therefore different meanings.

Before considering Wittgenstein's own illustration of this feature of ordinary language, we can draw out some of its implications by looking at the word 'row'. 'Row' is a sign that in use can have a different sound and completely different meanings. For example 'you row the boat', 'sit in the third row' and 'a row in a marriage'.

The word however, may be used metaphorically, dependent upon its literal meaning. So for example, literally, the word 'row' means disturbance, noise, commotion, free fights etc. But in the sentence 'there'll be a row about this', the meaning may be not that there will be noise, commotion etc. alone but that someone will be called to account, will be reprimanded.

In the light of the Family Resemblance doctrine, we might compare:

(a) a row in a classroom, where school boys are making a great deal of noise but where there is no violence or disagreement

(b) a row between two neighbours over the fence where there is noise, disagreement and may be violence

(c) a row in the Cabinet where there is disagreement according to a pattern of procedure, but no noise or violence.

'Row' has different uses and therefore different meanings.

The precise debate about Wittgenstein's doctrine of Family Resemblances continues amongst philosophers with little sign of agreement on his 'essential meaning'.[15] It is not our immediate concern and so we need not follow it. But one particular question must be pursued because it concerns this matter of the meaning of a word as its use. Much clearly depends on determining to what use the word is put in any particular context.

Wittgenstein's illustration of the Family Resemblance doctrine was the use of the word 'games'. He described the many different kinds of games that are played. He then went on to ask how we should explain to someone what a game is? 'I imagine we should describe *games* to him, and we might add: "This and *similar things* are called 'games'".'[16]

But consider the three following statements. A: 'This is a game of football.' B: 'He's a game little footballer.' C: 'She's on the game.' A is a straightforward use of 'game', part of an obvious 'family'. In B the word is used adjectivally, with a different but not unconnected relationship to A. C is a 'slang' usage, descriptive of prostitutes. The games they play are not part of the 'game family' however blurred the concept might be.

We have said that C is a slang expression, a figure of speech. Other examples of figures of speech would be 'the political game' or 'the marriage game' or even 'language-game'. Moreover we can 'make game' of someone. Others are employed to 'keep' game. These are all legitimate uses of the word 'game' but they are not all 'games' and as such part of the 'game family'. So what makes 'a' game a 'game'? R. Bambrough argues, 'of course games *do* have something in common. They *must* have something in common, and yet when we look for what they have in common we cannot find it. The simple truth is that what games have in common is that they are games'.[17] The concept 'game' may indeed have blurred edges but those who know how to use the language know when they are talking about games, and when they are using figures of speech. This is not to say that 'game' is a word with a simple referent. It is to say that its meaning in use has to be learnt.

Wittgenstein's point is that if you have learnt the English Language then you understand how a word applies to a multitude of individual instances, just as you understand that in using a word you do not draw all the various possible distinctions between its different shades of meaning.[18]

We shall follow this procedure. Instead of looking for a definition of knowledge, first, we shall examine the various uses of the word 'know'. This may reveal that in this case Wittgenstein's theory of Family Resemblances does not apply and we can say quite clearly what knowledge is. On the other hand we may discover that he is right and that the concept of knowledge is too complex to allow of a single definition. The uses of the word 'know' and its cognates will be dealt with in the following chapters under the following headings: inferential knowledge, immediate knowledge, knowledge by acquaintance and description, falsification, knowing how and knowing that and 'objective knowledge'.

3

Inferential Knowledge

I propose in this chapter to give an account of what is usually termed 'inferential knowledge'. We all make knowledge claims. We draw inferences on the basis of evidence. It is this use of 'know' and its cognates that I am now going to examine.

A. J. Ayer has argued that there are three conditions, each necessary and together sufficent, of knowing that something is the case; namely, 'first that what one is said to know be true, secondly that one be sure of it, and thirdly that one should have the right to be sure'.[1] 'I know that P' logically implies these three conditions. Let us take them in turn:

1 To know P implies that P is true. We cannot know what is not the case. The 'cannot' is a logical cannot. It does not make sense, for example, if I say, 'I know the desk on which I am writing is made of wood, but it is made of plastic' (provided that whatever is made of plastic is by definition not made of wood). This is tantamount to saying 'I know P, but not P.' That statement is contradictory and therefore false. A correct use of the word 'know' logically implies that what is known is true. Someone might claim to know something which turns out to be false. Upon being shown that his claim is false, if he is a rational man, he will no longer claim to know it. But he will not say, 'I used to know it, but now I see that it is false and so I know it no longer.' He will simply say 'I never knew it.'

2 To know P is to be sure that P. Sometimes this is expressed as 'believing' that P.[2] Again take the example of my writing at my desk. It does not make sense to say 'I know this desk is made of wood, but I am not sure that it is.' Being sure necessarily follows from knowing.

3 Ayer's third condition was 'having the right to be sure that P'. This must be more than a repetition of being sure that P, or believing that P. It concerns reasons, evidence, entitlement to be sure. Ayer says that it is a matter of correct reasoning, of following

one of the 'accredited routes' to knowledge. 'I know that P' logically implies 'I have the right to be sure that P.' Consider the claim, 'I know that this desk is made of wood, but I have no grounds for saying this.' The claim makes no sense to us because anyone who says 'I know' is logically saying 'I have evidence.' To say 'I know that the table is made of wood but I have no evidence for this' is to say 'I know P but I do not know P.' In order to know it is logically necessary to have evidence for what you know. Thus having the right to be sure is part of the definition of knowledge.

John Hick says of Ayer's definition of knowledge that 'if knowledge is so defined that we are only knowing when, as well as being sure and having the right to be sure, that of which we are sure is in fact the case, then knowledge is elevated into something that we may have but can never know that we have'.[3] This is the case because there is no independent guarantee that P apart from the grounds for P. Hick's question is about the possibility of certainty. Because Ayer's definition does not admit of certainty then Hick prosposes that the word 'know' should be defined with a more 'practical use'. But it has been shown above that Ayer's definition relates directly to a proper use of the word 'know' and what that use implies. Knowledge, by definition, cannot be erroneous. But claiming to know and knowing are distinct. In fact knowledge claims may be erroneous and when they are they cannot be cases of knowledge at all. Ayer is very careful to point out that the right to be sure may be earned in a number of different ways. But these ways are in no sense part of the definition of knowledge, 'just as it would be a mistake to try to incorporate our actual standards of goodness into a definition of good'.[4]

Thus nothing is lost or gained by admitting the logical impossibility of absolute certainty in some cases. It is true that one can be absolutely sure of some knowledge claims. We can know, for certainty, the truth or falsity of analytic propositions; for example, 'All bachelors are unmarried men.' If true such statements are tautologies; if false they are contradictions. They can only be tautologies or contradictions as a result of the meaning of the words used in them. So this kind of 'certainty' has restricted application. It is about the meaning of symbols or words and not things.

But in other cases where there is not the possibility of demonstration of this symbolic kind all we can ever have is the right to be sure. From this we infer a conclusion and claim to know it. It is always logically possible that we may be mistaken. What we considered good grounds, or a properly accredited route, may prove to be insufficient or inaccurate. It is an empirical fact that no one can be absolutely certain of what they say.

This is true of all knowledge claims, except the tautologies we have already mentioned. It is true, for example, of 'scientific' knowledge.[5] Here knowledge is a matter of a collection of hypotheses that have been extensively and well tested for falsification and which, at present, have escaped falsification and constitute together a related unity. But it is not logically inconceivable that some new discovery might throw some, or indeed, all of these hypotheses into question. A proper use of the word 'know' on the scientist's lips, or anyone else's for that matter, involves the ability to produce evidence. But the scientist, as scientist, admits the principle of tolerance. He can never know that what he says is true. He can only say that his hypothesis has so far escaped falsification.

E. L. Gettier has challenged this account of inferential knowledge by suggesting that the three conditions do not constitute *sufficient* conditions for the claim to know P.[6] He argues that it is possible for a person to be justified in believing P where P is false. To illustrate this he describes two men, Smith and Jones, who have both applied for the same job. Smith believes he has strong evidence for the fact that Jones will get the job, and Jones has ten coins in his pocket; the evidence could be that Smith has been told by the Company's Executive that Jones will get the job, and that Smith himself has just given Jones ten coins.

The proposition 'Jones is the man who will get the job' therefore entails 'the man who will get the job has also ten coins in his pocket'. Smith seeing the entailment is justified in his belief of the latter statement.

But Gettier argues, supposing in fact Smith gets the job, and that unknown to himself he also has ten coins in his pocket. Then the proposition 'The man who has ten coins in his pocket will get the job' is true, though the proposition 'Jones is the man who will get the job', from which Smith inferred the true proposition, is false. So all of the following propositions are true.

1 The man who has ten coins in his pocket will get the job.
2 Smith believes that (1) is true.

3   Smith is justified in believing (1) is true. He has reasons for
    so doing.

But it would be untrue to claim Smith *knows* that he will get the
job. (1) is true because of the ten coins in Smith's pocket, a fact of
which Smith was unaware. Smith based his belief in (1) not upon
this fact but on the fact that Jones had ten coins in his pocket.

This is Gettier's attack on the view that knowledge is justified
true belief. Here in the story of Smith and Jones we have a case of
justified true belief. It is true that the man with ten coins in his
pocket will get the job. Smith believes this and moreoever is justified
in so believing.

If anyone were to question Smith's justification, he might reply
'What more could be asked?' He has the Company Executive's assurance that the job is Jones.' Here is what any would count as evidence. In fact, as later events prove, the evidence is misleading.
But from the proposition 'Jones will get the job', for which he has
good evidence, Smith is entitled to infer from 'Jones is the man
who will get the job, and the man who will get the job has ten
coins in his pocket' the proposition 'the man who has ten coins in
his pocket will get the job'. This is logically derived from a belief
which Smith is justified in holding. So his belief that 'the man who
has ten coins in his pocket will get the job' is supported (a) by a
sufficient amount of empirical evidence and (b) by the validity of
the inference he has made. This is justified true belief because, in
fact, a man with ten coins in his pocket does get the job.

The truth of the proposition is preserved by the fact that Smith
has ten coins in his pocket. But it was Smith who, against all the
evidence he was entitled to go on, got the job. He did not take into
account the fact that he had ten coins in his pocket, perhaps he
did not even know the fact. In any event it did not figure in his
correct conclusion that the man with ten coins in his pocket will
get the job.

So here is a curious conclusion. Smith, with justification, has
believed that the man with ten coins in his pocket will get the job.
It is true that the man with ten coins in his pocket will get the job.
But there are two men with ten coins in their pockets. Smith took
the man with ten coins in his pocket to be Jones, and not himself.
If we had asked Smith, 'who is the man with ten coins in his pocket
who will get the job?' he would have answered with justification,

'Jones'. In this he would have been mistaken. So we cannot say that Smith *knew* that the man with ten coins in his pocket would get the job. This is not a case of knowledge although the conditions of justified true belief are fulfilled.

In this way Gettier has shown that Ayer's account of knowledge is unsatisfactory.[7] Justified true belief will not suffice as describing the conditions to be fulfilled in an account of what it is to know anything. Therefore, we shall take note of this common use of the word 'know', that is, what is entailed in such 'knowledge' claims, and the critical limitations indicated, and go on to look at other uses of the word which might give rise to a definition of knowledge which is more adequate than Ayer's.

Before moving on it is worth noting that the inferential form of knowledge claim features in religious discourse. We shall indicate later such claims in the Bible both with reference to past and future events in history which are taken to be evidence and supposedly good grounds for knowledge claims about God. It is of course, quite another matter as to whether such claims are justified but there can be no doubt that religious language does contain knowledge claims of this sort about God.

4

Immediate Knowledge

I have just argued that knowledge by definition implies the possiblity of giving grounds for knowledge claims. Where a claim to knowledge has no grounds, or perhaps only poor support, we must say that this is not a case of knowledge, only a matter of weak or wise belief. It has been assumed that following a knowledge claim it is always possible to ask 'How do you know?' in expectation of an answer. H. H. Price has asked whether this assumption is warranted in all cases.[1]

His primary illustration concerns travellers by train to Basingstoke. Consider the two statements made by passengers A and B. A: 'I know that I am worried about the late arrival of this train.' B: 'We know that he is worried about the late arrival of this train.'

In the case of B this might be an illustration of a knowledge claim by inference. From A's furrowed brow, his wringing of his hands, his shuffling feet, his questioning of the guard and his constant looking at his watch, his fellow passengers infer that he is worried about the train's late arrival. If they are sure of this and if in fact it is true that A is worried, then B's statement fulfils what Ayer would have regarded as the necessary and sufficient conditions of a knowledge claim by inference. This would be the case although many philosophers would question inferences drawn from any implied relationship between observable behaviour and a statement of mind. One need not entail the other. But most would accept the behaviour described as reasonably good grounds for making the claim. B and his friends have evidence.

But what is the case with A's statement? This is clearly not a matter of inference. The statement 'I infer from my behaviour that I am worried and therefore that I know I am worried' sounds odd. But it does not sound odd to say 'I am worried', or even 'I know I am worried.' How do you know you are worried? Certainly not by inferring such from your behaviour. Price claims that this is a case of direct or immediate knowledge. The question 'How do you know?' admits in this case of no answer, save 'I just know.'

21

If this claim were to be judged against Ayer's definition of inferential knowledge it would fail. Its only ground is the putative immediacy of the experience, a ground that it is impossible to verify or falsify. This is because the knowledge claim is personal in the sense that it is about myself. It is of the form 'I know this about myself, I am worried'. Indeed we do not often say 'I know I am worried', we just admit 'I am worried.' The state we are in is that of being worried. The experience of such is immediate and personal. This form of knowledge therefore is never about things other than myself in the world. It is about myself as I am.

Price describes the distinction between A and B's statements as on the one hand A's 'noticing an occurrence' and, on the other, B's 'asserting with conviction to a proposition'.[2] B cannot know in this sense what A is feeling. He can only infer and make from observation a knowledge claim. A is directly aware of what might count as evidence. A has an experience that is personal. B cannot have A's experience. The 'cannot' is a logical cannot.

This use of 'know' is therefore very limited. It is restricted to claims an individual can make about his own condition. It is not a matter of accepting a proposition, but rather of noticing some actual event or state of affairs internally. The claim to knowledge may take propositional form but as such it is only descriptive of present personal experiences, e.g. 'I know that I am worried.'

Price argues that immediate, non-inferential knowledge is the necessary foundational knowledge upon which other knowledge claims, by inference, can be built. 'Unless there were some propositions which we just know to be true, without having and without needing any reasons . . . the other sort of knowledge, when it does make sense to ask for reasons, could not possibly exist.'[3] While Ayer's definition of inferential knowledge results in probability, Price holds that this immediate knowledge is certain in character.

But it must be said again that the use of 'know' in the immediate sense described by Price relates only to personal states of affairs and experience. We cannot know immediately things about the world.

Some have claimed that it is possible to know things about the world, by intuition. Such a claim may have the quality of immediacy about it. It is conceivable that a person who claims to know something by intuition could say, 'I have these intuitions and from them I infer certain thing.' It might be claimed for example, 'I have religious intuitions and from them I infer the existence of God.' However, I would judge such claims to be unusual.

It is more usual for the claim to know anything by intuition to be one that makes no inference and offers no evidence. Indeed it makes sense for the intuitionist to reply to the question 'How do you know that what you claim to know is the case?' with the assertion, 'I just know it, I don't need to have any evidence.' In this sense knowing by intuition is comparable to knowing immediately.

Should anyone be convinced that all knowledge is of the order of inferential knowledge, then they will object that knowledge by intuition is bogus precisely because of its refusal or inability, to give evidence. The claim to know by intuition can never fulfil the third condition of inferential knowledge as described, say, by Ayer. Indeed, the claim to know by intuition is an admission that reasons for being sure cannot be obtained and that evidence will not be forthcoming.

However, it would not be correct simply to equate knowing immediately with knowing by intuition. This can be illustrated thus. It is conceivable that someone should answer the question 'How do you know this is right?' by replying, 'By intuition.' But if some-one were to ask 'How do you know you are worried?' it would be unusual to reply 'By intuition.' He would simply say 'I just know it.'

The difference between immediate knowledge and claims to know by intuition is best drawn out in this way. The person who claims to know something by intuition claims intuition as an answer to the question 'How do you know?' His claim relates to knowledge of things in the world. By contrast, the claim to know immediately is not related to things in the world as such, only to my own state of mind. The question 'How do you know?' is unanswerable in terms of evidence. Because the state of mind is personal, only personal testimony can answer. Thus the person who claims immediate knowledge knows that he is not entitled to claim knowl-edge of anything beyond his own state of mind. But it is this that the intuitionist wishes to do, without giving evidence. Psycholog-ically knowing by intuition may have the quality of immediacy about it. Some people speak of seeing the answer to their problem 'in a flash'. But in logic 'by intuition' is falsely given in answer to a proper question related to the grounds of the knowledge claim. The question of grounds is not a necessary one with regard to the logic and limits of immediate knowledge.

Claims to know immediately are restricted in use to first person singular subjects. However, in such claims it is essential to consider the context and the particular force of the statement beginning 'I know'. Price has succeeded in showing that the first person singular assertion 'I know directly or immediately that . . .' is of a different form to inferential knowledge. It cannot fulfil the third condition of inferential knowledge and, in fact, does not have to for its proper use.

We have thus far considered inferential and immediate knowledge. Religious believers make knowledge claims of both forms. There are those who claim to know God inferentially, i.e. from the beauty of nature or the events of history for example, and there are those who claim to know God directly and immediately in their experience. The problem regarding the first kind of claim, to which we shall come to in due course, is whether the evidence appealed to justifies one in inferring the existence of God.

People do, of course, refer to their own experience as part of the evidence of God. As they refer to the beauty of nature, so they refer to what they 'feel in their heart'. What they 'feel in their heart' is then regarded as some kind of objective fact from which the existence of God can be inferred. Furthermore, it is sometimes argued that since there is such a form of knowledge as immediate knowledge, then it is possible to have immediate knowledge of God. It is not so much the case that one says, 'I have religious experiences and I have no way of accounting for them unless God exists.' This would be a matter of inference. But on the analogy of the man in the train to Basingstoke who does not infer from his feelings that he is worried, the religious believer knows he knows God, not by inference, but immediately. 'The awareness of God as personal will is given immediately in the impact of unconditional value itself, so that the religious man says, not that God is a necessary postulate in order to make sense of such absolute resistance to his will, but that He is a "consuming Fire", or that "He is living and powerful and sharper than a two-edged sword".'[4]

So we might draw a distinction between the person who infers from the fact of religious experience that God exists, and the person who claims that because it makes sense to talk of immediate knowledge it is legitimate to speak of the immediate knowledge of God. The objection to this latter is that, according to the account of immediate knowledge given above, immediate knowledge can logically only be knowledge of one's own mental states. One's own mental state may be that of feeling something which one calls the experience of the peace of God. But, of course, nothing follows from the fact that I have an experience which I call 'the peace of God' as to whether God exists in fact, or that there is anything other than my feelings to which the expression 'the peace of God' has application.

5

Knowledge by Acquaintance and Description

In the two previous chapters, concerned with inferential and immediate knowledge, the use of the verb 'to know' has been considered in relation to propositions expressed in clausal form, 'I know that P.' However, the verb is not always followed by a clause. It may also govern a noun in the accusative case, 'I know A.' Objects or persons may be 'known' as well as propositions, for example, 'I know Exeter', 'I know John.' Philosophers describe this use as knowledge by acquaintance.[1]

Bertrand Russell noted the distinction which has just been drawn between knowledge of propositions and knowledge of objects or persons; he differentiated them as knowledge of 'truths' and knowledge of 'things'. He further distinguished in knowledge of things, knowledge by acquaintance and knowledge by description.[2] He was not the only philosopher to draw the distinction but we shall use his work to illustrate what is involved.

Russell stated, 'I am *acquainted* with an object when I have a direct cognitive relation to that object.'[3] Direct immediate awareness characterizes knowledge by acquaintance. But what are these 'objects, or things', of which we are directly aware? Russell's list began with sense data. 'In the presence of my table I am acquainted with the sense data that make up the appearance of my table.'[4] Its roundness, hardness and colour are apparent to me in the presence of my table. Then, memory is a source of knowledge by acquaintance. I can remember the excitement of moving to our new house. Further, knowledge by introspection is included in the list. By this Russell means our consciousness of particular thoughts and feelings. By acquaintance I know that I am happy at the family news I heard by post this morning. It will be seen that, for Russell, knowledge by acquaintance includes what in the last chapter we referred to as immediate knowledge. Russel also included Universals amongst

26

things which are known by acquaintance; he referred to the awareness of Universals as 'conceiving' and to Universals of which we are aware as 'concepts'.[5]

Russell contrasted knowledge by *description* with knowledge by acquaintance. According to him we know physical objects by description. Physical objects are logically different from sense data. We know other people's minds, according to Russell, by description. This stands in contrast with knowing our own minds, in the sense of our own thoughts and feelings.

By knowledge by description Russell means knowing that there is something appropriately described in the form 'the so and so'. We know that there is one object and no more having a certain property.[6] Knowing by description is therefore indirect. It is a matter of exclusive identification. We know that a definite description applies to some particular things. Knowledge by description is always reducible by analysis to knowledge that something is the case. According to Russell's analysis of definite descriptions, the meaning of 'the black table' is 'there is an X such that X is a table and X is black'.

By description we may know that X is the man in the iron mask, but not be acquainted with X. We may know that Paris is the capital of France, but not be acquainted with Paris. Some cases of knowledge by description give us little or no knowledge at all. For example, one man must be the most long lived of men. But you add nothing to my knowledge by saying that there is one man who can be described as 'the most long lived of men'. The statement involves only universals. We can make no judgements concerning this man which involve knowledge about him beyond the description already given.

Such considerations might leave us with the impression that knowledge by description is independent of knowledge by acquaintance. In fact knowledge by acquaintance and knowledge by description are not independent because what is known by description is ultimately reducible to knowledge by acquaintance. Russell argued that knowledge by acquaintance was 'foundational' of all knowledge. If there were not this foundation it would be possible to talk meaningfully and 'knowingly' about a whole system of beliefs that had no substance at all. For example, we may talk of knowing fairies by description, and Tinkerbell in particular. But there must be something which we can empirically verify if such statements or systems are to deserve the title of 'knowledge' or even of 'rational belief'. Empirical testing, in the last analysis, is a matter of knowing certain things by acquaintance, by being aware of them through our senses. So 'knowledge by description is only possible if some of the descriptions mention entities known by acquaintance'.[7] Or as Russell said, 'Every proposition which we can understand must be composed wholly of constituents with which we are acquainted.'[8] Knowledge by description is important because it enables us to pass beyond the limits of private experience.

Russell's case was that sense data, memory, introspection and universals were the objects of knowledge by acquaintance. The question may be raised as to whether this knowledge by acquaintance amounts to anything at all.[9] Russell's argument is that knowledge by acquaintance is a matter of direct awareness. This is not knowledge of physical objects. They can only be known by description. But it can be argued that in these terms knowledge by acquaintance is 'essentially contentless' because any attempt to say what one knows by acquaintance must be expressed in the language of description. It would follow that there is no such 'thing' as knowledge by acquaintance since what one knows must be identified under description.

But what does this criticism amount to? People do use the word 'know' directly with an accusative, describing acquaintance with a person or a thing. But when all the descriptions have been given is there not a sense in which to say 'I know A' is to mean more than 'I am able to describe A'? We have already seen that knowledge by description can be expressed as a proposition, i.e. knowledge that something is the case, or knowledge about someone. By contrast knowledge by acquaintance is a relational expression e.g. A knows B. Knowing that B is not a matter of acquaintance. Knowing B is.

Again we may ask, what does this amount to? For A to know B implies B's existence. It makes no sense to say 'I know B, but it is not the case that B exists'. Moreover, encounter, which is the way to acquaintance, must be real encounter between A and B. To know B by acquaintance A must have met B. Further it implies that A knows certain things about B as a result of the encounter. It makes no sense to say 'I know B, but I can't tell you a thing about him'. Knowledge by acquaintance implies knowledge by description.

Some have tried to draw a distinction between personal knowledge and knowledge in propositional form. But there is no basis for calling knowledge by acquaintance personal and not propositional. The contrast which should be drawn is between direct and indirect knowledge. If we are acquainted with an individual then there will be certain truths about him which we necessarily know; there will be other truths about him which we do not necessarily know. This may be described as the contrast between direct and indirect knowledge.[10]

The personal relationship between A and B, which is referred to when we speak of A knowing B by acquaintance, can never therefore be exhaustively described. Statements may be made by A concerning what he knows about B. A may be able to give very full descriptions of B's appearance, character, intelligence, language etc., but even when this knowledge is given in all its entirety it does not fully describe what A *means* when he says he knows B. By this he does not mean simply that he can describe B, though it has been argued that in some way he must be able to do that. He means something relational which in the last analysis cannot adequately be expressed in words.

To sum up then, how are we to understand 'A knows B' in the sense of knowing by acquaintance? There are four important features of this use of 'know'.

1   Knowledge by acquaintance has first-hand quality about it, necessarily. It is a relational experience and as such personal. This is not to say that it is private. It must admit of some description.

2   Because it has this first-hand quality, knowledge by acquaintance is non-transferable. A can know B. C can know B. But C cannot be acquainted with B as A is acquainted with B. Both A and C can know the same things about B. But they are both individually and differently acquainted with B.

3   Knowledge by acquaintance admits of development and degree. It is dependent upon familiarity, the ability to recognise and identify. A may know B while they are students together. Yet fifty years on at a reunion they may not recognise one another at all. Upon being reintroduced however, their memories will recall knowledge and their 'acquaintance' will be renewed.

4   Knowledge by acquaintance can never be equated with knowledge by description however exhaustive that knowledge by description may be.[11] The experience of knowing a person by acquaintance always lies beyond just knowledge by description although it makes no sense to claim knowledge by acquaintance where there is no

possibility of description. No amount of description, however, can equal knowledge by acquaintance. In this sense knowing by acquaintance and knowing by description are distinct.

Religious believers speak of knowing God by acquaintance. It is in this sense that the children of Israel are said to know God in some Old Testament passages. We shall come later to explore the nature of this religious knowledge claim, considering in which ways the knowledge by acquaintance claimed can also meet the requirement of knowing by description.

6

Falsification

In my analysis of inferential knowledge claims I drew attention to the importance of evidence. We come to this matter again with the challenge of falsification and in particular, to the question of evidence, demonstration and proof in the case of religious assertions. Are religious assertions cognitively meaningful? And can they be verified or falsified?

Much recent debate on these questions has sprung from Antony Flew's celebrated essay *Theology and Falsification*.[1] The thrust of this essay lay in the tautology, 'that to assert that such and such is the case is necessarily equivalent to denying that such and such is not the case'. Flew agrees that religious statements look like assertions that something is the case, but questions whether this is really so. After his adaption of John Wisdom's parable of the Gardener he goes on to claim that we can discover whether a genuine assertion is being made or not by attempting 'to find out what he (the religious believer) would regard as counting against, or as being incompatible with its truth'. According to Flew, if there is nothing that counts against the statement, or is incompatible with it, then it is cognitively meaningless.

The crucial passage in Flew's essay runs:

Now to assert that such and such is the case is necessarily equivalent to denying that such and such is not the case. Suppose then that we are in doubt as to what someone who gives vent to an utterance is asserting, or suppose that, more radically, we are sceptical as to whether he is really asserting anything at all, one way of trying to understand (or perhaps it will be to expose) his utterance is to attempt to find what he would regard as counting against, or as being incompatible with, its truth. For if the utterance is indeed an assertion, it will necessarily be equivalent to a denial of the negation of that assertion. And anything which would count against the assertion, or which would induce the speaker to withdraw it and admit that it had been mistaken, must be part of (or the whole of) the meaning of the negation of that assertion. And to know the meaning of the negation of an assertion, is as near as makes no matter, to know the meaning of that assertion. And if there is nothing which a putative assertion denies then there is nothing which it asserts either; and so it is not really an assertion.[2]

Flew is in effect saying here that a necessary condition of the cognitive meaning of any statement is that the statement has verification or falsification conditions. This is, of course, different from saying that it has truth conditions. I shall return to this important distinction when it is more fully discussed below.

However, it is important to note at once that 'being incompatible with' and 'counting against' are not the same thing at all.[3] 'Being incompatible with' has reference to the truth, or rather the falsity, conditions of any statement. If a statement has truth conditions then it will have falsity conditions. This is to say that there is something which is the case if it is true as distinct from something which is not the case if it is false. For a statement to be cognitively meaningful there must be some conceivable state of affairs which is incompatible with it.

'Counting against' has to do with verification conditions. This is a matter of what it would take to falsify a proposition. 'Being incompatible with' and 'counting against', or truth conditions and verification conditions, must be differentiated because it is conceivable, as I shall show in due course, that a statement could have truth conditions but not have verification or falsification conditions.

Leaving these considerations aside for the moment, Flew's argument as it stands has been challenged, for example by Professor Basil Mitchell.[4] The implication of Flew's paper was that the religious believer would not allow anything to count against his assertions. Basil Mitchell, however, suggests that this is not the case. He argues that 'the theologian surely would not deny that the fact of pain counts against the assertion that God loves men'.[5] The theologian often discusses 'the problem of evil'. It is a problem for the Christian theist precisely because it does count against his belief that God loves all men. However, it is another matter to say that it counts against this belief *decisively*. Nothing counts against religious belief decisively; should it do so it would be 'a failure in faith as well as in logic'. In this sense 'God loves all men' is an assertion that is not conclusively falsifiable, but the fact of evil counts against it.

But this may simply be to indicate the fact that the truly religious man is like Job, he holds his beliefs come what may, (Job 13:15). It is conceivable that Job should not trust God but none of the terrible things that have overtaken him have brought him to this point. This stubborn conviction is a feature of religious belief. If justification of it is called for the believer might claim that what goes on in this world, though it looks as though it disproves the existence of a loving God, will be seen eschatologically not to do so.[6] The religious believer may argue that the evidence should be seen as a whole before forming a judgement. Things at present may count against belief in God but we cannot do the whole sum now. Only in the hereafter will we be in a position to know what it all adds up to.

However, let us come now to the distinction between on the one hand truth or falsity conditions, and on the other hand verification or falsification conditions and their respective relationship to cognitive meaning. To ask whether theological assertions are meaningful is not the same as asking whether they are falsifiable. Flew's test qualification for membership in the class of assertions was that any assertion must be equivalent to denying its negative. There is no reason why theological assertions cannot pass this test. To assert that God loves the world involves denying that God hates the world.

If the assertion 'God loves the world' has any meaning, then we must be able to conceive of a state of affairs which is God loving the world as distinct from some state of affairs which is God not loving the world. If we cannot conceive of any such state of affairs then, I shall argue, the proposition 'God loves the world' has no cognitive significance. But to say that we must be able to conceive of some state of affairs which is God loving the world, as distinct from some other state of affairs which is God not loving the world, so that 'God loves the world' really does mean the same as 'It is not the case that God does not love the world', is different from saying that we know of procedures by which we could show that it is not the case that God loves the world. It is one thing to be able to conceive of this state of affairs. It is another thing to conceive of a way of testing whether this state of affairs exists or not.

An important distinction must be drawn between the *criteria* of meaning for any assertion and questions of *evidence* that warrant the assertion being made. This distinction is important when the question of knowledge is raised in connection with meaning. R. S. Heimbeck argues that the criteria for any assertion are the conditions defining or determining the meaning of a cognitive sentence.[7] Critera are truth conditions and to know the truth conditions for P is the same as knowing the criteria for the meaning of P; and to give the truth conditions is the same as giving the criteria for meaning.

However, this is not the same as evidence. Evidence relates to the conditions under which we would know or have reason to believe that P is true or false. Evidence implies verification conditions and procedures. The distinction is this: it is one thing for P to be conceivably the case and it is another thing for us to know that P is the case.

Heimbeck's illustration of all this is simply that if Mrs Jones is pregnant, it means that Mrs Jones has a foetus in her womb, that being the necessary and sufficient condition of pregnancy. Having a foetus in the womb is a truth condition of being pregnant. We might say it means being pregnant. To know the meaning of 'Mrs Jones is pregnant' is to understand that if Mrs Jones is pregnant, then she has a foetus in her womb. However, *to know the meaning of* the assertion 'Mrs Jones is pregnant', is not *to know that* Mrs Jones is pregnant. To know that Mrs Jones is pregnant requires evidence which is the result of certain verification procedures or tests. The proposition 'I know that Mrs Jones is pregnant' logically implies the propositions (a) it is true that Mrs Jones is pregnant and (b) I have good reason to believe that Mrs Jones is pregnant.

If an assertion is meaningful it must have truth conditions as distinct from verification conditions. But what is it to say we know something? A statement has cognitive meaning if it will contribute to our knowledge on the assumption that it is true. It does contribute to our knowledge if we know that it is true. So the relation between meaning and knowledge is that if I say I know something then what I know must have both truth conditions and verification conditions. This is to say, there must be something which is the case if what I know is true, as distinct from this not being the case if what I claim to know I do not really know because it is false. Moreover, if I claim to know something then I must have grounds for this claim. If there are no good reasons for making the knowledge claim then it is disqualified as knowledge. Knowing therefore implies verification conditions being fulfilled. Those conditions provide what counts as evidence. Thus we can say that having verification conditions, which imply verification procedures, is a necessary condition of knowledge claims.

There may be disagreement as to what counts as good reasons for the claim. If, as Flew says, every assertion has its price, then part of the price of any knowledge claim is the designating of what the claimant counts as evidence. His opponent may challenge whether what he offers really is evidence. In other words they may debate the checking procedure.

However, it is not the case that should any statement not have any means of verification then that statement is necessarily meaningless. It is truth conditions as distinct from verification conditions which are the necessary condition of meaning, that is, criteria and not evidence. Thus a statement may be meaningful to us, even though we do not know how to test it for truth or falsity.

Flew later admitted that he was not alive to these distinctions in his original essay.[8] But he still has a challenge for the religious believer. He argues that if nothing is allowed to *count* conclusively against religious belief then what is its relevance to life in this world? Religious believers claim that belief in God is highly relevant to life. But if nothing that could conceivably happen would be interpreted by the religious believer as falsification of what he believes about God, what difference is there between a believer and an unbeliever which is in any way relevant to the life we live? Flew is not merely asking what it means to believe in God. He is asking for an explanation of what it means to believe in God in this world if there is nothing in this world that would make a man disbelieve in God. It is because he hears no answer that Flew claims that religious beliefs lack relevance.

But in what is Flew using the word relevant? Suppose there is a scientist at work in his laboratory who has decided that although he is going to perform many tests, nothing is going to count against his hypothesis. One might well ask of this man, what is the point of putting something to the test if you are not going to allow anything to count against it? His laboratory work in this sense is irrelevant.

But to conceive of what the religious believer says when he claims that religious belief is relevant to life in this world in the above terms, I submit, is entirely to miss the point. What is it to talk about the relevance of religion? A religious believer will say that if you believe what he believes, and if you believe it very firmly then the difference between you and an unbeliever will not be that the unbeliever is prepared to conduct his enquiries by the light of evidence and that you are not, but that you are committed to certain ways of action, to certain ways of interpreting life, as he is not, which make all the difference in the world between him and you. The commitments which one has, the ways of interpreting life which one adopts, are highly relevant to life in the sense that they do make a great deal of difference to the way one lives. Flew's mistake is to imagine that being a religious believer living out his beliefs is like being a scientist entertaining a hypothesis in his laboratory.

In fact, believing in God is not the same as a scientist's entertaining of a hypothesis. We shall enquire further into what the nature of belief is in due course. We note, now, however, that religious believers do claim to know God, to know that he exists, to know that he is love, even to know God personally. Let us take the example, 'I know that God loves the world.' This is a knowledge claim. I showed above that it is a necessary condition of cognitive statements that they be meaningful. Is 'God loves the world' a meaningful assertion? I claim it is at least a genuine assertion on Flew's grounds because it is clearly a denial of the statement 'God hates the world.' But to ask about its meaning is to ask about its truth conditions, the criteria of meaningfulness of this statement. The truth conditions would be that God really exists, that he is concerned deeply for the well-being of all men and is not disinterested in the state of the world etc.

But is the statement 'I know God loves the world' true? This is to ask not about criteria, but evidence or grounds for the assertion. The religious believer may give his reasons, such as his own religious experience, the life of Christ, the beauty of the world, the religious claim to eternal blessedness etc. The unbeliever would not find this evidence conclusive. He might point to his own lack of religious experience, the uncertainty about the historic Jesus, the cruelty in the world, etc. The fact is that what the religious believer offers as evidence is ambiguous. Are ambiguous grounds good enough for a knowledge claim? I shall come to the question of evidence again.

It is important to notice here, however, that although the putative evidence for God is ambiguous, the religious believer goes on making knowledge claims. The 'knowing' is an essential part of his religious faith expressed in language. He says 'I know' because this is the language he uses about God, reinforcing as it were the weaker confession of faith 'I believe'. But this is not a knowledge claim according to evidence. It is a commitment word, describing a relationship in which the religious believer feels himself to be.

Thus we might argue that 'knowing God loves me' is akin to 'knowing my wife loves me' in that in both cases the acknowledged evidence is ambiguous. But in fact neither are the sort of knowledge claims which consist in having conclusive evidence at all. To ask for conclusive grounds or evidence in these cases is to misunderstand the language of personal and religious relationships.

7
Knowing How and Knowing That

One further common use of the verb 'to know' is in statements claiming to know how to do something; for example, 'I know how to swim', 'He knows how to fly an aeroplane.' In recent years it is Gilbert Ryle who has commented most on this theme.[1]

Ryle was critical of the 'intellectualist' who claimed that intelligence was some special faculty exercised internally as thought. On this view, thinking was the pathway to knowledge. Knowledge was expressed in considered propositions. Such thoughts might be applied practically. But 'doing things' was not a matter of intelligence. Intelligence 'steered' wise action. Thus there was a distinction between theory and practice whereby theorizing was not an act of 'doing'. According to this concept, knowing how to do anything was dependent initially upon knowing that certain things were the case, or that certain theories applied. Ryle argued against this notion, that acquiring truth was some kind of mental event and that minds somehow had to discover the truth before they could apply it.

The intellectualist's case was that intelligent actions are true theory put into practice. Therefore an intelligent deed was really two actions. First there was the thought, then followed the application. Ryle argued that there was no gap between intelligence and practice corresponding to the familiar gap between theory and practice. An intelligence performance need incorporate no 'shadow-act' of contemplation. There is no 'ghost in the machine'.[2]

Against this Ryle asks what we mean when we describe a certain action as intelligent. His answer is, 'an action appropriately performed'. Those who perform well, and are responsible for their performances, have displayed intelligence. To do something intelligently is not to do two things, i.e. theorize and then practice. It is to do one thing well. It is to 'know how'. It is not a question of thought and practice.

Ryle's interest in this topic arises from his studies in the Philosophy of Mind. Our concern is with the analysis of the use of the word 'know', but we shall continue to follow Ryle's analysis leaving aside any other philosophical considerations. Ryle's case is that 'knowing how' is logically prior to 'knowing that'. Knowing a rule or principle is essentially knowing how to apply it. It is one thing to consider reasons, quite another *to* reason. In considering an argument, 'knowing a rule of inference is not possessing a bit of extra information but being able to perform an intelligent operation. Knowing a rule is knowing how'.[3]

What is involved in knowing how? Ryle makes three points.

1   'When a person knows how to do things of a certain sort, his knowledge is actualized or exercised in what he does.'[4] That he is intelligent is revealed in his deeds. Knowing how to do something is expressive and not abstractly theoretical.

2   But when anyone is able to do something well, i.e. knows how to do it, his actions are governed in some way by principles, rules, or criteria. It is always possible to explain why he succeeds. Ryle's case is that these rules are not primary. There is a difference between knowing the rules and knowing how to apply them. 'The propositional acknowledgement of rules, reasons or principles is not the parent of the intelligent application of them; it is step-child of that application.'[5] The very formulating of rules is a matter of 'know-how', as is their application. So Ryle describes rules as spectacles. We see through them, we do not look at them. Ryle's main point is that we could not consider principles of theory unless we or others had already intelligently applied them in practice. 'Rules, like birds, must live before they can be stuffed.'[6]

3   Principles certainly can be deduced from knowing how, say, to drive a car. Ryle suggests that the expression of such principles falls naturally into the imperative mood; e.g. 'Switch on, depress the clutch, put the car into gear, release the brake' etc. Such statements are unnatural in the indicative. However, imperatives are not true or false. Thus rules or maxims are not true or false, though they may be good or bad in their expression or use. The rules for driving a car cannot be affirmed or denied in themselves.

The usefulness of these maxims is found in teaching. They provide useful guides for those who are learning how to act.[7] 'Learning how' is different from 'learning that'. It is possible to learn the maxims of good argument and yet not be a good debater. To know the rules is to know the appropriate way to argue. It is not the same as being able to argue, i.e. correctly to apply the rules.

Ryle argues that 'knowing how' to behave is exhibiting correct behaviour. Knowing how to drive a car is a matter of being able to drive well. Thus to say that X is shrewd, or intelligent, is to credit X with a certain dispositional excellence. We are describing his character.[8] In fact it is conceivable that a man might know how to behave well without being able to give advice on good behaviour. But then knowing how to give advice is not the same as knowing how to behave. Rules and maxims are important for those who are still learning.

This leads to a further distinction. We can be instructed in rules and truths but skilful use of techniques and methods requires practice and discipline. Under instruction we strive for mastery of the method. This is not to say 'knowing how' is a matter of unconscious ability. Drill and habit are not the same as responsible discipline. 'Drill dispenses with intelligence, training develops it'.[9]

In this regard, understanding is part of 'knowing how'. It is possible to say 'I can do X, but I don't know how I do it'. The confession of ignorance in ordinary speech reveals the distinction between knowing how to do something and merely being able to do it. If anyone has no understanding of how they accomplish a certain feat it is inappropriate to say they *know* how to do it.[10] If they have learned to do this deed then it is appropriate to say they know how. But what they have learnt is a certain technique. They have mastered a method. There is understanding, but 'the knowledge that is required for understanding intelligent performances of a specific kind is some degree of competence in performances of that kind'.[11]

'Knowing how' is essentially an activity. Thus we might understand philosophy, not as a science, but as a discipline.[12] The philosopher is the master of a method. He has learnt a technique and by its application advances our knowledge. At least, he does if we can follow him, if we know how to follow him. No amount of 'knowledge-that' can ever be built up to the status of 'knowing-how'. There is a gap between theory and practice. But both may be learnt.

Let us consider now the three following cases:

1   'Fishes know how to swim.' Thus we might use the word 'know'. Such use does not imply or require that fishes understand

what they are doing. No one would suggest that they know how they perform this action. But they do swim and we say 'fishes know how to swim'. They do not know that anything is the case. They know no facts. Thus in this case 'knowing how' is directly equivalent to 'being able to' and has no cognitive significance. In a cognitive sense, fishes do not 'know' how to swim. They simply swim.

2   'I know how to swim.' The necessary and sufficient condition for the truth of this statement is my ability, when I am in water and out of my depth, to swim and not to drown. It is not necessary that I should understand any theoretical principles; nor is it necessary for me to be able to explain the workings of my actions to another. Yet, part of this exercise includes the simple notion that I can swim because I work my arms and legs in particular ways. I know that if I do this I shall swim. If I do not do this I shall drown. Unlike the fish, however simplistic it may be, my 'knowing how' includes some 'knowing that'. But no amount of 'knowing that' can amount to 'knowing how' to swim. Thus 'knowing how' implies principles expressible as 'knowing that' but is not equivalent to 'knowing that'.

This point leads to a further distinction. Suppose a boy on his first visit to the swimming baths had been pushed accidently into the water and instead of drowning somehow managed to keep afloat and come to the side of the bath in safety. He might say 'I was swimming, but don't ask me how I did it.' This would be a confession of ignorance. No knowledge claim is made. But it would be possible to deduce maxims which in theory explain how he did it. Thus we can distinguish between a person who knows how to do something and may or may not be able to draw maxims explaining in some way his action and an observer who may or may not be able to perform the action but can draw maxims, possibly more effectively than the participator who 'knows how'. 'Knowing how' in this use implies the possibility either by the participator, or by the observer, of telling how something is done by reference to 'knowing that' certain things are the case. But this is different from. . .

3   'He taught me to swim'. For anyone to teach another how to swim he must know something of the principles of swimming. It is not necessary that he should himself be able to swim. It is only necessary for him to know what swimming is and what principles are involved. By reason of physical deformity he himself might be unable to swim. But he knows how it is done. This is a purely cognitive use of the word 'know' and can be fully expressed in

terms of knowledge that certain things are the case. 'Knowing how' in this sense does not equal 'being able to'. 'Knowing how' is equivalent to 'knowing that'. The teacher cannot perform the action himself in the case I have described. But he can tell others what to do. This is his 'know how', but it is reducible to 'knowing that'.

What is the relevance of all this to religion? What is religious 'knowing how'? This we shall explore later in greater detail with reference to the biblical material and in the final chapter. However, in the light of the above, the following observations and indications are appropriate.

First with regard to that meaning of 'knowing how' that is directly equivalent to 'being able to' and that alone, it seems to me that there is no religious significance in a claim of this form and content. The mere performance of certain religious actions is not necessarily of any religious significance. I shall draw attention later to the prophetic condemnation of ritualistic religion that was a mere thoughtless recital of the liturgy. Such action only indicated the absence of the knowledge of God.

However, there is more to be said in the second case where 'knowing how', while not being equivalent to 'knowing that', nonetheless implied 'knowing that'. Most examples of religious 'knowing how' come into this category. The religious man serves God, with understanding. He 'knows how' and he 'knows that'. The interesting questions that arise, however, centre on the issues of how much 'knowledge that' does a religious believer have to have for his 'knowledge how' to be proper. If we speak of someone serving God, what is it for them to be aware of what they are doing? In what sense does the practice of religion deepen understanding of what they are doing? Living religion implies understanding, but what is the nature of this understanding and in what way does it relate to saying what is being done, i.e. educing certain maxims? Let us take the case of prayer. How much understanding is required of the believer in such wise that he does offer prayer and therefore knows how to do it as opposed to offering vain repetitions and indicating thus that he does not know really what he is doing? And is it possible for the observer to explain the action of the person praying by deducing maxims, thus helping the person who knows how to pray to understand better what he is doing? Or will he only grow in his understanding of prayer by the practice of prayer?

This leads to the third consideration, illustrated in the relation between the theologian and the religious believer. It is possible for a man to be an expert theologian but not be a practising religious believer. But if the theologian cannot, shall we say, pray, what is it that he can teach about prayer? Can he teach someone to pray in such wise that they will soon be better at this than he? Can this 'knowledge that' relating to 'knowledge how' itself be understood outside of the act of participation? These are questions we shall come to later.

8
Objective Knowledge

There is a use of the word 'knowledge' which is specialized as in the title to this chapter. It is associated with the name of Sir Karl Popper. In order to make its meaning clear I shall have to say something about (1) Popper's understanding of the growth of knowledge, (2) his notion of World 3 and objective knowledge and (3) his distinction between science and non-science.

(1) First then, the growth of knowledge. The traditional approach of the scientist to his work has been that of observation and experiment leading to the promulgating of assured results. He conducts experiments which he controls and observes as carefully as possible and from his findings emerges perhaps an hypothesis which is a scientific 'law' if tests secure the hypothesis. It is observation therefore that is taken to be the basis of scientific knowledge. On this basis of 'proven' experiments science *is* knowledge , the aggregate of assured results, to which further knowledge is added as it is discovered.

There have been well known difficulties with this approach. David Hume indicated the most important as the problem of induction. It matters not how many observations of B following A there are because there is no logical entailment to be deduced between A and B by observation. This philosophical problem cast severe doubts on science's putative sure foundation.

Popper believes he has solved the problem.[1] He regards '*all laws or theories as hypothetical or conjectural; that is, as guesses'*.[2] He understands that no scientific theory or 'law' can be verified because of the problem of induction. Such a 'law' however can be falsified if it is properly formulated. Empirical generalizations such as 'All swans are white' are not verifiable but an observation of one black swan logically enable us to state 'not all swans are white'. Thus Popper argues that scientific 'laws' can be tested not by the amassing of observed evidence but by the systematic attempts to refute them.

However, it is possible, without contradiction, to reject a certain item as evidence. One could insist that the black swan is not a swan at all because it is a bird of some other species. A saving hypothesis can always be introduced. Doubt of some sort or another can always be cast. For this reason Popper argues that hypotheses must be formulated as unambiguously as possible in order to expose them to refutation, if that can be done.[3]

The formulating of a hypothesis is the response to a problem. It is an attempt at explanation or solution. Thus we come to a crucial formula in Popper's thought.

$$P_1 \rightarrow TS \rightarrow EE \rightarrow P_2$$

P_1 is the problem. TS is the trial solution or hypothesis, EE is the process of error elimination, the attempts at refutation and P_2 is the resulting situation. P_2 is not the same as P_1. P_2 is a new situation with new problems. But this is the growth of knowledge, from problem to solution to problem. It is an evolutionary concept.

Popper is critical of what he calls the common sense theory of knowledge.[4] This is the theory that if we want to know anything all we have to do is to open our eyes and look around. It is assumed that our various senses are thus sources of knowledge through which we fill up our minds like a bucket.[5] Knowledge is therefore *in* us, stored in our minds. It is formulated into ideas, expectations and beliefs, all in the mind of the knowing subject. Popper argues that there is knowledge in the subjective sense, but this consists basically of expectations and dispositions. There is, however, more importantly, knowledge in the objective sense, '*human knowledge, which consists of linguistically formulated expectations submitted to critical discussion*'.[6]

Popper also indicates another feature of the theoretical element in observation. We do not begin our observations *de novo* as it were. It is a condition of observation that we know what we are looking for. This is a matter of some importance in discussing religious belief. Religious presuppositions are the conceptual load of religious questions. This matter of conceptual loading is not unique to religion. For example, questions posed using the concept of causation look for answers in terms of causation. Popper expressed this point as follows.

. . . we do not stumble upon our experiences, nor do we let them flow over us like a stream. Rather, we have to be active: we have to *"make"* our experiences. It is we who always formulate the questions put to nature; it is we who try again and again to put these questions so as to elicit a clear-cut "yes" or "no" (for nature does not give an answer unless pressed for it). And in the end, it is again we who give the answer; it is we ourselves who, after severe scrutiny, decide upon the answer to the questions which we put to nature . . .[7]

What Popper is saying is that you cannot (logically) have an experience which is not conceptually 'made'. This is illustrated in the case of Samuel hearing his name called while he slept at Shiloh (I Samuel 3). Eli told Samuel to reply 'Speak, Lord: thy servant hears thee.' It is possible that one of Eli's sons, less religiously perceptive than his father, might merely have told Samuel that Eli often talked in his sleep and the best thing to do was to ignore him. A different concept means a different experience and response. This theoretical element is important in the structure of religious experience and belief. We shall return to it later.

The scheme outlined above is the expression of Popper's understanding of the growth of knowledge. The place of error elimination, of criticism, cannot be over-estimated. The growth of knowledge proceeds from life's problems and our attempts to solve them. It is impossible to propound simply on the basis of observations a theory or hypothetical solution. Theory is prior to observation. This must be so because otherwise we would not know for what were looking. All observations are interpretations and explanations of the facts observed. The critical evaluation and examination of theories is, therefore, the *sine qua non* of the growth of knowledge. In our testing of theories we are not looking for 'certainty' of a subjective kind. We are looking for a theory which answers a problem that interests us, that is compatible with other information we possess and that is testable because it has a high information content.

Popper holds that the attempt to understand the world is an open task. The theories we work with must all be open to criticism. This is the only possible approach for reasonable men. 'Our powers of reasoning are nothing but powers of critical argument.'[8] It is by critical argument and enquiry that the work of science is directed not towards strengthened beliefs but towards the growth of objective knowledge.

(2) We now turn to examine Popper's notion of World 3 and objective knowledge. He understands problem solving as a 'primal activity'. All things living are possessed of 'inborn expectations'. In this way Popper's theory of knowledge is coterminous with his theory of the evolution of knowledge. He argues that the most important development in problem solving is language. It is partly the use of language critically that makes us human. We have used language to express answers to our problems, often in the form of myths. At birth everyone enters into a heritage of myths, all of them man made yet not the creation of the one newly born. In this sense we all enter a world of ideas that is essentially autonomous.[9]

Popper distinguishes between what he calls World 1, World 2 and World 3. World 1 is the material world of everyday things; tables, carpets, cars etc. World 2 is the subject world of our own minds. This consists of states of mind or consciousness, dispositions, reactions and behaviour. In sharp distinction is World 3 which is knowledge in an objective sense. World 3 is not the subjective act of thinking. It is the objective content of thought, expressed in language as products of the mind.

Thus Popper understands World 3 as the world of ideas, arts, ethics, religion, language, etc., all preserved in World 1 objects such as books, libraries and galleries. World 3 is the product of human minds and yet is independent of every human mind. The important invigorating factor in World 3 is criticism. Thus the dogmatic closed minded attitude frustrates the growth of knowledge. Knowledge is not the passing on of assured, unsullied truth. Criticism is the scientific rational method necessary for the growth of knowledge.

In this sense Popper holds that we can never actually know anything if certainty is implied. Certainty is not important. What matters is our openness that allows us, if need be, to the most radical of intellectual transformations. Yet, we do study 'something'. Knowledge is objectified in World 3 publications. These are the answers given to problems. They take a variety of forms. Therefore, when we study something in World 3, say a religion, or mathematical theorem, or scientific hypothesis, the important thing to ask is 'What problem is being faced here?' or 'What are these people trying to answer when they say this?'. It is not enough just to find out what they said.

Only in this way are we in a position to offer criticism. While 'knowledge' remains in our heads it remain uncriticizable. But this

is not the case with whatever inhabits the public objective World
3. Moreover, what is in World 3 is testable. This is not possible with
the private states of mind of World 2. '"I know", considered as a
statement about me, asserts my disposition to do and say and
believe certain things, and also claim justification for this; but none
of that is knowledge in the objective sense.'[10]

Let us see how all this might apply to theology. Suppose the
theologian is concerned to demonstrate the existence of God. He
is particularly interested in certain attempted refutations of the
ontological argument that he feels are inaccurate. So he goes to the
library to read Anselm and others. He tries to see just what it is
that Anselm was saying and why he was saying it. This takes him
to other sources that convince him that Anselm has been misinter-
preted. So, on the basis of these texts, he writes an article proposing
a new solution by way of indicating the errors of others. His paper
is answered, critically and carefully. There is a dispute about translation that involves other scholars, and so on. Popper would no
doubt hold that the scholars would be concerned not with their
own beliefs but with the objective knowledge of World 3.

The example of the theologian raises the question of the 'status'
of the problems we discuss. Suppose someone were to ask the
theologian 'Does all your talk of God refer to anything?', he might
reply, 'Yes, it refers to God, the Father, Almighty, Maker of heaven
and earth'. Then comes the question of the nature of this 'referring'
and the meaning of religious language. Here we turn to the third
matter in considering Popper's thought, his distinction between
science and non-science.

(3)   I indicated above the importance of falsification in Popper's
thought. He argues that falsifiability is the criterion of demarcation
between science and non-science. He understands the aim of science to be the finding of *'satisfactory explanations,* of whatever strikes
us as being in need of explanation'. He goes on, 'The question,
"What kind of explanation may be satisfactory?" thus leads to the
reply: an explanation in terms of testable and falsifiable universal
laws and initial conditions. And an explanation of this kind will
be the more satisfactory the more highly testable these laws are the
better they have been tested.'[11] If an explanation of a problem is
given that fits every conceivable state of affairs then it has no infor-
mative value and no observations can be properly claimed in support of it. There is no observable difference between its being true
and its being false. Therefore, according to Popper, it conveys no

scientific information. It should be remembered that, for Popper, epistemology is the theory of *scientific knowledge*.[12] If any knowledge claim cannot be tested, i.e. falsified, then it cannot be held to be scientific.

This sounds like logical positivism. But Popper was called the 'official opposition' in the Vienna Circle[13] and offered a trenchant criticism of positivism in *The Logic of Scientific Discovery*. It is crucial to note that by referring to falsification Popper is offering a criterion of demarcation between science and non-science, not between sense and non-sense. Popper is no anti-metaphysician. In fact, he argues, that it is out of metaphysics that science has emerged. Metaphysical statements may be both meaningful and true. Popper does not hold that the statement 'God exists' is just meaningless noise. He would say it is a statement which has meaning and could be true but it is not scientific because it cannot be falsified, and that is all. Commenting on myths he says

> At the same time I realize that such myths may be developed and become testable; and historically speaking all – or very nearly all – scientific theories originate from myths, and that a myth may contain important anticipations of scientific theories...I thus felt that if a theory is found to be non-scientific or "metaphysical" (as we might say), it is not thereby found to be unimportant or insignificant, or "meaningless", or "nonsensical". But it cannot claim to be backed by empirical evidence in the scientific sense – although it may easily be, in some generic sense, the "result" of observation.[14]

Popper's work provokes much discussion because of the independence of his approach, the clear force of his arguments and the obvious wide range of implications. All this debate is beyond my immediate interest and I shall simply concern myself with two questions related to religious belief and talk of God.

The first can be phrased thus. Can theology be regarded as part of World 3? In the sense previously described I think the answer is 'yes'. There is a corpus of material called Christian theology, for example, upon which it is possible to set an objective examination. The student's answers would be right or wrong as a matter of fact.

This would require no 'belief' in the content of theology. It is not logically impossible for an atheist to engage in theological work and become proficient in it. The theological talk may be understood as an attempt to reply to certain questions and the various answers relate to historical, philosophical and textual studies. Thus the theologian has, by his industry and critical appraisal, knowlege of theology.

It might be argued, however, that the atheist who studies theology is a rare animal and perhaps is only interested in the history of ideas which he explores as an historian. It is more usual that the theologian be a believer in the existence of God and that it is this basic commitment that gives reason to his study of theology. He believes he is studying something or someone. This is a matter of belief. Thus there is a contrast between knowledge of theology and religious belief.

Popper does not believe in belief.[15] He is interested in ideas and theories and it is of no interest to him whether anyone believes in them or not. Beliefs may relate to expectations or dispositions or explain way of behaviour[16]. But Popper is interested in objective knowledge and rejects any epistemology that centres on belief and understands knowledge as a species of that gene.

The religious believer, however, may express his belief in propositional form, for example, 'God is the creator of the Universe.' Here is an idea that as Popper would say might 'interest' us. It appears to be a hypothesis. It is an idea that a theologian or anyone else might explore, write up and deposit in World 1 libraries as a contribution to World 3 knowledge. But two conditions for objective knowledge claims according to Popper are their openness to critical discussion and possible falsification. Can the religious believer's theory be tested?

But this brings us back to the meaning of the religious believer's assertion of God as creator. Is it intended by him to be a scientific hypothesis given in answer to a problem that interests him, i.e. how the world came to be? Religious believers would answer 'No'. The meaning of this statement is not to be understood as a form of scientific hypothesis. This is not the meaning of religious language. The religious believer is not living with a hitherto unfalsified hypothesis. The meaning of the religious statement is its commissive force in the religious man's life. Thus the believer in speaking of God as creator is not asserting a 'fact' in any scientific sense. He is not making that sort of statement at all. He is making a religious statement, i.e. one in terms of God whose existence is neither verifiable nor falsifiable. The believer's statement 'God created the heavens and the earth' is not a scientific assertion according to such an account of religious belief, neither according to Popper, because it cannot be falsified.

Some theologians, however, are at pains to indicate that religious statements are fact asserting. John Hick, for example, argues that religious language presupposes the extra-linguistic reality of God.[17] But if this is so then the question of the justifiability of such statements can be raised and with them Popper's request for a formulation of the hypothesis in such wise that attempts at falsification are possible.

Hick argues that religious claims are indeed will be verified or falsified eschatologically.[18] He asserts in this that religious language must be understood in its own terms but that its own terms permit of and lead to questions of truth or falsity. Either God is or is not a matter of fact. This is a bold claim and we shall look at it more closely.

Hick's theory of eschatological verification is a reponse to Flew's falsification challenge, described in the parable of the gardener. He accepts verification as a valid criterion of factual meaning and argues that the 'core' of verification is the removal of ignorance or uncertainty concerning the truth of P. P would be verified if there were no longer room for rational doubt. Verification relates to the subject matter under discussion, e.g. the logic of 'table' determines what must be done to verify statements about tables, and likewise for 'god'.

Part of the concept of God in the Christian tradition includes the theme of eschatology. Thus Hick offers his parable of the two travellers, one of whom looks for the celestial city. The parable describes the choice between theism and atheism as a real one so that the universe envisaged and explained by the theist is different from that of the atheist. There are a whole host of philosophical problems surrounding this notion of eschatological verification. They find their focus in the question as to what it would be for anyone who had no physical body nonetheless to have 'experiences'. Can we conceive of such a case? These are real problems but do not concern us here.

Hick is careful to claim, however, that this notion of eschatological verification is not offered as an attempted logical demonstration of theism. He offers the concept only to show that it makes sense to speak of religious statements as factual assertions.[19] He acknowledges that the existence of God does not have the status of a tentatively adopted hypothesis in the believer's mind, not even of one to be verified after death. The holding of a hypothesis is not the nature of faith, yet the faith statement is fact asserting.

So Hick is really offering a defence of religious belief as being meaningful according to the nature of the verificationalist's challenge. He is not willing nor attempting to claim that religious belief is a matter of science. There are no empirical tests available to falsify the hypothesis scientifically. But more important, the religious believer's faith is not a matter of holding a hypothesis about God and the world at all.

So in answer to our original question, 'Can theology be regarded as part of World 3? – the answer is 'Yes' if by theology is meant the disciplined work upon the problems and answers offered by theologians within the many systems of religious belief. But if by theology is meant 'religious belief' and this is understood as the first order commitment by those who talk of God then the answer is 'no' both from the point of view of Popper and from the point of view of the religious believer. When the religious believer says 'I believe in God' or even 'I know God' he is not first entertaining a hypothesis; and the meaning of his assertion will not be found by asking for an scientific justification for his views. Thus religious statements are non-scientific but not necessarily therefore nonsense.

This leads to our second question as to whether theology can admit of criticism to the extent that science can. Criticism, in Popper's understanding of knowledge, is the *sine qua non* of the growth of knowledge. It is the attitude of the rational man who holds all his beliefs and theories open to critical evaluation and discussion. This view is powerfully expressed by an admirer of Popper, W. W. Bartley.[20]

The rational man, being shown that a belief he holds is erroneous, abandons that belief. It is a sign of his being rational that he adopts this open-minded attitude to all his convictions. So Bartley's description of such a man is of '. . . one who holds *all* his beliefs, including his most fundamental standards and his basic philosophical position itself, open to criticism; who never cuts off an argument by resorting to faith or irrational commitment to justify some belief which has been under severe critical fire'.[21]

Whether this can be done as a matter of psychological fact is an interesting and disputable question. But Bartley's point is whether there is anything, as a matter of logic, that we cannot be open-minded about. Can a Christian hold all his beliefs open to questions and remain a Christian? Bartley says:

. . . theologians have argued that not only to abandon allegiance to Christ but even to subject that allegiance to criticism, is to forsake Christianity. But for a comprehensively critical rationalist, continued subjection to criticism of his allegiance to rationality is explicitly part of his rationalism.[22]

Bartley argues the case that a democracy, by democratic means, can give up democracy, i.e. by voting for a totalitarian state. This is a perfectly conceivable state of affairs. But is it conceivable that a rationalist could have good reasons for giving up rationality? Is there not something odd about that language? And would it not also be logically odd for a Christian to give up his belief in Christ for Christian reasons? Isn't there in this sense a logical stop on the comprehensiveness of the critical rationalist?

Bartley's point against religious belief seems to be the closed nature of religious commitment. The religious man, he suggests, as the religious man, cannot be open-minded. Again, leaving aside the psychological questions, there are two points to make.

The first is simply to say that a man may give up his religious beliefs. As a matter of fact some do just this. They might do so because they no longer find the reasons for belief in God compelling as once they did. They once made a religious commitment, but now for what seems to them good reasons, they have given it up. There may be very strong psychological pressures that prevent this action, the decision may be of the greatest magnitude and pain for the one concerned. But is is not logically impossible that he should give up Christian belief for what he counts as good reasons.

The second point is this. Within Christian discourse the concept of open-mindedness can properly function. It is not necessarily the case that Christianity must be conceived of as a series of propositional statements in a particular fixed form essential to Christian belief. This is not to say that a Christian can get along without propositional statements in the account of his beliefs. It is to say that there is nothing fixed nor final about the form of these statements.[23] It can be argued that Christian 'truth' can be more dynamically understood. The fundamental assertion of Christian belief is that God is revealed in Jesus Christ. But it is not impossible for a Christian's concept of God to develop or be revised. All that the Christian believes about God within this framework-reference of Christ can be held open to criticism.

If Bartley now were to ask for a fundamental criticism of the 'framework of reference of Christ' I would argue that indeed it is not possible for anyone to give up this point of reference and be a Christian. That is not logically possible. He may, of course, give up being a Christian, but not for Christian reasons.[24]

Thus I would argue that there is nothing to prevent the religious believer, in logic, maintaining a sharply critical attitude. Indeed by such means within Christian belief he may increase the Christian's knowledge according to Popper's scheme for the growth of knowledge. But this does not lead to the claim that it is scientific knowledge. Religious statements may be as subject to criticism as scientific hypotheses. But this of course does not make religion science.

One of Popper's central assertions has been to insist that we misconceive of knowledge when we think of it as something going on or residing in someone's head. We are misunderstanding the nature of knowledge if we think of it in the traditional subject and object terms. Popper, as we have indicated, thinks of knowledge as something objective in World 3, the world that is our common inheritance. Thus knowledge, being the answers to many problems that have interested man from the beginning, is stored in world I repositories ever waiting our present critical appraisal.

It is possible to think in these terms of the 'deposit of the Faith'. Here are statements about God and his relation to man recorded in World 3. This deposit is quite autonomous. It is handed on through the generations. There is the concept of *Torah* in the Old Testament, there are references to 'the Faith' in the Pastoral Epistles, cf. I Timothy 4:1, Titus 1:9. In this sense the faith is objective. It is there to be enquired into. And because men have always enquired into it, it has a dynamic character. The 'deposit' is always changing as each generation contributes its understanding.

This understanding of 'the Faith' is, I think, different from the emphasis of some Christian churches. These, as the guardians of true doctrine, have emphasized the authoritative teaching role. But the understanding of 'the Faith' as some kind of religious World 3 allows for a greater level of criticism and development. Thus the knowledge of God is not some fixed or final thing but has a more dynamic quality.

How much of this can be found in the Bible? We shall look later at the biblical material. Yet it is not unimportant to note the developing importance of written material in the Old Testament and the development of doctrine in these writings as I have indicated above.

In this brief expression of Popper's thought, I have concentrated on three aspects (1) that knowledge 'grows' (2) that it is objective and (3) that science and non-science can be clearly differentiated. Can religious belief or the knowledge of God relate to these issues?

I think it can. I see no reason why the knowledge of God should not grow and develop. Certainly I cannot think of anything in the nature of religion that prevents this development. It seems to me to be both conceivable that a religious believer should grow in understanding and that increasingly there should be more known of God. I am not here arguing for a concept of progressive revelation or anything of the sort. I am merely suggesting that there is nothing in religion, as religion, that denies the possibility of growth or evolution in the knowledge of God.

I have already indicated above that I think that the knowledge of God, the theological deposit of the faith, can be viewed objectively. In this sense theology can be part of World 3.

I have argued further that theology is not necessarily the same as religious belief and that religious belief is not science. Popper's distinction between science and non-science was falsifiability. Thus the religious believer who says that God exists is not offering a scientific hypothesis in making that assertion. However, part of the essence of falsifiability is openness to criticism. One might draw a contrast between criticizable and dogmatic knowledge. Does religious knowledge have to be dogmatic, in the sense of being uncriticizable? I do not think so. I would argue that it is a sign of rationality in religious belief that the believer holds all his assertions open to criticism.

Therefore, it seems to me, there is nothing in the nature of religious belief, in the matter of the knowledge of God, that denies that such knowledge can grow, be objective, or be criticized.

9

On Certainty

Thus far I have isolated and examined the ordinary uses of the word 'know'. I have indicated the necessary and sufficient conditions for these various uses. However, I do not now claim to have exhausted the meaning of the word 'know'. I take to heart Wittgenstein's warning, 'One is often bewitched by a word. For example, by the word "know".'[1]

This quotation comes from his last writings, published posthumously, under the title *On Certainty*. Towards the end of his life, Wittgenstein was encouraged by Norman Malcolm to reflect upon two of G. E. Moore's most famous essays.[2] *On Certainty* is not a polished finished work but rather the fascinating reflections of Wittgenstein on the problem of knowledge and certainty. The discussion is subtle and sensitive. It is of interest here because Wittgenstein is concerned with what the word 'know' may mean. I do not intend to attempt a summary of the whole work, nor to consider its many implications. There are, however, three themes in particular that relate to my argument. These are the meaning of doubt; the relationship of language games and knowledge; and the question of whether 'knowing' is a state of mind. I shall examine these three in turn.

The Meaning of Doubt
It is part of Wittgenstein's purpose to persuade the sceptic that some propositions about the external world have the same epistemological status as mathematical propositions (651).[3] What would it mean to doubt the proposition 'That is a chair?' Wittgenstein said that doubt, like knowledge, needs grounds (458). Universal doubt is logically impossible because a doubt that doubted everything would not be a doubt (450, 232) and in any event presupposes certainty (115). Our very testing of any proposition is dependent upon something being the case which is not doubted (163, 341). Moreover, doubting must find some expression in practice, otherwise it is an idle exercise (120, 247, 117).

56

Wittgenstein argues that there are some propositions which are impossible to doubt, for example, those of the form $12 \times 12 = 144$. But he wants to say that it is also correct to claim certainty for empirical propositions, for example, 'This is my hand.' If one were looking at one's hand it would be unreasonable to doubt the proposition 'This is my hand.' What would constitute grounds for reasonable doubt in this instance? 'There are cases where doubt is unreasonable, but others where it seems logically impossible. And there seems to be no clear boundary between them' (454).

It does not follow, of course, that because there are propositions which we cannot doubt there are propositions about which we cannot be mistaken. Wittgenstein draws a distinction between making a mistake, for which there is a reason, and a false belief or mental disturbance which is a cause (71–5). To doubt everything is not an error as such but just craziness (217, 674–5) and this is understood as we consider that the procedures for talking someone out of a mistake are quite different from talking anyone out of mad belief (257, 330–4).

However, Wittgenstein lists some propositions of a form which he believes we can neither be mistaken about nor doubt. For example, he is sure his friend doesn't have sawdust in his head; to have doubts about this would be madness (281). He cannot doubt but that he has two hands (125, 245). There can be no doubt but that he is living in England, everything tells him so (419–21). But even so, Wittgenstein points out that to claim certainty and deny doubt concerning these propositions is not the same as saying that they can be known.

Language-Games and Knowledge
It is further part of Wittgenstein's understanding of doubt that doubt presupposes mastery of a language-game. To doubt any proposition requires that we must understand that proposition, which means we must be able to participate in the language-game in which that proposition is at home. Wittgenstein takes it to be an empirical fact that words do have meanings (114, 306, 486). One of the meanings of the phrase 'I know' Wittgenstein understands thus, that 'I know that that's a hand' means 'I know the language game of hand' (371). 'I know this is my hand' is at home in those language-games where there is no doubt about the existence of 'hand'. Indeed, absence of doubt belongs to the essence of the language-game (370), doubts about existence are excluded by the nature of the language-game

(24) and doubts about existence of hands, or anything, only work against the background of a language-game.

Thus following Wittgenstein here we might argue that the statement 'I know that was the work of God' may be a perfectly proper statement made by someone who understands the language-game of religious belief. But if someone were to say that they doubted whether or not God existed this would be a statement of doubt outside the language-game of religious belief. The religious believer cannot deny the sceptic the right to his doubt but he is entitled to ask the sceptic what such a doubt is like. It cannot be like a religious assertion because doubt about God's existence is excluded in the language-game of religious belief.[4] Doubt comes from outside the game. This is not to say religious believers do not have their doubts about God. It is only to say 'that absence of doubt belongs to the essence of the language-game, that the question 'How do I know. . .' draws out the language-game, or else does away with it' (370).

Wittgenstein, agreeing with Moore, argued that there are certain empirical propositions that cannot be doubted, these propositions 'stand firm' (112, 116, 151). These are fossilized or foundational and their acceptance makes enquiry possible. As such they are features of our 'world picture, our inherited background' (94). Such propositions are not learnt by experience, rather, they function as rules for a game we can learn. These propositions, empirical and logical, form the foundation of all operating with thoughts (401). These are not propositions about the world, they are the propositions which make up our world picture. These are the unmoving foundations of the language-game (403, 446, 524). But it is important to note that Wittgenstein does not believe these propositions provide *grounds* for language-games.[5] Giving grounds comes to an end, in action (204, 110, 559). What then do we mean when we say we know these empirical propositions?

The Meaning of 'I Know'
Wittgenstein drew attention to the fact that all the propositions Moore offered are in no way cases of special knowledge. If Moore knows them then we all do (84, 100, 462). But in these cases the affirmation 'I know' is misleading and superfluous (58, 100, 587, 401). Special circumstances may give 'I know' a use but these would be unusual circumstances and would not be enough to refute or answer the sceptic. (23) But outside these peculiar circumstances Wittgenstein argues that propositions of the form 'I know that P'

are senseless, i.e. where P is a foundational proposition. 'If "I know etc" is conceived as a grammatical proposition, of course the "I" cannot be important. And it properly means "There is no such thing as a doubt in this case" or "The expression 'I do not know' makes no sense in this case".' And of course it follows from this that 'I *know* makes no sense either' (58). We may understand 'I know that P' as an expression of a mental state, thus making what Wittgenstein calls an *utterance* (510). But what is the value of this? Saying one knows does not prove one knows (487–9), the possibility of doubt and knowledge always go together (10). Wittgenstein argues that it is not the case that knowledge is a mental state on which we report when we say 'I know.' Belief and knowledge are not different kinds of mental states at all (42, 308).

Two things in summary are of special importance for us from this work of Wittgenstein. One is the importance of learning the meaning of words and being able to participate in language-games. Teaching children to use words correctly is bringing them to knowledge because knowledge concerns participation in a language where words have meaning as an empirical fact (527). In this sense knowing what mathematics is means doing mathematics and knowing what religious belief is means participating in religious language. Knowledge may mean more than this, but it means at least this.

The other emphasis is that of the importance of action. All questions about grounds of knowledge do come to an end. But they do not end in some assured, clear and distinct idea. The end is an ungrounded way of acting or participating in a form of life (110).

Are we now in a position to give a definition of 'knowledge'? I think not. I have shown that there is evidence of Wittgenstein's 'family resemblance' doctrine. It seems to me that after this analysis we are left not with the essence of 'knowing' but a variety of quite proper uses of the verb 'to know' and a number of characteristic features of 'knowledge'.

I have indicated in my analysis the qualifications relating to each usage of the verb 'to know'. It will be important when we consider the claim to know in religious language to apply these qualifications correctly. But the way the word 'know' is *used* will be the key to understanding its meaning and to the necessary and sufficient conditions for its proper use.

So what progress has been made thus far in elucidating the concept of the knowledge of God? I have demonstrated the fact that in everyday language the concept of knowledge is complex because the use of the word 'know' is various. These various uses are proper each within certain limitations imposed by the particular logic of the knowledge claim being made. So we are not left with a complete unitary definition of knowledge.

I intend now to go on and see if the various forms of knowledge and knowing I have indicated can be matched with what is said of knowledge of God in the Bible. It may be that the variety of ways of knowing are present in Old and New Testaments and that therefore the concept of the knowledge of God in the Bible also has a complex character.

10
The Knowledge of God in the Old Testament

I propose in this chapter to examine some of the claims to know God made in the Old Testament. I shall do this in two ways (1) I shall take my previous analysis of the various uses of the word 'know' to the Old Testament to see whether the claims to know God correspond to any, or all, or none of these forms. (2) I shall concentrate my attention upon claims to knowledge using *yada'* and *da'at*.

I wish to make it clear that there are two things I am not attempting to do:

1 I am not attempting to describe the Old Testament concept of the knowledge of God. My work may well provide data for such a study, but that is not my direct purpose here. Having described the conditions of the normal usage of the word 'know', it is my limited intention only to ask whether the claims to know God in the Old Testament reflect this variety of use.

2 Although I shall concentrate upon *yada'* and *da'at* I shall not restrict myself to texts that include these words. But since *yada'* is usually translated 'I know'[1] it is obviously appropriate to concentrate on it. However, it is not my purpose to describe or define the meaning of *yada'* as in a 'word study'. I am citing only those uses of *yada'* that are associated with God and it is basically these claims that are my interest.

It is well known that *yada'* is used in the Old Testament in a variety of contexts. It can refer to 'blows' (I Sam. 14: 12), childlessness (Isa. 47: 8), sickness (Isa. 53: 3) and many other experiences, for example, divine punishment and retribution (Jer. 16: 21, Ezek. 25: 14).[2]

It may also have sexual connotations; a man may 'know' a woman (Gen. 4: 1; Judg. 19: 25) and a woman 'know' a man (Num. 31: 17). It is used on nearly 200 occasions with reference to man's knowledge of God. It is also used of God's knowledge of man.

As I said above, within this wide range of use *yada'* is usually translated 'know'. However, there are some instances where this translation does not fit the sense and so other meanings have been proposed on the basis of words in cognate languages. D. Winton Thomas has made a special study of *yada'* and has concluded that in a number of cases an identification of an Arabic root *wada'a* with the meaning of 'make quiet', or 'make submissive', or 'subject to humiliation', is the more appropriate and correct.[3]

My purpose in raising the question of translation now is but to reinforce a previous argument. Philological studies have become increasingly important and helpful in the task of understanding the Old Testament in recent years. Before the increased knowledge, which has come through philological research was available, a text which was 'difficult' in translation because of its form, or the unusualness of a word, might become more understandable if textual emendations were made. But with the increasing knowledge of other cognate languages, it was seen that the difficult hebrew text might be better elucidated by philological rather than textual treatment.[4]

In an ideal situation the meaning of all the words in a text should be established so that an accurate and proper exegesis can be given. But since our knowledge of the meaning of words is not complete we do not live in an ideal exegetical world. I have already indicated that *yada'* means 'know' but that it has a wide variety of uses and possible meanings. Simply to discover the 'root' is not necessarily to discover the meaning of a verb, though no one would deny that such a 'discovery' would be important.[5] All I am arguing is that the meaning of a word in one passage is not the same necessarily as in another. There are 'shades' of meaning. Some words have double meanings. Some verbs have two 'roots' which lead to ambiguity and ambiguity may be deliberate as well as unintentional.[6] It is also important to note that the meaning of a word cannot necessarily be shown with certainty from the cognate languages. To say this is not to adopt a position of scepticism. It is simply to be cautious and to stress the need of corroborative evidence where possible.[7] Neither is this to say that context alone can be our guide in understanding the meaning of any particular word. It is to say that determining whatever 'root' meaning of any verb is present depends upon the sense of the passage, i.e. upon exegesis. To repeat what I have said before, it is the sentence that is the bearer of meaning and therefore it will be the exegesis of texts which include *yada'* rather than a precise study of *yada'* that is my concern in assessing the various Old Testament claims to know God.

I begin therefore by asking whether there are any claims to know God of an inferential form.

INFERENTIAL KNOWLEDGE

My earlier analysis of inferential knowledge described three necessary and together sufficient conditions for a knowledge claim. These are (1) that what is claimed is true, (2) that the claimant believes, or is sure of, his claim and (3) that he can give reasons for his claim. These three conditions do not describe what knowledge is. They merely indicate conditions that must be fulfilled in a proper knowledge claim of this form. Claiming to know and knowing are not the same thing at all and it is with knowledge claims that we are here concerned.

When anyone makes an inferential knowledge claim it is always appropriate to ask him 'how do you know?'. We look for an answer giving reasons why he considers himself entitled to be sure. This entitlement may take different forms as befits the nature of the claim. If the reason given is inappropriate then the claim fails. If the reason given, the evidence cited, etc. is appropriate then the claim is justified.

So my concern in this Section may be expressed in the question, 'Are there claims to know God in the Old Testament for which the Old Testament writer would claim to be able to give evidence?' I believe there are. It is not my purpose to discuss whether these claims are justified or not. I only wish to examine claims to know God that appeal to evidence, taking note of the sort of thing that the Old Testament counts as evidence.

Basically the appeal in the Old Testament is to historical evidence, to things that have happened, or to events yet to take place. For this reason, although the distinction is in some way artificial, I shall first consider (1) claims that cite as evidence events that have taken place; then I shall examine (2) claims that appear in the future tense, (3) I shall ask whether anything other than history is taken as evidence for the knowledge of God in the Old Testament and (4) I shall offer my conclusions.

1 *Appeals to History*

It would be difficult to over-emphasize the importance of the Exodus event for the Old Testament understanding of God. For example, it is understood in Deuteronomy 4: 35 that the purpose of the events is to make God known. 'You have had sure proof that Yahweh is God.'[8] The invitation to the Israelites is to reach into days gone by, beginning even with creation (verse 32) and to ask whether any other actions have been as powerful as those that Israel has experienced. In their past there have been deeds performed that 'cannot have been in vain'.[9] All of this is taken as evidence and leads to the insistence that the people may be sure (verse 39) that Yahweh is God.[10] The appeal is to the past as evidence of Yahweh's actions. Indeed the claim is that he did these things in order that he might be known as God, and there is no other. To the question, 'how do you know Yahweh is God?', the answer would be 'because of what he has done'.

The response of Jethro in hearing news of the escape from Egypt is of a similar pattern. 'Now I know that Yahweh is the greatest of all gods because he has delivered the people from the power of the Egyptians who dealt too arrogantly with them', Exodus 18: 11. That Yahweh is the greatest of all gods is a basic confession of Israel's faith.[11] The reason given here for the assertion is news of the deliverance from Egypt. Some scholars suggest that Jethro, priest of Midian, comes to the mountain of God to make a covenant with Moses and thereby to recognize the power of Israel's God of whose deeds he had already heard (verse 1).[12] Others deny this, suggesting that the celebration described is an act of worship.[13] The sacrifice at which Jethro presides (verse 12) is a rejoicing in the presence of Yahweh. He is not introduced to someone previously unknown. He recognizes the action of one known and worshipped before. Now, however, on the evidence of the Exodus even more is known of the power and greatness of Yahweh.[14] In fact, whatever position is adopted here, the knowledge claim is related to the recounting of the events of the Exodus. Jethro 'knows' that Yahweh is the greatest of all gods *because* of what he has done.

Remembering the Exodus is a feature of a number of the Psalms. Psalm 106 includes reference to the rebellion of the people by the Sea of Reeds. 'Yet Yahweh delivered them for his name's sake and so made known his mighty power', verse 8. The thought is that in acting Yahweh revealed something of himself. At Psalm 103: 7 Yahweh is said to have made known his way to Moses and to have shown the Israelites what he could do. Although the psalm has a personal emphasis it rests on the experience and expresses the faith of the fathers. Thus present conviction about Yahweh relates to what has been experienced and seen of him in the past,[15] a theme to which I shall return.

A third reference from a psalm Psalm 9: 16, takes up again this thought of Yahweh acting to make himself known. The appeal is to the past and the overcoming of enemies in which Yahweh executes judgement. 'Now Yahweh makes himself known.' It may be that the psalm is commenting upon the experiences of the Egyptians.[16] In any event, it is by acting and therefore in history that Yahweh indicates who he is.

So foundational are these events surrounding the Exodus for Israel's understanding of Yahweh that the didactic Deuteronomist can be imperative. 'Know then that Yahweh your God is God', Deut. 7: 8. What is particularly to be known is that Yahweh keeps covenant and it is within this relationship, and in the light of the Exodus just recalled, that the call to know is issued. It may have the sense of 'understanding' in this context. It certainly is related to the command to be obedient (verse 11), a feature of Israelite knowing I shall develop more fully later. But the explicit appeal again is to the Exodus as revealing the choice and power of Yahweh, the basis of the covenant.[17]

After the escape from Egypt there came the wilderness wanderings. These the people of Israel remembered in their worship, especially at the Feast of Booths. Leviticus 23: 34ff records elaborate ordinances for the festival. In verses 42–3 there comes an injunction for the Israelites annually to live in booths for seven days so that they and their descendents may know how God brought the people out of Egypt and led them through the wilderness.[18] The intention is that the people should 'relive' in the cult the one time situation in the desert.[19] Thus each generation will acquire the important knowledge of what Yahweh has done and thereby learn who he is. Without this *remembering* of history there is no knowledge of Yahweh.

The purpose of the stones at Gilgal is to be a reminder to the people of how Yahweh acted for them at the crossing of the Jordan, 'thus all people on earth will know how strong is the hand of Yahweh', Joshua 4: 24. Some suggest that the story reflects the work of the Deuteronomist redactor stressing that the miracle at the Jordan is the means Yahweh used of showing that he is God.[20]

It may be, however, that this is no 'mosaic of redactions',[21] but records the fact that the Israelites adapted a celebration of the re-enactment of creation at the pre-Israelite sanctuary of Gilgal by laying stress on Yahweh's acts in history. In any event the 'knowing' is realted to what has taken place in Israel's history. Again, at Micah 6: 5, the prophet calls the people to remember certain incidents, the Exodus, the work of Aaron and Miriam, the plans of Balak and Balaam, 'in order that you may know the triumph of Yahweh'. It is not, of course, that the prophet calls the people to remember these incidents for their own sake, as past history, but for their significance in terms of Yahweh and his choice of Israel and for what is said, taught and understood about them. The thought that Yahweh is in control of events and that what happens takes place because he wishes thereby to reveal his power and presence is something we shall develop more fully a little later when considering knowledge claims relating to future events. But we may illustrate it here with reference to Ezekiel 20: 26. The prophet seems to want to affirm God's sovereign will over his people, even in the evil they perform. Yahweh may use their wrong-doing to bring them to recognize who he is. 'I made them surrender their eldest sons to them (the idols) so that I might fill them with horror. Thus they would know that I am Yahweh.'[22] It has been suggested that this refers back to Exodus 22: 29, understood as a temptation of Yahweh through which he prepares the people for judgement in which he is made known.[23] It may be that Ezekiel so strongly asserts Yahweh's control that he finally attributes Israel's continuing sinfulness to Yahweh's deliberate misleading of his people by giving them evil laws to a greater purpose.[24] Almost out of revulsion the people turn to Yahweh. If this is so then the one who wrote these lines must have had a very strong religious passion for Yahweh. But again, the only point to which I draw attention is that it is perfectly conceivable in the Old Testament that events in history, in people's existence, can be 'evidence' of Yahweh. This theme is present in Ezekiel 20: 1–31. The exiles are admonished for their idolatory and are reminded of the disobedience of their forefathers. The story is told of Yahweh's choice, verse 5, [25] and how he made himself known in the land of Egypt.[26] He further made himself known in bringing them out of Egypt, verse 9, where the stress is on Yahweh acting 'for his name sake'.[27] Again, the deeds of Yahweh are understood to be purposeful, i.e. to make known his will and power.

All of the above are related to events in history, events which count as evidence of Yahweh's presence and power. The evidence is there for all to 'see'. We shall come across a number of instances where 'knowing' and 'seeing' are obviously related concepts. Thus in Psalm 46, after some statements about God, his strength, faithfulness and presence (verses 1–7) there come two verses that begin with the invitation to 'come and see what Yahweh has done' (verse 8). From this there follows the injunction, 'Let be then: learn that I am God', verse 10. It may be a matter of dispute as to whom the words are addressed but the appeal is to look and see and therefore 'know'.[28]

Finally in this section concerned with claims to past events I draw attention to two more personalized incidents. First in 2 Kings 5: 15, after having bathed in the Jordan and been made clean of his leprosy Naaman declares, 'Now I know that there is no god anywhere on earth except in Israel.'[29] For Naaman this is an experience of the power of Israel's God; his cleansing is evidence of that power. A similar appeal to personal experience, though of a less obviously dramatic character, comes from Manasseh. He is in disgrace in Babylon and there prays to Yahweh. As a result, so the account goes, he is brought back to Jerusalem and restored to the throne and 'thus Manasseh learnt that Yahweh was God', 2 Chron. 33: 13.[30] Manasseh was a poor king and the Chronicler makes the inference that between captivity and restoration there stands the prayer of the King and the activity of Yahweh. This activity and experience of Yahweh is the ground for the knowledge claim, although it may be more accurate to understand that it was because Yahweh had brought humiliation through the Assyrians (verse 11) as much as through the repentance and restoration that Manasseh learnt who Yahweh was.

2 Appeals to Future Events

There are a number of passages where there is a straightforward promise of unusual activity, the end of which will be that God is known. The account of the final plague in Egypt is one such. This plague of the first born does not have the same literary pattern as the others.[31] It is asserted that when the plague strikes Egypt, Israel will remain unscathed. 'Thus you shall know that Yahweh does make a distinction between Egypt and Israel', Exodus 11: 7. Who is the 'you' that shall do the knowing? The hebrew text gives the plural, but the Samaritan text and the Septuagint both read the singular form. It seems clear that in verse 8 Moses is addressing Pharoah,[32] and so the most likely meaning is that Moses is declaring the word of Yahweh to Pharoah who will come to know the choice of Yahweh by reason of what is going to happen.

Later in Exodus 16, probably part of the Priestly narrative, [33] there are murmurings against Yahweh. Moses declares (verses 6 and 8) that, in the evening as the people receive the gifts of God and in the morning, as they see the glory of Yahweh accompanying them on their way, they will know that the Exodus from Egypt was the work of Yahweh, verse 6. The repetition of 'evening and morning' suggests the predicted times of the appearing of Yahweh's glory. What is to be 'known' in the provision of food is that Yahweh has done all this, that he has brought the people out of Egypt into the wilderness.

Joshua 3 is an account of the miraculous crossing of the Jordan. In verse 7 the divine commissioning of Joshua as Moses' successor is reaffirmed. The purpose of the miracle is to make it clear that as Yahweh was active through his servant Moses, so now his servant is Joshua. There are 'explicit parallels'[34] between Moses and Joshua as Yahweh chooses a charismatic leader through whom he proposes to guide the people. The miraculous event will let the people know that as Yahweh was with Moses so he will be with Joshua. The event will be ample evidence.

In Judges 6: 11–24 there occurs the story of the call of Gideon and his encounter with the angel of Yahweh.[35] Why then does Gideon later ask for proof of his calling? (Verses 36–40). It may be that Verses 36–40 is the conclusion of Verses 11–17.[36] Or it may be that this is a different account of the call described in Verses 11–17.[37] In any event a miracle is asked for by Gideon as proof of his calling. 'If there is dew only on the fleece and all the ground is dry, then I shall be sure that thou wilt deliver Israel through me, as thou hast promised', verse 37. The miracle happens and is repeated this time with the fleece remaining dry on wet ground. This is the stuff of saga, serving the purpose of emphasizing the power of God in Gideon's enterprise. Again God is conceived of as one who by his action works miracles or signs.

I Samuel 6: 1–9 concerns the return of the Ark to Israel under the guidance of the Philistine priests.[38] The proposed return of the ark is associated with a guilt offering following the plague of rats. It is what would count as the unusual activity of the cows, in going towards Bethlehem rather than returning to their young, that is taken to be a sign that Yahweh has sent the plague upon the Philistines. 'Watch it: if it goes up towards its own territory to Beth-shemesh, then it is Yahweh who has done us this great injury; but if not, then we shall know that his hand has not touched us, but we have been the victims of chance', verse 9. If the cows behave normally there are no theological undertones to the situation, it could have happened to anyone.[39] Such an event, however, could be understood as a sign as an aid to decision.[40] It is of the nature of the simple assertion, 'if this happens, then we shall know'.

Finally among these uses of *yada'* in conjunction with 'unusual events, there is Numbers 16, the account of the death of Dathan and Abiram. It again suggests that a knowledge claim may be confirmed or disproved by following events. The claim in question is that of Moses as Yahweh's messenger. Moses declared that this can be proved. 'This shall prove to you that it is Yahweh who sent me to do all these things, and it was not my own heart that prompted me. If these men die a natural death and share the common fate of man, then Yahweh has not sent me; but if Yahweh makes a great chasm, and the ground opens it mouth and swallows them and all that is theirs, and they do down alive to Sheol, then you will know that these men have held Yahweh in contempt', verses 28–30. The sudden demise of the two doubters will settle the issue not merely in the sense of getting rid of the opposition but in demonstrating Moses' true status. We might ask whether the precise prediction of the miracle in verse 30 belongs entirely to the original form of the narrative or whether the later writer has not wanted to leave the impression that Moses knew everything before it happened.[41] In any event Dathan and Abiram, the two Reubenites, disappeared without trace. (The purpose of the story may simply be to explain their disappearance). This fact, in the account as we have it, following upon the pronouncement of Moses, is taken to be sure proof of the fact that Moses is called of Yahweh. This is something that men may know. The 'proof' is there in history.

There is one particular phrase, occurring in a number of different forms, to which special attention must now be given. The formula occurs often in the Priestly narrative, Deutero-Isaiah and Ezekiel. W. Zimmerli who has made a particular study of this phrase, calls it the 'formula of self-representation', *(Element der Selbstvorstellung)*.[42] The phrase appears in a number of forms. With *yada'* it combines in what Zimmerli calls the 'formula of acknowledgement'

(*Erkenntnisformel*).[43] Although the form may alter, the meaning of the phrase remains consistent in that 'the profession of God occurs only on the basis of his activity in history'.[44] It is not surprising therefore that it should be prominent in the Exodus tradition and with this I begin.

Exodus 6 sees the beginning of the Priestly narrative. It is in verse 7 that there occurs the 'recognition formula', [45] 'You shall know that I, Yahweh, am your God, the God who releases you from your labours in Egypt.' Through the events which will soon take place, Israel is to be led to an understanding of God which at present is beyond her. The coming chain of events is the means of providing that understanding. It is not just that the event will be recognized as Yahweh's action. It is that Yahweh will somehow be recognized in the event and acknowledged as God. It is quite clear, however, in keeping with what I have already indicated, that the historic event is the point of reference in the knowing of Yahweh.

The formula is repeated in Exodus 7: 5. 'When I put forth my power against the Egyptians and bring the Israelites out from them, then Egypt will know that I am Yahweh.' It is a feature of the use of the 'formula' that the knowledge of Yahweh in his deity is not intended for Israel alone. Here the Egyptians will 'know'. The purpose of the plagues (verse 3) is to demonstrate the control Yahweh has of the total situation. His power is over Pharoah who refuses to listen (verse 4) and who hardens his heart against Yahweh, at the instigation of Yahweh, as part of his purpose. Through the coming events the Egyptians will 'learn'[46] that the will and power of Yahweh is supreme, that he alone is worthy of the title 'God'.[47] Exodus 7: 17 against explicitly declares the purpose of the plagues. 'By this you shall know that I am Yahweh.'[48] Now it is Pharoah who will come to know that Yahweh is God by Yahweh's own actions and that is their purpose.[49] The display of power, in the context of Pharoah's present knowledge, will be decisive.

It is part of Zimmerli's argument that the words 'I am Yahweh' are part of a prophetic form. It is for this reason that he associates Ezekiel with the cultic prophets and I shall later indicate that the phrase theologically has a much wider frame of reference than the notion of inference being employed here. Some argue that the phrase's history goes back to an early stage in the development of prophetic speech forms.[50] This may be the case in I Kings 20. In the narrative the prophet, who is unidentified, promises that Benhadad and his army will be overthrown by King Ahab and in this victory ' you shall know that I am Yahweh', verse 13. The overthrow of the Syrians will be an event therefore of theological significance for Israel because it will be an act of Yahweh in which he will reveal his power. The 'formula' is in use again in I Kings 20: 28. Israel is to understand the victory as a new self-manifestation of Yahweh. He alone will be seen to God, both in the hills and the valleys. The victory will be won not by reason of superior military strength but because Yahweh has decided on victory.[51] This is knowledge related therefore to a clear objective sign, namely the defeat of the Syrians.

I return once more to the Exodus story. The Priestly narrative at Exodus 14: 4 reiterates all the emphases already made. 'I will make Pharoah obstinate, and he will pursue them, so that I may win glory for myself at the expense of Pharoah and all his army; and the Egyptians shall know that I am Yahweh.' The sense is given that Yahweh is in control to some great purpose. He hardens Pharoah's heart. He will win glory for himself and Israel and Egypt will recognize whose is the victorious power, who alone is God. The appeal to knowledge is inseparably related to the events of history.

Two references in Deutero-Isaiah continue this theme. Isaiah 45 again indicates events with a purpose. Cyrus the Persian is declared to be Yahweh's anointed. Yahweh will go before him and do great things for him, 'that you may know that I am Yahweh', verse 3. Although it is stated in verses 4 and 5 that Cyrus has not known Yahweh, the full purpose of Yahweh's use of the foreign king is described in verse 6, 'so that men from the rising and the setting sun may know that there is none but I: I am Yahweh, there is no other'. In what is to take place men will recognize the presence and activity of Yahweh, Israel's God, the only one involved in the action. To serve his purpose he uses the king of a foreign power.[52] Whether Cyrus did ever come to acknowledge Yahweh is doubtful but he may be understood as a representative of the great powers of the earth whom Yahweh intends should one day acknowledge him. This is the purpose of the exercise. It is not the 'conversion' of Cyrus that is at stake but that over the whole world men are to know that Yahweh alone is God.[53]

The same forward look is expressed in Isaiah 52: 6.[54] Following a brief recitation of historical events there follows, 'But on that day my people shall know my name; they shall know that it is I who speak; here I am.' 'That day' may refer to the release from Babylon, by which Israel is to recognize and acknowledge again Yahweh's presence and power, or it may refer to some other future event. It is because Yahweh's motives and presence are not recognized that the enemy scoffs. But events to come will change all that.

From the many occurrences of the 'formula' in Ezekiel I shall only draw attention to four here. Where it appears in Ezekiel it is associated with words of judgement. The actions of Yahweh in history, of redemptive judgement, are performed in order that Yahweh may be known for who he is and that his presence and power may be recognized. The 'objective' of God's action is to confer a new knowledge of himself, the recognition of the all-prevailing almightly power and the exclusive rights of the divine Lord.[55]

The hill country sanctuaries which were outlawed in Josiah's reforms of 621 are referred to in Chapter 6 where the 'formula' appears in verses 7, 10, 13 and 14. In the destruction of these sanctuaries, those upon whom the judgement of Yahweh will fall will recognize the terrible delusions of which they have been victims and thereby come and give Yahweh his due.[56] The destruction will reveal the ineffectiveness of the idols, and in contrast, the power of Yahweh. The desolation to come will indicate both the judgement and presence of Yahweh.

In 22: 1–15 the sinful crimes of the people of Jerusalem is evidence that Yahweh is not 'known' by the people. But this living in sin will not continue for ever because Yahweh will act. 'I will sift you in the sight of the nations, and you will know that I am Yahweh', verse 16. There are alternative readings to 'I will sift you' with the meaning of 'I will profane myself', or 'I will let myself be profaned', or 'you will be profaned'. It may indeed be that the profanation involves Yahweh.[57] In contrast to his earlier concern that his name should not be brought into disrepute (20: 9) Yahweh will now allow himself to be shamed in the scattering of his people and the wretchedness of Jerusalem, in order that Israel might realize her wickedness and again acknowledge him as God. The text would then mean that there is no other way of Yahweh to bring his people to know the holiness of his being but by this act of self-sacrifice.[58] The event of judgement would be the vehicle of knowledge. The perspective of Ezekiel goes beyond imminent judgement, however, and I quote two further references which relate to acts of redemption and the final victory of Yahweh. 'These are the words of Yahweh God: O my people, I will open your graves and bring you up from them, and restore you to the land of Israel. You shall know that I am

Yahweh when I open your graves and bring you up from them, O my people', 37: 12ff. In the event of restoration Yahweh will finally be known. His judgement is not the final word. 'They will know that I am Yahweh their God, because I who sent them into exile among the nations will bring them together again on the soil of their own and leave none of them behind' 39: 28.

The phrase 'I am Yahweh' is an important one in the Old Testament. It is not easy to say precisely what it means, but I think that, certainly in the references I have cited, three features are important. First, the phrase has to do with Yahweh's presence. In the assertion of the phrase Yahweh somehow 'presents' himself. Second, the phrase also is related to the recognition of Yahweh in action. Putting it crudely, where the phrase is used it implies that Yahweh is here and he is doing whatever is being done. These two elements are, of course, related for his action is but the expression of his presence. But there is a third consideration that goes beyond this. Although the concept of 'monotheism' is always debatable when applied to the Old Testament, this phrase implies a strong monotheistic emphasis in that it suggests that Yahweh is the only God. The later references to Cyrus would be evidence for this. It may be therefore that the phrase means that Yahweh is the only One, *the* God. It may be, in this sense, that the phrase has an important 'ontological' significance in the Old Testament. Since he is the only one who has any effect, the only one who acts, then Yahweh is the only God who exists. The phrase sometimes is reduced to 'I am he.' It may be that what this means is that he, Yahweh, is the existent one.

Before making a summary statement I shall indicate, as further support for my case that appeals to evidence for God is conceivable in the Old Testament, some references to prayers calling on God to act in order that he may be known. For example, this is a feature of Soloman's prayer in I Kings 8: 59-60. It is a prayer for the blessing of Yahweh, 'so that all the peoples of the earth will know that Yahweh is God'.[59] Elijah's prayer at Mount Carmel is a more direct request for evidence of Yahweh's power; 'At the hour of the regular sacrifice the prophet Elijah came forward and said, "Yahweh God of Abraham, of Isaac, and of Israel let it be known today that thou art God in Israel and that I am thy servant and have done all these things at thy command. Answer me Yahweh, answer me and let this people know that thou, Yahweh, art God and it is thou that hast caused them to be backsliders"', I Kings 18: 36–7. What is at issue here is not just a trial of strength between rival prophets but the question of whether Yahweh or Baal is 'God'.[60] Elijah calls Israel again to her historic status in the covenant relationship by contrasting this faith with the impersonal nature cult of Canaan.[61] The prayer is that in response to Yahweh's act of power the people should again acknowledge and serve him alone, having recognized or 'known' him through the prophet's word and in the consuming of the sacrifice.[62]

Hezekiah's prayer that all the kingdoms of the earth may know that Yahweh alone is God appears in both 2 Kings 19: 19 and Isaiah 37: 20. It is expressed in the conventional language of Temple prayer and is part of an edifying legend concerning the good king Hezekiah. The burden of the prayer is for the deliverance of the people from their enemies, the Assyrians, which will demonstrate Yahweh's supremacy and power over boasted rivals. Such a victorious event will convince any who doubt the claims of Yahweh to be God alone. Psalm 59 also includes a prayer for deliverance from enemies which will reveal Yahweh's power, verse 13. In their destruction by Yahweh the wicked will learn that Yahweh rules in Israel, and even to the ends of the earth. Psalm 67 is a prayer for the realization of God's blessing, not for selfish reasons of national interest or self-preservation but out of a desire to see God's power and authority acknowledged by the whole world.

3 *Inferences from other than History*
All of the above amply demonstrate that there was a clear connection for the Hebrew between the events of history and the knowledge of God. Now I ask whether anything other than history is indicated evidentially as part of the knowledge of God.

As far as the use of *yada'* is concerned the concentration upon history is virtually exclusive. The most obvious sphere from which the existence of God may be inferred one would think would be nature. But this is not a predominant theme at all. The natural world is fully recognized (though not in these very unhebraic terms) but is not used with *yada'* as 'evidence' for God.

The natural world is thought of in the Old Testament as a means of revelation.[63] This is evidenced in Psalm 19 that speaks of the glory of God being 'told out' by the heavens. The psalm is essentially one of praise in which the heavens personified offer adoration to their maker. The 'knowledge' in verse 2 that night shares with night is information secretly passed continually on, 'each night informs the next that there is an almighty creator in the shining of the moon and stars'.[64] This is in no sense a matter of inference, of arguing from the world to God, but rather 'the world proclaims itself before God as a created thing'.[65] In this sense the beauty and order of the world are understood as evidence of Divine power and wisdom, e.g. Psalm 90: 2, Proverbs 8: 22ff etc. That God is the creator and that creation is aware of this is the 'common knowledge' of the Old Testament.

Psalm 135: 5 uses *yada'* and this is followed by reference both to natural and historic events which are understood as the actions of Yahweh. These tell of his greatness. 'Nature' in this sense is not understood as something objective from which inferences may be made. Rather the Old Testament speaks of God active in what we call nature. He rebukes the sea, Psalm 106: 8, he causes waves and winds etc. In this way 'nature' is 'historized'. It is seldom 'personified' as being apart from God, in the same way as 'history' in the Old Testament is not a concept independent of God.

If, however, we look beyond the use of *yada'* then there is more evidence in the Old Testament that God stands behind nature and can use it for his purposes. Amos 5: 8, Job 38, 39, 41, Psalm 104, Isaiah 40: 12, 26, Hosea 2:8 and many other references support this belief. What we do not find in the Old Testament, however, are direct claims to know God based upon the fact of nature by way of inference.

4 Conclusion

What then can be said of claims to know God in the Old Testament where appeal is made to evidence? In summary I shall make five points:

(a) It is quite clear from the above that the Old Testament appeals to history in the matter of the knowledge of God. Certain events are primary data in hebrew religion. Moreover, it is understood in the Old Testament that some future events will have the power to convince, even to prove, that what Israel says about Yahweh is true. The natural world, or rather natural events in history, is also thought of as a vehicle for God making himself known. But it is clearly history rather than what we call 'nature' that is the Israelite's chief interest. This is not to say that Israel was uninterested in creation, for that would be untrue. It is simply to say that the knowledge claims relate more to historic events than to anything else. History, or rather events in history, may be understood as 'evidence' for God. This is an argument used in the Old Testament. To the question 'How do you know Yahweh is a great God?', in so far as he would understand the question, the Israelite would reply 'see what he has done'. The close relation between verbs to see and to know in the text is evidence for this.

(b) However, it is my judgement that the events of history are not used by Israel to infer God's existence at all. It does not seem to me in the cases I have cited with *yada'* that there is any attempt to move from the world or history to God *de novo*. God is presupposed throughout the whole. The one who acts at the Red Sea is already known. So what is inferred is not the existence of one unknown but the characteristics are of one already known, at least to some.

(c) This fact, that God is presupposed throughout whole Old Testament, raises an issue that must be mentioned here, but will be developed later. It is that Israel told the story of her history not so much to prove anything by inference but to instruct. The emphasis on 'teaching' can hardly be over emphasized. Many of the references cited in this chapter could well come in a later chapter on knowledge by description where I shall argue that what the Israelites know of God they know because they were taught these things; Joshua 4: 24 and Psalm 46: 10 would be particularly good illustrations of this point. If it is true to say that the answer to the question 'how do you know Yahweh is God?' is answered by saying 'because of what he has done'; it would also be appropriate within the Old Testament for someone to answer, 'because we have been taught about him'. It is in one sense that teaching makes inferences possible.

(d) Therefore, in the context, although *yada'* may allow the sense of knowing things about God by way of inference from what he has done, it also has the sense of acknowledgement. Such acknowledgement, as I shall go on to show, it not just a matter of intellectual inference making (even if it is that at all), it is a matter of response, worship, obedience, of recogniton that there is no power like Yahweh, no God like him in all the earth.

(e) So the 'knowing' in event, especially when it has a future reference, has also the sense of experiencing. The event will be an experience of Yahweh's power. Remembering the event becomes an encounter situation in which Yahweh is 'met' and known by acquaintance. This would particularly be the case if Zimmerli is right in his analysis of 'the formula of acknowledgement' and of its possible use in the cult. But this is to anticipate my next section.

KNOWING GOD BY ACQUAINTANCE IN THE OLD TESTAMENT

In Chapter 5 I drew attention to the distinction between knowledge by acquaintance and knowledge by description. I argued that the distinction was one between direct and indirect knowledge. To know anyone by acquaintance was to have a direct cognitive awareness of that person. I argued that there was a logical connection between knowledge by acquaintance and knowledge by description but that what knowledge by acquaintance means could never be reduced to knowledge by description however accurate and comprehensive the description might be. The experience of knowing by acquaintance was always beyond description.

So knowledge by acquaintance is personal, but not private. The experience of being acquainted is not transferable but can in some part be described. Knowing by acquaintance admits of development and degree. Those who make claims to know by acquaintance are therefore claiming personal cognitive awareness of someone. They claim that because of the experience they have had they 'just know' the one with whom they claim to be acquainted.

Now my question is, 'Are there any claims to know God in the Old Testament that are of this nature?'. I shall argue that the answer is 'Yes'.

I begin by departing from my practice of citing references with *yada'* and indicate three passages where the concept of God is such that an encounter between God and man is experienced. First there is the call of Moses, Exodus 3: 1–6. As we have the story, God identified himself as the God of the Fathers and began to give Moses his charge. The story implies that an encounter took place between Moses and Yahweh. The second incident is the call of Isaiah. Here Isaiah claims to have seen Yahweh. It is for this reason that he is in despair. What is described for us in account in Isaiah

6 is an experience of God, again an encounter. Third comes another prophet's call, Jeremiah 1: 41–50. As we have the story, a conversation with God takes place and Yahweh is again conceived of as one who meets and communicates with his chosen servant.

If it is objected that I have drawn attention to rather special passages I reply by saying, first, that I shall give further evidence by referring to less spectacular and individualistic encounters with God. But second, all I wish to show is that the Old Testament does think of God as one who encounters men, with the result that they might say they just know him. God is conceived of as one who speaks, who calls and commands. The naïvete of the form of such stories should not blind us to the essential concepts underlying them which testify to the biblical conviction 'that God may be known to men because he desires to be known and because he has chosen to reveal himself to them'.[66]

Now I turn to further claims using *yada'* where, in some cases, an intense experience of Yahweh is indicated. Such an experience may come in the form of a dream as Jacob had at Bethel, Genesis 28: 10–19.[67] The story has the form of a sanctuary foundation legend indicating to the reader the correct understanding of a particular place and its significance.[68] The dream is of a ladder from earth to heaven with angels ascending and descending and Yahweh standing by. Clearly the dream is understood to be an encounter of some kind with God but the eventual confession of Jacob is 'Truly Yahweh is in this place, and I did not know it.' The stress in the story is not on the form of the appearance of Yahweh but upon the words spoken.[69] The purpose of the story is not in the first instance to establish that Jacob 'knows' Yahweh but relates to its form as an aeteological sanctuary foundation legend. It is thus understood that here Jacob met Yahweh and that it is at Bethel that Yahweh can be 'met' again. It is an encounter that takes place but the form of the meeting is played down in the sense that there is no description of Yahweh. We shall have cause to note again the carefulness of language used in such incidents.

Another encounter is recorded in Judges 13, the entire chapter being given over to the story of the birth of Samson. The angel of Yahweh appears to Manoah and his wife although at first he is seen only as a man (verse 16). It is only later when the angel disappears in the flame of the offering that Manoah knew that he was the angel of Yahweh, verse 21. The crucial question, as far as this book is concerned is, are the Angel of Yahweh and Yahweh identical in such wise that for anyone to have met the Angel of Yahweh, as Manoah did, they must have met Yahweh himself?

Opinions vary among scholars on this issue. Some argue that the Angel is the visible manifestation of Yahweh,[70] that his appearance denotes the appearance of God Himself in human form.[71] Others stress the Angel's role as one through whom Yahweh communicates with mankind, although to see him is as dangerous as seeing Yahweh himself because he is virtually indistinguishable from Yahweh.[72] A. R. Johnson offers as the reason why the Angel is frequently indistinguishable from Yahweh Himself 'the oscillation as between the individual and the corporate unit with the conception of God'.[73] Thus Johnson argues that Manoah was confronted by an extension of Yahweh's complex personality. However, it is important to notice again the veiled nature of Yanweh's appearing.

It is my opinion that the form of the story is such that an encounter between Yahweh and Manoah and his wife is described. In this sense the Old Testament can understand a direct communication between Yahweh and people. It is not the case that Yahweh is invisible but that it is dangerous to see him and that only to special persons or for special purposes does he make himself visible.[74] In this sense the story has a hidden meaning and the initiated would know the answer to Manoah's question, 'What is your name?' (verse 17).

The Angel again appears in Numbers 22, the story of Balaam's ass. The repeated insistance of Balaam that he must obey Yahweh and not speak without learning what Yahweh has to say to him is of importance because, and this may be part of the point of the story, Balaam is a foreigner who clearly was held in high esteem as one of Israel's neighbours who nonetheless acknowledged Yahweh. In the story Yahweh's messenger appears in human form but is not recognized by Balaam. The ass sees the angel and by the action of Yahweh speaks to Balaam. This miracle of Yahweh indicates how directly and unusually he acts in the affair. Balaam recognizes Yahweh because Yahweh opens his eyes. It is therefore an encounter but the story includes no claim to know Yahweh other than the original presupposition that Balaam acknowledges Yahweh and seeks to be obedient to his will.

The emphasis in these stories is not so much on Yahweh revealing himself in personal relation as of making clear or confirming his will or promise. Although there is an identity between Yahweh and the Angel it is important to note it is the angel, the anthropomorphic form, that is mentioned. This may well indicate a certain reserve in the Old Testament about all speech of meeting Yahweh or Yahweh revealing himself and that therefore the communication of his will and word is in a form that preserves his separateness. The fact that the form of communication may seem to us unreal and incredible, e.g. Yahweh making Balaam's ass speak, is of no immediate concern. It may not 'fit' our thinking, but there is 'a cohesion of Old Testament thought on such matters',[75] and this relates to the concepts of God and his relationship to the world that are employed in the Old Testament.

Direct communication from Yahweh appears again in the call of Samuel. There was a time when Samuel 'had not yet come to know Yahweh', I Samuel 3: 7. Those were the days when the word of Yahweh was seldom heard and no vision was granted (verse 1). Eli, out of his experience and perception, is able to tell Samuel what is happening when he hears the voice and what is the appropriate response. Samuel could only imagine one source of the voice since he had had no experience himself of communication from God. Therefore we may understand that knowing Yahweh in this sense means an experience of a disclosure of the word of Yahweh.[76] Hearing the word of Yahweh is the most significant concept in the passage.[77] Knowing Yahweh means both Yahweh's readiness to speak and human readiness to listen and, as I shall later emphasize, obey.

This is primarily a case then of hearing the word of Yahweh. As such it is part of a 'tradition' in the Old Testament where, as I have already indicated, certain men of God, e.g. Moses, Gideon, Samson, Isaiah, Jeremiah etc. are called to a special obedience. To the chosen there is given this more direct experience of God.

This is not simply the case with Samuel but illustrates something important in the Old Testament concept of God and of what constitutes knowledge of God. Theophanies and dreams are of great importance in the Old Testament. But, although there is an emphasis on seeing, there is little attempt made at description and the main emphasis is upon the words uttered. Two features are predominant in all the cases I have cited, i.e. the encounter with Yahweh and the hearing of his word. 'Knowing Yahweh' in these cases therefore involves encounter with Yahweh, may even involve seeing someone, but certainly concerns the hearing of his word.

As well as these theophanies and special cases of 'calls' there are other references where claims are made to know God directly. First,

three references in Deuternomy. In 11: 2 the claim 'This day you
know the discipline of Yahweh' begins a recital of history. It is
typical of the Deuteronomistic approach that the story of God's acts
in history is told for its educational aspect.[78] Here *yada'* means
'experience'. The 'knowing' refers to the experience which the
people of Israel have lived through, experience of the almighty acts
of God. They are acquainted with the action and education of
Yahweh. Memory is a source of knowledge by acquaintance. By
telling the story they educate their children and themselves. 'Knowing' for the Hebrews means experiencing the difference anything
makes and they are acquainted with the difference Yahweh has
made. In the story the next generation is acquainted with Yahweh
also.

In 11: 28 the appeal is to past experience. Israel is called to remain
loyal to Yahweh and not to follow other gods 'whom you do not
know'. This does not refer to any possible agnosticism. It is, in the
context, a reference to gods Israel have not experienced and which
therefore have no claim upon Israel's obedience. These gods are in
no way part of Israel's past. It is, however, part of Israel's history
that they did turn aside and did acknowledge the gods of their
neighbours, 32: 17, 'gods whom your fathers did not acknowledge'.
Does this mean 'gods with whom your fathers had never been
acquainted?' I suggest that this is an appropriate reading. The
emphasis is on the history through which Israel has lived. The
history has been dominated by the action of Yahweh and in that
history the other gods have had no active part. In that sense they
have not been experienced or known. What Israel is acquainted
with is the acts of Yahweh in history as these references from
Deuteronomy stress.

Other passengers may be cited of a similar nature, stressing something of Yahweh or from Yahweh that the people have or are
experiencing.

First, in Psalm 89: 15, 'happy the people who have learnt to
acclaim thee, who walk, Yahweh, in the light of thy presence'.
Some scholars[79] suggest that the 'knowing' involves knowing the
festal shout in worship, i.e. the people know what to say and how
to participate in the cult. On the other hand it may mean more
than knowing this. It may also involve the experience of being
overwhelmed by the goodness and majesty of Yahweh.[80] If this
were so then it would reflect some sense of encounter with Yahweh
that leads to recognition and praise. Those who so respond know

God's favour, they walk in the light of his presence. The experience of worship would be an experience of encounter as Yahweh manifested his presence in the cult.

There are five other passages to which I wish to draw attention that shed further light on any possible knowledge of God by acquaintance in the Old Testament. The first of these comes from one of the 'Trial Speeches' of Yahweh, calling the nations to court with their gods. 'My witnesses, says Yahweh, are you, my servants, you whom I have chosen to know me and put your faith in me and understand that I am He', Isaiah 43: 10. Does 'know' here mean acquaintance? C. Westerman implies that it does when he asserts that 'what the prophet has in mind is a fully personal knowledge such as comes only from encounter'.[81] The basis of this assertion is the argument that 'that I am He' is a cry made in personal encounter whose significance depends in each case on the circumstances. The present circumstances are defeat and exile for the Israelites. But the promise of Yahweh is that he can and will act to build a future out of the ruins of the past. That He can do this is what Israel is to know, have faith in and understand. 'Wherever Israel knows that God is truly God, she may become his witness: for the one thing which she is to attest is that she has encountered the God who is truly God.'[82]

This is not quite the emphasis in Jeremiah 31: 34. In the time of the new covenant which Yahweh will make with Israel – 'no longer need they teach one another to know Yahweh; all of them, high and low alike, shall know me says Yahweh'. The emphasis here is upon the covenant relationship in which each man will do God's will from his heart.[83] This does not mean a highly personalised religion as some have suggested Jeremiah introduced.[84] New Covenant it may be but it is still made with Israel in which *all* shall know Yahweh. There is of course a strong stress on 'inwardness' and a going beyond just outward conformity to the tradition. Yet the result is not individual relationships with Yahweh, 'but all men in the covenant community will live in the personal knowledge that Yahweh is their Lord'.[85] The outlook of the prophet is eschatological, an increasingly important feature in the Old Testament concept of the knowledge of God. The new covenant is a convenient name for the creation of a new type of man.[86] But I suggest the emphasis remains on acknowledgement and obedience expressed in the phrase 'I will become their God and they shall become my people.' Knowing Yahweh means understanding this and obeying Yahweh's will. What the prophet looks forward to is the day when this will describe the life of all men.

Two texts from Hosea follow on this theme. In 2: 20 there is the promise 'I will betroth you to myself to have and to hold, and you shall know Yahweh.' The language is that of wedlock, personal and intimate. But it is between Yahweh and the people. 'Knowing Yahweh' is what is expected of the covenant people, the whole response of Israel to the acts and words of Yahweh. Again the outlook is eschatological. As H.W. Wolff says . . .

The outcome expected from Yahweh's payment of the bridal price is described: Israel will acknowledge him as the generous Lord of her life. *Yada'* should be interpreted in view of its other uses in Hosea; what Yahweh has painfully felt to be absent in Israel (2: 10, 15; 4: 1, 6; 6: 6) shall be no longer. Now there will be acknowledgement of and thankful response to Yahweh's gifts.

His covenant relationship with Israel, which was to have been legally abrogated as a result of Israel's separation from God (2: 4) would be restored by Yahweh's eschatological action and again become legally binding in all respects.[87]

The other text from Hosea I wish to comment on at this moment is 13: 4. 'But I have been Yahweh your God since your days in Egypt, when you knew no other saviour than me, no god but me.' This is part of an oracle of judgement leading up to the specific accusation in verse 6 – 'and so they forgot me'. 'Know' here again means experience. Israel's history is the revelation that Israel has no other God because no other helper has been part of her history, there has been no *experience* of the benefits and presence of another.[88]

Finally, one further reference where Moses is described as being in conversation with Yahweh. Exodus 33, following the story of the Golden Calf, faces the problem of how Yahweh can go on with this sinful people. The issue is one of sin and atonement. It has been suggested that in verses 12–17 we have an ancient liturgy with Moses as the intercessor.[89] The crux of the matter is 'if your presence will not go, do not make us go forth from here'.

Verse 13, is part of Moses' prayer. 'If I have indeed won thy favour, then teach me to know thy way, so that I can know thee and continue in favour with thee, for this nation is thy own people.' It seems that what Moses is requesting is covenant knowing, a mutuality of the knowing relationship between Yahweh and Moses.

Yahweh's 'knowing' of Moses means his choice of Moses. Moses asks to know Yahweh's ways so that he can know him. This is a step in obedience, a covenant response after the pattern of that already indicated in Hosea. It is not just a personal knowing that is involved for the request ends 'for this nation is thy own people'. So again there is the emphasis that knowing the ways of God and also his demands is part of what the Old Testament means by knowing God,[90] but the story further illustrates the concept of personal relationship between God and man that the Old Testament conceives of as perfectly possible.

Is there then any sense in which we can speak of knowledge of God by acquaintance in the Old Testament? As I said earlier, my answer to the question is a qualified 'yes', and I suggest the texts I have cited are evidence for that claim.

It does seem to me that the Old Testament assumes some direct communication between man and God and God and man. The theophanies to which I have drawn attention are evidence of that. However, the qualification is that such experiences of God are described in careful veiled terms that 'play down' any thought of a person to person encounter and stress rather the command of God to which men are required to be obedient.

Yet I suggest there is person to person encounter implied in these passages. Although the emphasis is upon hearing the word of Yahweh, it is not just the case that a message is given. There is also an emphasis on 'seeing' and on 'seeing someone' in these stories. It is a moment of encounter.

It is part of the bible story that to certain individuals, for specific purposes, Yahweh makes known his presence and his will. Again the caution is there because we go too far if we suggest that Yahweh revealed himself at Sinai, or Bethel, or in the Temple at Jerusalem, if by revelation we mean full self disclosure. There is a hiddenness of God in such incidents. This may indicate something important about the nature of God, the experience and concept of God operating in the Old Testament. But it is enough to be cautious about any unqualified talk of knowing God by acquaintance in the Old Testament. 'Knowing Yahweh' after all is not quite the same as having direct knowledge of another person and this is recognized in the Old Testament.

All of the above assumes that the philosophical distinction between knowledge by acquaintance and knowledge by description stands. It assumes that there is something over and above knowing someone that is more than expressible in our description of the various effects they have upon us. I shall examine this issue in the final chapter. My purpose of raising at least some doubt about the distinction at this point arises from the fact that, what is understood to be experience of God in some of the passages I have cited in this chapter, is inconceivable without those who have had the experience having previously been taught about God. As I have said before in any proper understanding of the Old Testament the importance of teaching cannot be over-emphasized. Teaching involves the passing on of knowledge, knowledge by description.

Therefore, although I suggest that the Old Testament does conceive of the possibility of direct communication between God and man, indeed it asserts that it happens, experience of God involves being part of a community where God is already known, by description. And it is learning what is known that enables anyone to participate in the life and worship of God's people, therein to experience God.

I turn therefore to knowing God by description.

KNOWLEDGE OF GOD BY DESCRIPTION IN THE OLD TESTAMENT

The contrast I drew earlier between knowledge by acquaintance and knowledge by description I suggested was the contrast between direct and indirect knowledge. I argued that knowledge by acqaintance was foundational of knowledge by description in the sense that whatever was to be described had first to be known by someone as a matter of acquaintance. Knowledge by acquaintance involves being aware of someone directly. When we express what we know, we do so in descriptive terms. Knowledge by description is important because it allows us to pass beyond the confines of our own experience. It is something we can share with others and their descriptions of what they know by acquaintance adds to our knowledge.

In the previous section I argued that there are instances in the Old Testament of people knowing God by acquaintance. They encounter his presence or hear his word, see visions or receive 'messengers'. Now I ask whether there is knowledge of God by description in the Old Testament. I shall argue that there is.

If fact, when we come to the question of knowledge by description in the Old Testament we come to a very important aspect of the knowledge of God. All that the Old Testament says about God is knowledge by description. It gives accounts of what might be called 'encounter situations' but necessarily whoever is known by acquaintance in such situations is described in the telling of the story. Many of these 'encounter situations' are remembered and retold for their 'educational' value. I have already drawn attention to the importance of education in Israel. It is basically in what I have called indirect knowledge, or knowledge by description, that the people of Israel learned who God was and how they were related to him. I shall return to this point later.

It is as well to remember that the concept of God in the Old Testament is many sided. This is not surprising considering the wide span of history covered in the Old Testament story and the many experiences through which the people of Israel went which are inseparable from their understanding of God. So, as I shall illustrate, there are many different things said about God by way of description. Sometimes a particular way of speaking about God is modified or abandoned. Certainly, by way of contrast, some things popularly said about God are denied by the prophets as being incorrect statements about God. It is not my purpose to say whether these descriptions are true or false, even if that were possible. All I wish to indicate is that there are some things it makes sense to say about God in the Old Testament because these are understood by the people of Israel accurately to describe the one who is their God. Conversely there are some things that are not said, or cannot be said, of God because he is not like that in the tradition and thought of the Old Testament concerning God.

In my discussion of theophanies in the previous section, I drew attention to the fact that very little attempt was made at all to describe the person encountered in the experience. However, it is the case that, where any reference to what is seen is made, the form perceived is that of a man.[91] This may not surprise us since if the Israelite's view of himself was as 'higher' than the animals the 'form' of God could scarcely be less than human. However, to say this is perhaps to indulge twentieth century rationalism. As I argued, the theophanies must be understood not simply in terms of the words spoken but a full recognition of the claim to have *seen* someone. In any event, the way of speaking of God anthropomorphically is more prominent in the earlier writings of the Old Testament and, although it is modified,

it is never completely abandoned. [92] In certain passages God is conceived of, or perceived as, having the form of a man. He has eyes
(Ps. 33: 18), ears (Ps. 18: 6), hands (I Sam. 5:11), feet (Deut. 33: 3) etc.
In the theophany described in Exodus 33, Moses is not permitted to
see Yahweh's face, but he can see his back (verse 23).

Along with the above we must set the anthropopathisms of the
Old Testament. God can be angry (Ps. 7: 11), he can repent (Jer.
26: 19) he can hate (Isa. 1: 14), he can love (Jer. 31: 3) etc .

These are ways in which the Old Testament speaks about God,
with the features and feelings of a man. But it would be quite wrong
to imagine that these references alone constituted a description of
God in the Old Testament. For, along with this anthropomorphic
way of speaking there went the insistence that God is God and not
man, Hos. 11: 9. There was the clear injunction that there was to
be no image making, no attempts made at depicting God, Exod.
20: 4. Thus we must understand that there are imposed limits on
anthropomorphic language in the Old Testament. It is acknowledged that there is an essential dissimilarlity between God and
man.

So there are other ways of talking about God, other things that
can be said about him, in the Old Testament. These reflect what
we might call his transcendence, the fact that if Yahweh is known
at all it is because 'he comes to the world from his secrecy'. [93]

Thus God is holy (Isa. 6: 3), he is the living God (Ps. 42: 2; Jer.
10: 10), he has no equal (Isa. 40: 25), there is no god like Yahweh
(Isa. 41: 4), he is one in his being (Deut. 6:4), he is eternal (Gen.
21: 34; Ps. 90: 2), he is the fountain of life (Ps. 36: 9) and his ways
are not as man's ways (Isa. 55: 9). He is omniscient (Jer. 16: 17; Job
34: 21–2) and omnipresent (Psalm 139: 7–12).

God is conceived of as a personal being (I Sam. 17: 26; 36). He
is wrathful against the heathen (Zeph. 3: 8) and also on occasion
against Israel (Is. 5: 25; Num. 25: 11). Yahweh is Israel's God (Is.
45: 3) who marches at the head of armies (Num 10: 35ff; I Sam. 17:
45). He is the *ba'al* of his people (Isa. 54: 5).

He is the only God (Isa. 43: 10), God of Gods (Isa. 44: 5). He is
the creator (Isa. 40: 12), maker of heaven and earth (Gen. 2: 4) and
all mankind (Gen. 2: 7; Job 4: 17). He is Lord of nature (Isa. 41:
18–20), he grants rain (Deut. 28: 12), commands winds and waves
(Exod. 14: 21), performs miracles (Isa. 42: 18), directs the course of
history (Is. 40: 23–4). He is almighty (Gen. 17: 1; Exod. 6: 3) the
most high (Gen. 14: 18), the Ancient of Days (Dan. 7: 9) and nothing

is too hard for him (Jer. 32: 27). He is also known as Father (Deut. 32: 6; Jer. 3: 4; Mal. 1:6; Ps. 68: 5).

All of the above is part of the Old Testament 'picture' of God, illustrating some of the ways in which he is conceived. To have been taught these things is to know Israel's God by description. These particular descriptions are not cast in the form of knowledge claims, they do not use *yada'*. For this reason I shall conclude this section with reference to claims to knowledge by description where the verb 'to know' is used.

First, Exodus 6: 3, 'God spoke to Moses and said, 'I am Yahweh. I appeared to Abraham, Isaac and Jacob as God Almighty. But I did not let myself be known to them by my name Jehovah'. This is an encounter situation that is described, it being the Priestly account of the call of Moses. The giving of the new name is to be understood as a new disclosure. Something more and very important is known *about* God. God was already known. But now more is known and the giving of the name means a new revelation.[94]

Other instances using *yada'* are Psalm 48: 3, part of a festival psalm celebrating the saviour of Zion, where God is known as or for a tower of strength. I have already mentioned Is. 45: 3 where Yahweh is in conversation with Cyrus and is described as 'Israel's God' and the one who calls Cyrus by name.[95] Israel is said to know Yahweh's greatness (Deut. 11: 3), his fame (I Kgs. 8: 43), that God tests the heart and plain honesty pleases him (I Chron. 29: 17). Job knows that God will not hold him innocent (9: 28) and Zophar knows that God exacts from you less than sin deserves (Job 11: 6). In his heart Job knows that his vindicator lives (19: 25) and that God can do all things, which means he is unique (42: 1).

The psalmist knows that God is on his side (56: 9). He can pray that his enemies should know that Yahweh is God most high over all the earth, something he presumably knows himself (83: 18). He knows Yahweh's decrees are just (119: 75), again that Yahweh is great, above all gods (135: 5) and that he will give the needy their due and justice to the down-trodden (140: 12).

All of these passages are part of the concept of God in the Old Testament. They are what it makes sense to say of him and form the ground for contradicting those who say otherwise, what it does not make sense to say of Yahweh (Isa. 29: 15). These passages I submit 'describe' God in the Old Testament. He is not described as any thing in the world is described, for part of the Old Testament understanding of God is such that although he acts in the world he is not part of his creation. This has been well expressed by R. de Vaux when he says, 'Yahweh was a God who could not be seen and therefore could not be represented. This does not mean he was thought of as purely spiritual being (such words would mean nothing to the Hebrew mind). It is recognition of transcendence.'[96] This point is echoed in the Old Testament concept of God as hidden (Isa. 45: 15; Ps. 89: 46). But to know this is to know something about God, and this is part of the description of God who is known in the Old Testament.

I return to the important point I made earlier by drawing attention again to the concept of *Torah* in the Old Testament and the obvious importance given to teaching in the Jewish religion. The teaching given was more than moral and liturgical instruction, more than history. It was the story of God's way with his people, the disclosure of his will and purposes, the claims he made, the choice he made. There was a content to Israel's theology, a description of god as he was known. This description, like the objective knowledge described by Sir Karl Popper,[97] was independent of every Jew, yet the inheritance of every Jew.

To be taught these things about God was to have knowledge of God. It is understood in the Old Testament that there is much more to 'knowing God' than just being able to speak about God within the tradition. But, as I shall comment upon later, it is this knowledge, rather than any particular 'acquaintance experiences', that is foundational for most of the people of Israel. Indeed there is an important logical sense in which unless they are taught these things about God experiences of God will be denied to them.

KNOWLEDGE AND OBEDIENCE

Knowing God in the Old Testament means acknowledgement of Yahweh, Israel's God. This 'acknowledgement' involves worship, service and obedience. It is this fact to which I wish to draw attention now. We have already seen that, although 'knowing God' for the Old Testament person was an intellectual matter, it was not that alone; 'Knowing God' was also a practical affair. In this sense 'knowing' was living in a particular way according to particular beliefs, insights and convictions. Thus knowing Yahweh in the Old Testament involves obeying Yahweh, and it follows from disobedience that God is not known.

This is straightforwardly illustrated by reference to Jeremiah 22: 16. The passage is part of a judgement against Jehoiakim who was indulging himself while the nation is weak. His father lived more simply and in other ways fulfilled his obligations to God. Thus, 'He dispensed justice to he lowly and poor; did this not show he knew me? says Yahweh'. Here the knowledge of God is seen as a moral rather than intellectual matter. 'In ancient Israel, knowledge that did no issue in appropriate action was not true knowledge at all; genuine knowledge involved the whole of a man's personality – his mind, his feelings, and his deeds.'[98]

This is further illustrated in Psalm 36: 10. 'Maintain thy love unfailing over those who thee, and they justice towards men of honest heart'. The parallelism of the verse suggests that those who know God are men of honest heart. Certainly 'those who know thee' would include those who recognize Yahweh's authority. A number of scholars suggest that this is the terminology of covenant.[99] One has drawn attention to the use of *yada'* in ancient near eastern covenants.[100] He shows that the sense of acknowledgement and obligation is fundamental to the use of *yada'* in such contexts. Whether in fact it does have such technical usage in the Old Testament is not vital to the point that knowing does include obeying, recognition and worship. The experience of living in covenant relationship with God, accepting and fulfilling all the obligations involved is an essential content and descriptive of what knowing God in the Old Testament means.

The covenant obligation is evidence in the use of *yada'* in connection with exhortations to keep the Sabbath. In Exodus 31: 13 the Sabbath is described as a sign that in every generation Israel may know that it is Yahweh who hallows them. The same theme occurs in Ezekiel 20: 12 and 20. The Sabbath took on increasing inportance during the exile as a means of preserving religious identity. Participating in a form of life that acknowledged Yahweh in deed and word is part of what keeping covenant means and of what knowing God means.

In this sense doing evil, disobeying God's will, disregarding the covenant claims, is a matter of not knowing God. For example, 'Eli's sons were scoundrels and had no regard for Yahweh', I Samuel 2: 12. They were poor priests who were concerned not with the correct performance of their office but with their own profit. They were indifferent to their responsibility to God and to those who looked to them for teaching and instruction. It is obvious from their actions that they do not know God. Failure to acknowledge Yahweh that expresses itself in wickedness is described in Jeremiah 9: 3, 6 and, in the language of the wisdom literature, in 4: 22. Psalm 79: 6, Exodus 5: 2, Hosea 8: 1–3 are other references that support this point that knowing and obeying Yahweh are allied if not almost identical activities. There cannot be one without the other. But as F. G. Downing comments 'This is not the same as saying, "If you 'know' God, you will obey him"; it is that the only way to "know God" is to obey him in your dealings with people and things, and in the manner of your worship.'[101] It is in this sense that 'knowing God' in the Old Testament is a very practical matter.

All of this suggests that there is a proper 'attitude' required for the knowing of God. This is indicated further in Isaiah 11: 2, 'the spirit of Yahweh shall rest upon him, a spirit of wisdom and under-standing a spirit of counsel and power, a spirit of knowledge and the fear of Yahweh'. The combination of knowledge and reverence suggest that a right relationship and awareness of God is required. 'The knowledge of God means to "cease" from idolatory and sin, to "turn" to Yahweh and to "seek" him, to "adhere" to him, and "fear" him; it means to exercise love, justice and righteousness.'[102]

In Proverbs 1: 7 the fear of Yahweh is declared to be the beginning or chief part of knowledge, but fools scorn wisdom and discipline. The phrase, 'the fear of Yahweh is the beginning of knowledge', appears, with minor variations four other times in the wisdom literature, Proverbs 9: 10; 15: 33, Psalm 111: 10 and Job 28: 28. Von Rad suggests that 'the fear of Yahweh' essentially means 'simply obedience to the divine will'.[103] Without reverence for Yahweh and submission to his will there can be no acquisition of wisdom. Thus the 'fear of Yahweh' does not mean being afraid but rather living in an attitude of awe and reverent submission to Yahweh. It means, in this sense, being religious and this is the prerequisite for know-ledge of God, which is more than adopting an attitude, it has to do also with understanding.

A consequence of this is that faith is not seen as in any way inferior or in opposition to knowledge in the Old Testament. 'On the contrary, it is what liberates knowledge, enables it really to come to the point and indicates to it its proper place in the sphere of varied, human activity.'[104] Faith is not so obviously a prominent concept in the Old Testament as it is in the New Testament. It does,

however, carry the sense both of fear and trust. It is response to
God. Thus faith, obedience, acknowledgement and knowledge of
God are all related.

In summary of all this, I have left until now the concept of the
knowledge of God in Hosea. I have done this because the theme
of the knowledge of God is a central one in Hosea and his use of
the phrase expresses and contains much of what has gone before
in this study. I shall examine six references in order to illustrate
what is involved.

Hosea 4: 1 'Hear the word of Yahweh, O Israel: for Yahweh has
a charge to bring against the people of the land. There is no good
faith or mutual trust, no knowledge of God in the land.' The prophet
then gives his evidence for this claim in the wickedness of the
people (verse 2). The case against Israel here is sins of omission;
neither faithfulness, nor devotion nor knowledge describe the
people. Elsewhere in Hosea the content of the knowledge of God
is outlined. J. L. Mays has suggested it has three features.'[105]

1   Yahweh as he was revealed in the Exodus is their only God,
13: 4;
2   His healing help saw the people through the history of their
beginnings, their wanderings in the wilderness, 12: 3;
3   It is Yahweh who gives the people the good things of the
land, 2: 8.

All this is denied by Israel in her going after the Baals. But to
know Yahweh is for Hosea to have faith. It is to be obedient and
keep covenant. But by their actions the people declare there is no
knowledge of God in the land.

It is this lack of knowledge that is the ruination of the people,
4: 6. The priests in particular are at fault here in that they did not
pass on this knowledge in instruction and therefore the people
have lost any sense of the reality of being the covenant people.
Hosea did not argue for the abolition of the priesthood, only that
the priests should mind their business for the good of the people.
Tragically it is Israel's false leaders who have finally separated her
from God, 5: 4. 'To know Yahweh' is Hosea's basic formula for the
relationship which Israel ought to have to its God under the covenant. Because she has not been properly taught, her return to Yahweh
(whom she no longer knows) is impossible because of her current
way of life.

There is a call to repentance in 6: 3, 'let us humble ourselves, let us strive to know Yahweh.'[106] It is what Yahweh requires of Israel. The scene is probably that of the Syrian–Ephraimite war and the peoples desperation is expressed in this time of danger. Verses 4–6 comes as a divine oracle, answering the song. In 6: 6 Yahweh declares, 'Loyalty is my desire, not sacrifice, not whole offering but the knowledge of God.' It appears that the people have not failed to respond absolutely. They do offer sacrifices. But this is not what God requires.[107] Loyalty is much more important to him, loyalty that expresses itself in obedience. This knowledge of God means an unqualified response to Yahweh as he was revealed in the Exodus and wilderness and the obedience which hears and obeys his instruction. Knowing is in this sense a state of being.[108]

With the Assyrian foe at the door the people cry for help, 8: 2. 'They cry to me for help: "We know thee, God of Israel". But Israel is utterly loathsome.' They cry out in the cult, but the point is that they do not know God and even in her prayers of lamentation Israel's misunderstanding of the knowledge of God shows itself.[109]

Those references from Hosea serve as a summary of what I have indicated of the Old Testament sense of knowing God as a whole form of life and being. It rests on the covenant love of God. It is expressed in obedience. It therefore means teaching and instruction. As H. McKeating puts it,[110] 'The Knowledge of God is a very comprehensive and rich phrase. It involves piety, the proper fulfilment of religious duties. It involves uprightness of moral life, probity, both at an individual and social level, and it involves spirituality, i.e. an inward conviction of the reality of God. Knowledge of God is something that can be taught. It is taught by giving instruction about the terms of the covenant; by reciting or explaining the law in which they are embodied; and by recounting the saving acts of God on which the covenant rests'.

SUMMARY

As I indicated in the introduction to this chapter it has been in no way my intention to offer a full account of the concept of the knowledge of God in the Old Testament. I wished to do only what I have done, namely to explore the various forms of 'knowing' to which I drew attention in Chapters 3–9, and to enquire whether they are present in the Old Testament with reference to God. I have shown that this is the case. I do not claim to have expounded *the* Old Testament concept of the knowledge of God; that would require a quite different study though not unrelated to the issues raised in this section.

My purpose, therefore, in this brief concluding passage is to draw attention to five features of the discussion whose particular significance will be seen in the argument of the final chapter:

1. Whereas we have found forms of inferential knowledge, i.e. claims that appeal to evidence, in the Old Testament, we have not found any attempted proof of the existence of God. The fact is that for the Old Testament as a whole, the existence of God is a conscious postulate that needs no proof. As such, being so fundamental, the existence of God requires no demonstration. The concept of God is just 'given' in the whole story.

2. In this above sense, therefore, God is always 'known' in the Old Testament. He 'controls' the story. All that happens, is said or done, takes place in an inescapable relationship to God. Thus although God is not inferred from anything else, the Old Testament makes inferences concerning God and his relationship to the world. Again, on the question of knowing by acquaintance, the encounters with God described in the Old Testament are not experiences of someone quite unknown but of one already 'known'. It is in this fundamental sense that Israel is acquainted with Yahweh, in this sense he is 'just known'.

3. So the whole of the Old Testament is lived out in the conscious or unconscious recognition of this concept, or better, in the presence of God. As we have seen, 'knowing God' therefore includes acknowledgement, obedience, worship, etc. Knowing God might be described as sharing a form of life. It is both intellectual, experiential and practical.

4. For this reason the cult and participation in acts of worship is an important feature both in the sense that in this way the people come to 'know' Yahweh as he manifests his presence and in the sense that participation in the cult and obedience to the *Torah* in life is part of what knowing God means. The whole concept of *Torah* and teaching in Israel's life can hardly be over emphasized. Knowledge of God in the Old Testament means knowledge of Israel's God. Hence the stress on history, tradition and the necessity of instruction.

5.   There is one feature of knowing God in the Old Testament to which I have not drawn attention. It is the fact that increasingly in the Old Testament the full knowledge of God is part of Israel's future hope. It is not permitted to men now and becomes part of Old Testament eschatology. The full revelation of God and his glory, as far as the Old Testament is concerned, is yet to come.

11

The Knowledge of God in the New Testament

In this chapter I shall examine a number of claims to know God in the New Testament. My approach will be similar to that which I have just taken on the Old Testament, namely to ask whether there are in the New Testament claims to know God by inference, by acquaintance, by description, and to ask whether there is any relationship between knowledge and obedience in the New Testament that corresponds to that in the Old Testament.

Let me underline again that it is in no sense my intention to attempt to set forth the New Testament understanding of the knowledge of God. Undoubtedly the material I am about to discuss would be relevant to such a study, providing some necessary data. But it is my intention here only to see whether the ordinary forms of knowledge claims I have already identified are reflected in the New Testament text with reference to God.

The basis of my selection of texts to be examined will be those using *oida*, *ginōskō* and *gnōsis* with reference to God. *Yadá* is normally translated by *oida* and *ginōskō* in the Septuagint. Some scholars have suggested that there are different shades of meaning in the two words.[1] They argue that, following classical usage, *oida* has the sense of simple, absolute and direct knowledge whereas *ginōskō* is relative and indirect. Other scholars, however, allowing such a distinction in classical greek suggest that, 'the distinction between *oida*, 'know' absolutely and *ginōskō*, 'come to know', cannot be pressed in Hellenstic Greek'.[2] Whether or not this is the case we shall be in a better position to judge after examining the various texts and their different forms of knowledge claims.[3]

I begin then with the question of whether there are claims to know God in the New Testament of an inferential form.

INFERENTIAL KNOWLEDGE

At the heart of inferential knowledge is the appeal to evidence. Anyone who claims to know something by inference may properly be asked to give reasons for the claim he makes. In answer he would indicate what he counts as evidence. He believes what he claims, with reason. There are some knowledge claims in the New Testament of this order. They appeal to evidence. They are not large in number and we begin with two, related to particular miracles.

The real point at issue in the story of the healing of the paralysed man is that of the authority to forgive sins.[4] Jesus takes this upon himself, to the horror of some lawyers, because the forgiveness of sins is understood to be God's prerogative alone. Jesus then proposes a test. 'But to convince you that the Son of Man has the right on earth to forgive sins' – he turned to the paralysed man – 'stand up, take your bed, and go home'; Matt 9: 6, Mark. 2: 19, Luke 5: 24. The command to stand and walk is the test observable by all. If this happens then it is evidence for the greater claim concerning the authority to forgive sins.

Is this a case of knowing God by inference? Much will depend upon the interpretation given to the title 'Son of Man'. Although there are several well-known interpretations,[5] none of them identifies the son of Man and God directly. This story, however, clearly implies some relation since it is understood that although the right to forgive sins belongs to God, the Son of Man has that authority. In the account as we have it, the Son of Man in verse 6 refers to Jesus himself.[6] He reveals his authority to forgive sins in the act of healing, his authority deriving not from men but from God. Should anyone question this then they have the evidence of the miracle.

The second miracle story is quite different. It concerns Peter's escape from prison as told in Acts 12. The author's intention seems to be to so emphasize the staggering nature of the escape as to make it well nigh incredible. The utter strangeness of the event, therefore, can only suggest to the reader the work of God. Indeed the story is so structured that what with Peter 'coming to himself' (verse 11) and the disciples not at first believing the story (verse 15) the stress is all on the divine activity.[7] Finding himself free Peter says, 'Now I know it is true . . . the Lord has sent his angel and rescued me . . .' (verse 11). Again the event is understood as evidence of God.

An appeal to evidence is made in John 10: 38, 'If I am not acting as my Father would, do not believe me. But if I am, accept the evidence of my deeds, even if you do not believe me, so that you may recognize and know that the Father is in me, and I in the Father.'[8] The tenses of the verbs suggest both a beginning of knowing at a certain time and the continuous state of knowing. What is at issue is the claim 'that the Father is in me, and I in the Father'. This amounts to blasphemy for the Jews, hence their readiness to stone him (verse 31). Jesus' reply is to point them to what he is doing. These deeds are evidence of the truth of the claim which they find so offensive. It's not that individual deeds in themselves will be convincing, it is the willingness to see God's loving plan and redeeming power in what Jesus has been doing as a whole that matters.[9] The claim is that Jesus alone knows the Father but through his works and death men may, or will, come to know the Father. The work the Son is about is the Father's work and it is 'in exercising the divine prerogatives of vivifying and judging that the unique Lordship of Christ is manifested'.[10] This is the appeal to evidence.

Activity as evidence of the truth of Jesus' claim is the theme in John 14: 31. 'He (The Prince of this world) has no rights over me; but the world must be shown that I love the Father, and do exactly as he commands; so up, let us go forward!' Jesus determines to be totally obedient to the Father so that the loving relationship between him and the Father may be seen for what it is.[11] If needs be he will submit to the Prince of this world, but it will not be a true submission for he will be doing nothing but the Father's will. It is not that the Prince of this world is in control at the Passion, but rather that Jesus is showing his obedience. So by the final act of death Jesus proves that he is the revealer.[12]

Three texts refer to events to come which, when they happen, will be evidence of the truth of words spoken. Matt. 24: 33, Mk. 13:29, Lk. 21: 31 refer to 'signs of the end'. 'In the same way when you see all these things, you may know that the end is near, at the very door'. To these we may add Luke 21: 20. Undoubtedly the evangelists saw such events as the fall of Jerusalem as having theological implications, their significance is eschatological. The knowledge they bring is that the 'end' is near.

A quite different approach to a future event is expressed in John 8: 28, 'Jesus said to them "when you have lifted up the Son of Man you will know that I am what I am". Jesus' passion will confirm

what he has already said about his identity. There is deliberate
ambiguity here. It will be his being lifted up to the cross that will
prove his obedience to the Father who sent him.[13] The 'lifting up'
is both to execution and exaltation, and this is 'Johannine irony'.
In lifting him up on to the cross his enemies assist him on his
upward way and in this very action his true nature will be known.[14]
Thus the appeal is to an event which will be seen to be confirmatory
evidence of what it is claimed is being revealed of God now.

The above references are evidence, I submit, that the New Testament includes knowledge claims that relate directly to particular
events in the past or yet to come. In this respect the New Testament
follows the Old Testament. But, again like the Old Testament, the
nature of the revelation between 'event' and what is understood
or claimed about it is not straightforwardly a matter of inference.
This I will return to later. However, I suggest that there are grounds
enough already to assert that 'events as evidence' is an argument
the New Testament understands and uses. And thus far I have not
drawn attention to the resurrection.

We would expect appeal to be made in particular to the resurrection and five texts illustrate this. First, John 12: 20, 'because I live,
you too will live; then you will know that I am in my father, and
you in me and I in you'. The New English Bible rather weakly
translates *en ekeinē tē hēmera* as 'then'. Many commentators[15] see
the phrase referring to the resurrection. It certainly belongs to the
language of eschatology, but the 'end time' is anticipated in the
day of Jesus' resurrection.[16] 'That day' will be a day of realization,
of 'knowing' the relationship of mutual indwelling of God and
man, made possible for John through recognition of Christ, as the
revelation of God, of Christ, who is inseparably one with God.[17]
So an event which falls within the time sequence is charged with
eternal significance for the disciples. As so often in John, although
the reference is to the historic event, the interest is mostly on the
inward apprehension of those concerned.

A more explicit appeal to the resurrection as proof comes in Acts
2: 36, 'Let all Israel then accept as certain that God has made this
Jesus, whom you crucified, both Lord and Messiah.' Of this, the
resurrection is the final guarantee. Peter builds up his argument
on the appeal to the scriptures and the word of witnesses to the
resurrection. So with scriptural testimony, joined to that of the eye
witnesses, the Apostle brings 'all Israel'[18] the certain knowledge
that God has made this Jesus the Lord and Messiah.[19]

Peter is, in fact, making more than an appeal to the resurrection. He is offering an interpretation of the life, death and resurrection of Jesus. In verse 22 the miracles are understood as those acts of God which come at the End Time. The cross, which appears to be so contradictory of Messiahship in the popular understanding, is now seen as part of the 'deliberate will and plan of God'. The empty tomb is taken to be a fact in contrast to David's tomb. The resurrection declares Christ to be greater than David who is understood to have foretold the event as a prophet. And the experience of this day of Pentecost is the seal of the promised Holy Spirit.[20] It is therefore more accurate to say that what we have from Peter is not so much as an argument with inferences as an interpretation of Christ. We shall have cause to return to this very important point.

But to continue with the theme of the resurrection event as evidence, a rather different reference comes in Romans 6: 3, 'have you forgotten that when we were baptized into union with Christ Jesus we were baptized into this death?' The emphasis here is upon union with Christ. Being 'baptized into his death' means the death of the Cross and 'being buried with him' is being laid in *his* tomb. It is not that the Christian's death and burial in baptism is some personal demise in a merely symbolic sense. The death and resurrection of the baptized man is the death and resurrection that he suffered in the Christ who died and rose as his representative.[21] It may be that Paul is referring here to the sacrament for pedagogical purposes,[22] but it will not do to say that the meaning of baptism is a purely symbolic affair. Here again we come to this point that, although there is obvious reference to events in history, it is not so much that inferences are made from such events as that they are understood and interpreted, and we might say 'lived in' in a particular way.

This is taken up later in 6: 8 'we know that Christ, once raised from the dead is never to die again'. The inference is straightforward. Christ, having died once will not die again. His resurrection life which is the work of God has that finality about it. The reference is clearly to the events of history. But the interpretation of the events in the context of Paul's discussion of baptism leads him on to remind his readers about the quality of their present life as Christians in Christ. The basis of the believer's new life is not his faith, it is the resurrection of Jesus Christ, in which the life of baptized persons is already a real, though hidden, present.[23]

The last of these five references to the resurrection is 2 Corinthians 4: 14, 'for we know that he who raised the Lord Jesus to life will with Jesus raise us too, and bring us to his presence and you with us'. Paul understanding the resurrection of Jesus as the action of God. It is God who raised Jesus to life and this, for Paul, is proof that he too will be raised with Jesus and brought into the presence of Christ at the parousia.[24]

According to the writer of I John, Christians know that God dwells in them because he has given them a share in the Spirit. This he believes can be verified. The issue is not just a theoretical one, it is a response to opponents to the faith. He is concerned with the difference between genuine and spurious claims to spirit activity. He provides a test. 'This is how we may recognize the spirit of God: every spirit which acknowledges that Jesus Christ has come in the flesh is from God and every spirit which does not thus acknowledge Jesus is not from God', I John 4: 2. What is being denied in this 'incipient Gnosticism'[25] is the Incarnation. No one can deny that Christ has appeared in the historical Jesus and say that he has the anointing of the spirit of God. The writer insists upon the historic claim, the event of Christ, to which the early Christian tradition bore testimony in its claim to know God.

The writer speaks of proof and evidence in I John 4: 13, 'Here is the proof that we dwell in him and he dwells in us: he has imparted his spirit to us.' This is the writer's answer to the question of how the Christian believer may be sure of the mutual indwelling with God the gospel proclaims. The answer is the gift of the spirit. It may be that he refers to the 'interior witness of the Holy Spirit, the awarness of a divine presence in our life'.[26] But the author is already aware of the dangers of the appeal to experience and that is perhaps why he moves in verses 14–15 to repeat the affirmation of Incarnation. The proof of the doctrine that God is love and that in love we dwell in him and he dwells in us is not made by reference to any philosophical argument about the nature of God. The proof consisted in a two-fold appeal; on the one hand, the experience of the Spirit which is the new objective happening in the believers' lives and on the other hand, the encounter some had in the flesh with the Saviour of the world.

I shall return to these claims related to events in my concluding comments. Now I turn to two further references in Romans that may suggest not inferences from history but from the nature of the world.

The first is Romans I: 19–20, 'For all that may be known of God by men lies plain before their eyes; indeed God himself has disclosed it to them. His invisible attributes, that is to say his everlasting power and deity, have been visible, ever since the world began to the eye of reason, in the things he has made.'

This is the only passage in Paul that might be termed 'natural religion'. It is not, however, the Apostle's intention to set up any kind of reasoned argument for the existence of God. Neither is it his purpose to infer the existence of God from the fact of the world. What Paul is concerned to show is that the Gentiles, like the Jews, had sufficient knowledge of God to be blameworthy.

The background thought of Romans 1: 18ff is that of Hellenistic Judaism, and often it is argued that Paul echoes the motifs and thought-patterns of the Wisdom of Soloman 12–13.[27] Such Hellenistic Judaism seeks to awaken a knowledge of God by observing the world. Because it stands in agreement with the reasonable understanding of the world open to every man, it presents a possibility of the knowledge of God to all men.

But Paul does not understand the knowledge of God in this way. It is not that he does not hold it a possibility open to all men. Rather he sees the knowledge of God as the reality under which all men in fact stand. For Paul the initiative always lies with God. Thus God himself discloses 'the knowledge of God' to the Gentiles. The reason why the Gentiles stand condemned is not because of their ignorance, but because of their knowledge. The question of how the knowledge of God 'occurs' is not one that concerns Paul here. It is sufficient for him to say it is 'disclosed'. The godlessness of men is therefore not an intellectual matter but a moral one in this passage. It is not the disclosure of the divine being that concerns Paul but the meaning of human existence. It is this meaning that the gentiles have failed to appreciate. 'Knowing God, they have refused to honour him as God', verse 21. Hence, having got the first principle wrong, as it were, their whole lives end in disorder and futility.

It is perhaps unwise to build too much upon these verses since this is the only occasion when Paul uses the phrase *gnōstov tou theou*. However, it does seem that Paul is not offering in this instance an inferential argument for the knowledge of God. He assumes that the possibility of the knowledge of God is available to the Gentiles by reason of the disclosure of God, but he does not teach that there exists a rational means of proving God's existence from the world.[28]

Lastly, in this section, Romans 8: 28, 'and in everything as we know, he co-operates for good with those who love God and are called according to his purpose'. There are well known textual problems here and the translation may be 'He, that is God, co-operates in all things . . . ' or 'All things co-operate . . . '.[29] Our concern is with the possibility of an inferential knowledge claim. Is Paul claiming that from 'everything' certain inferences can be made about God? Clearly this is not the case. It would not occur to Paul to look to 'everything' for the salvation of man. What he does look for and finds is God's co-operation with us in all things, even in things hostile to us.[30] The believer first anchors himself in what God has said to him of his love in Christ and then experiences life and the world in the way stated in 8: 23.[31] What the believer 'knows' may involve an appeal to history but is not in the first instance inferred from history. It has much to do with his whole outlook and therefore experience of life.

By way of summary I make five points:

1   It is quite apparent that, as far as the use of words for 'know' and 'knowledge' are concerned, the appeal to events in history is not so emphatic in the New Testament as it is in the Old Testament. However, an argument from the numerical use of words here may be misleading for there can be little doubt that just as the event of the Exodus is in some way determinative of the Old Testament concept of God, so the historic event of Jesus Christ is determinative of the New Testament concept of God.

2   There are no cases of inference in the New Testament where a move is attempted from the known to the unknown. In other words, as we saw is the case in the Old Testament, the fact of God is 'given', is 'just known'. So there is no attempt to demonstrate or prove the existence of God inferentially.

3   The events of the New Testament are taken to be significant in the sense that they are understood from the first to be acts of God and are taught and proclaimed as such. The resurrection, for example, is not understood as a strange event the explanation of which can only be the activity of God. The resurrection of Christ is announced as the act of God from the very first. This is how the event is understood and it is not a matter of inference at all.

4   The resurrection, the miracles, etc. can, however, be understood as divine confirmation, or evidence of the truth of the claims Jesus made or his followers made about him. This we saw was the case in Acts 2: 36. The resurrection is understood as a kind of guarantee or proof of Jesus' unique relationship with the Father.

His deeds bear witness to the same claim. Thus the words, deeds, death and resurrection of Jesus are understood as evidence for the claim that Jesus is the Son of God.

5   The proclamation of the New Testament is the proclamation of believers. The 'story' they tell is the story they live by. I have already drawn attention to the fact that they refer to events not simply to make inferences from them, although they do do that, but to commend their faith in God whom they assert 'stands behind' these events. It is in this context, where the thought of God is 'given', that inferences can be and are made. But there is no attempt made to establish, from the events themselves, the existence of God.

KNOWING GOD BY ACQUAINTANCE IN THE NEW TESTAMENT

The essential feature in knowledge by acquaintance is its directness. To know anyone by acquaintance is to have direct cognitive awareness of that person, and thus it is that claims to know by acquaintance find expression in the form of the verb being followed not by a clause but by a noun. Such claims have necessarily a personal quality. The experience of being acquainted with something or someone is not transferrable to anyone else. Both parties may have the experience, both may be able to describe and identify whom or with whom they have been acquainted. But they cannot have each other's experience of being acquainted because such experiences are essentially personal and relational.

Now my question is, are there claims to know God by acquaintance in the New Testament? This is to ask whether anyone claims to know God personally, to have encountered or met or experienced God in some way. I shall argue that there are such claims. To repeat what I have said before, whether such claims are true or not is not my immediate concern here. All I am concerned to show is that God is so conceived in the New Testament that it is possible for someone to claim to know him by acquaintance.

Like the Old Testament, the New Testament conceives of the possibility of some form of communication between God and man of a personal experiential kind. Thus there are a number of references to visions, or 'messages' being received, practically all of them confined to the Lucan writings. For example, there is the case of Zechariah in Luke 1; 11ff and his vision of the angel Gabriel.

Again in 24: 23 the story of the vision of angels at the empty tomb. Neither of these incidents involves a direct encounter with God.

It is a different emphasis in Acts 2: 17 where Peter's claim that what is being experienced is the fulfilment of God's promise and the outpouring of his spirit. The vision of Ananias, 8: 10, includes hearing the voice of the Lord, but with Cornelius, 10: 3, we are back to an angel of the Lord imparting the message. This is followed by Peter's trance, 10: 10ff, where a voice is heard that is taken by Peter to be the voice of the Lord. I have earlier drawn attention to the story of Peter's release from prison. Interestingly in 12: 9 Luke comments that Peter had 'no idea that the angel's intervention was real: he thought it was just a vision'.

Paul had visions. Acts 16: 9 records the call from Macedonia for help, a vision Paul took to be from God. Another vision is referred to in 18: 9. It seems, however, that Paul did not set too much store by these experiences. They were much less significant than the gift of love, I Cor. 12: 1–3. He certainly saw little value in boasting about them, 2 Cor. 12: 1. But the essential point that I am making is that the New Testament assumes that direct communication between God and man is possible. A feature of these experiences is, in nearly every case, that some personal instruction or direction is communicated, the medium of communication being the vision.

Paul may not have rated visions very highly but clearly the Damascus Road experience was of a different class. This was for him *the* moment of greatest significance. None of the accounts of the resurrection 'encounters' uses the words for 'know'. The theological problem they raise in this context is the relationship between whatever 'knowing God' means and whatever is meant by seeing, meeting or knowing the risen Christ. This is an issue to which I will return.

The distinction between first and second-hand awareness is apparent in John 4: 42. It comes at the end of the story of Jesus' conversation with the Samaritan woman. The other Samaritans say, 'It is no longer because of what you said that we believe, for we have heard him ourselves; and we know that this is in truth the Saviour of the world.'[32] This is a case of knowing, or claiming to know, something about Jesus. But in the contrast between 'hearing' and 'knowing' we have the difference between first and second-hand faith, between report and personal testimony.[33]

I turn now to three direct claims that the Son knows the Father. The first of these is Matt. 11: 27, 'Everything is entrusted to me by my Father; and no one knows the Son but the Father, and no one knows the Father but the Son and those to whom the son may choose to reveal him.' This is the only reference in the Synoptic Gospels to 'knowing the Father' and has been called the 'thunderbolt fallen from the Johannine sky'.

The parallel in Luke 10: 22 reads, 'Everything is entrusted to me by my Father; and on one knows who the Son is but the Father, or who the Father is but the Son, and those to whom the Son may choose to reveal him'.

This passage abounds in critical problems and there is a clear division of opinion as to whether hellenistic[34] or semitic[35] influences are predominant. Those who stress hellenistic influences suggest that the phrase reflects the Christology of the primitive Church while others, stressing the semitic characteristics of the saying claim either its authenticity or that 'it is the product of a Christianity which has remained very close touch with the mind of the historical Jesus'.

My concern is with the nature of the knowledge claim. Both versions of the logion begin with 'Everything is entrusted to me by my Father.' There is good evidence to suggest that *paradidonai* is a technical form for the transmission of knowledge and doctrine.[36] What Jesus has had entrusted to him and what he is to pass on to others is the revelation of God's purposes he has received. If this is so then there is good reason to suggest that the Father's 'knowledge' of the son implies the Father's choice of the son, a use of 'know' which figures in the Old Testament.[37] Correspondingly the son's knowledge of the Father is expressed in obedience, in fulfilling his part of the purpose of God, the knowledge of which has been entrusted to him. The Father–Son relationship would then be characterized by 'choice and response, authority and obedience'.[38] The relationship described in these terms does not necessarily imply the directness of knowing by acquaintance or the mutual indwelling of Johannine theology.[39] However, I suggest, that, whatever judgement is made about the authenticity of the saying, the Sonship that is implied is one of 'nature and being'. The language is parabolic but 'it is a parable drawn from the intimate language that a father and a son alone have of each other, which Jesus is using to desribe the *abba* relationship to God that he is claiming for himself'.[40] This judgement is sound even if we take Luke's form[41] as indicative that the saying is late. It is a father–son relationship, after all, that is being spoken of and unless we are to say that what is implied here is quite unlike what a father–son relationship involves then, taking the terms as they stand, we can say that Jesus, the Son, knew the Father directly, personally, by acquaintance. It seems to me that what is claimed in the New Testament for Jesus, or even perhaps by Jesus himself, is not simply that here is a man with new information about God but who knows God as no one else has quite known him before. It is because of this unique Sonship that he was privileged to admit others to know the Father also through his eschatological ministry.[42]

Thus this statement is an important one in understanding Jesus' mission. He knows the Father, because he is the Son. His 'knowing' is grounded in the Father's will, his 'choice' of the Son, and is demonstrated in the Son's obedience. This is undoubtedly part of what 'knowing' means here. Jesus passes on what he knows in his proclamation and deeds of the Kingdom. To know God, therefore, is to be the object of his choice and to respond to that choice in obedience. Jesus knows the Father already, others will come to know the Father through him.

Two other similar claims may be cited from John's gospel. The first is 8: 54–5 where Jesus replies to the Jews' charge that he is possessed by saying, 'If I glorify myself, that glory of mine is worthless. It is the Father who glorifies me, he of whom you say, "He is our God", though you do not know him. But I know him; if I said that I did not know him I should be a liar like you. But in truth I know him and obey his word.' The text again reflects the important relationship between 'knowing' and 'obeying', and part of the differences between Jesus and the Jews lies here. If they did know God, as they claimed to do, then they would recognize in Jesus the faithful representative who keeps God's word. However, the 'knowing' of the Father by the Son amounts to more than just the matter of obedience. The obedience flows from an identity of nature and will such as earthly sons, even the best of them, cannot know.[43]

Second, John 17: 25 is also a record of the claim that Jesus 'knows' God. 'O righteous Father, though the world does not know thee, I know thee and these men know that thou didst send me.' The world does not know God, 1: 10. But the Son, the incarnate word, knows the Father. Between Father and Son there is unique reciprocal knowledge, cf. Matt. 11: 27. The disciples know (i.e. believe and acknowledge) that the Father has sent the Son and that therefore the Son is the authorized agent and revealer of God. Knowing here, both for Jesus and the disciples, implies establishing some sort of personal relationship in which the decisive quality is love, 17: 26. But it is Christ's knowledge of God that is the means of the disciples' knowing of God. It is because the son knows the Father by acquaintance, i.e. directly and personally, that he can be the means of making the Father known to others.

Now I turn my attention to the claim that knowing Christ is to know God. I shall illustrate this trend in the New Testament first with three references from John. First, John 14: 7, 'If you knew me you would know my Father too. From now on you do know him; you have seen him.' There are textual variants here and it may be better to read with the verbs in the future, viz. 'If you have known me, you will know my Father also. Henceforth, you know him and have seen him.'[44]

Whatever reading is adopted, the meaning seems to be that either from this moment, or henceforth (i.e. at Jesus' departure) ignorance of God for Christ's disciples is a thing of the past. The disciples have not completely failed to know Jesus, as the Jews have done, 8: 19. But the questions the disciples ask indicate that they do not know Christ perfectly. All this will be changed at 'the hour'.[45] The claim is that to have 'seen' Christ is to know the Father. This is but to repeat an initial assertion of the gospel, 'no one has ever seen God; but God's only Son, he who is nearest to the Father's heart, he has made him known', 1: 18. In fact only one person can speak of direct vision of God, 6: 46. This is the quality of knowledge Christ has and he mediates it to others. John continually draws a contrast between the disciples and the unbelieving world. Thus with regard to the Spirit, 'the world cannot receive him, because the world neither sees nor knows him; but you know him because he dwells with you and is in you', 14: 17. Here again is the theme of mutual indwelling, the experience of 'knowing'. The claim is that it is the indwelling of the Spirit in the disciples that perpetually mediates the knowledge of Christ, which is the knowledge of God. The experience of the Spirit is both corporate and individual,[46] and to live in this experience is to know God, for 'knowledge and vision of the Father of the Son and of the Paraclete are equipollent'.[47]

The third text I wish to cite from John with this claim that knowing Christ is knowing God is 17: 3, 'This is eternal life: to know thee who alone art truly God, and Jesus Christ whom thou hast sent.' The notion that the knowledge of God is essential to salvation sounds as though this is a gnostic intrusion. But this is not the case. It is a theme found in the Old Testament, e.g. in Hosea, 4:

6; 6: 3; 6. In John, although it is affirmed that the *knowledge* of God is 'life' the same result follows from *believing*, 20: 31, which again suggests an Old Testament emphasis in which knowing and believing are not species of a different genus but are correlated. However, it cannot be denied that 17: 3 does relate eternal life to a correct appreciation of the Father–Son relationship. But this is only to understand that faith has an intellectual content.

R. E. Brown makes two observations upon all this which mark off this assertion in 17: 3 from gnosticism. (1) For John, the knowledge of God in which eternal life consists has been mediated by something that happened in history and that this knowledge is salvific in that it frees men from sin, 8: 32. (2) The understanding of eternal life is that it is not reserved to some future state, but is granted to men on this earth.[48] This last point is of some interest because it also goes beyond the Old Testament which came to regard man's knowledge of God as a matter of promise, but here it is asserted to be the present possession of believers. The 'form' of knowing operating here has intellectual content but is more than intellectual apprehension. We are again in the realm of relationships. The claim is that of 'knowing' God but this claim cannot be severed from knowledge of his Son, 14: 7; 20: 31.

Neither can it be separated from the Christian community. This is a feature of the New Testament which to overlook would be most misleading. It is pertinent to draw attention to it here, because of particular features in John's gospel. These I can indicate by returning for a moment to two texts already cited.

I have already argued that John 14:7 is evidence of the New Testament theme that knowing Christ is to know God. But what is it to know Christ? Clearly more is implied here than knowing him, that is being acquainted with him, as a human being. What that 'more' is can be drawn out in this manner. Jesus said, 'If you knew me you would know my Father too. From now on you do know him; you have seen him.' C. K. Barrett sees the whole discourse dominated by the departure and return of Jesus, his return being with his Father to the believers, to the waiting disciples. The spiritual presence of Jesus, and the ministry of the Holy Spirit are secured only through the death and departure of Jesus.[49] It is therefore 'from now on', that is, from the moment of the completion of Jesus' work, that the disciples will 'know' the Father.

The stress on the community of believers in which the Father, the Son and the Spirit are known is reflected in 14: 17 with its theme of mutual indwelling. The 'knowing' is something the disciples share by reason of the presence of the Spirit in the Church. Only now, after Jesus has gone, do they know the real presence as the Spirit takes 'the things of Christ' and declares them, 15: 26; 16: 14.

It follows from this that knowing God by acquaintance in the light of these references from John can only mean recognizing the whole work of God in Christ which is related to the 'realization' of the life eternal through Christ in the fellowship of the Church. Acquaintance as direct awareness comes by the teaching of the church, its fellowship in love and the individual commitment or belief of the disciples who shares the life of the new age.

Thus far, with the exception of Matt. 11: 27, I have concentrated attention upon John. Now I turn to three texts from Paul which will give not a different but complimentary sense of knowing by acquaintance.

First then, 2 Cor: 5;11, 'With this fear of the Lord before our eyes we address our appeal to men.' What does 'knowing the fear of the Lord mean?' The phrase follows the assertion in verse 10 that we must all appear before the judgement seat of Christ. Holding this conviction Paul therefore lives his life knowing that he must one day render an account of his service. 'Knowing the fear of the Lord' therefore does not necessarily refer to any special and particular experience or experiences but rather to Paul's way of understanding his life. He knows the fear of the Lord because he is a believer. The reason, therefore, for my drawing attention to this text is not that it is a case of knowing God directly by acquaintance , but that it reminds us that all the experiences of life are context dependent and conceptually loaded and that Paul's 'knowing' in this text cannot be divorced from his believing, and his participation in a particular form of life.

In Ephesians 3: 18–19, the Apostle speaks of knowing the love of Christ; 'with deep roots and firm foundations, may you be strong to grasp, with all God's people, what is the breadth and length and height and depth of the love of Christ, and to know it, though it is beyond knowledge'. Here it is asserted that there is more to the knowledge of God than just possessing information. To experience the love of Christ is more than just an intellectual matter, indeed the love of Christ exceeds our capacity of comprehension. But for the Apostle to know the love of Christ is to know what is deepest in the nature and purposes of God as he has experienced this through Christ in the Christian community.

Finally, Philippians 3: 8, 'I would say more: I count everything sheer loss, because all is far outweighted by the gain of knowing Christ Jesus my Lord, for whose sake I did in fact lose everything.' This is the only place where Paul speaks of knowledge of Christ. For Paul, the knowledge of Christ is the knowledge of one who loves and knows himself to be loved, hence the intimate 'Christ Jesus my Lord'.[50] A. E. Harvey expresses it well when he says:

> Only here does Paul speak in such intimate and personal terms of "knowing his Lord", and we must ask, in what sense did Paul "know" Jesus? Not, it seems in the sense that he was acquainted with Jesus on earth – if he had ever in fact seen Jesus, he attached no importance to it. His "knowledge" was more of the kind associated with many popular forms of religion, in which the supreme object of all rites and ceremonies was to "know" the deity in a mystical sense. For Paul, this meant not so much knowledge about God as a relationship with him, such that "to know" God" was almost equivalent to "being known to him". It involved our experience of the power – the reality and efficacy – of Jesus' resurrection, a sense of solidarity with Jesus in suffering, and the hope of ultimately sharing in the glory.[51]

Is God known by acquaintance in the New Testament? I suggest the answer is 'Yes', but, as was the case with the Old Testament, there are some qualifications to be made. I began this section with reference to certain visionary experiences reported by Luke. That these be understood as visions requires that the New Testament conceives that communication between God and man is possible. In this sense God must be 'known'. The emphasis in the visions was upon the messages given and received. However, there is a big gap between talk of receiving a message and knowing the originator of the message, a gap too large to allow that 'I know God' by acquaintance' follows from 'I have had a vision.' For whatever reason, the New Testament, as I indicated by its absence of words for 'know' in such stories, does not attempt this move.

However, it is the claim of the New Testament that Jesus 'knows' God and that this 'knowing' is conceived of in terms of personal relationship. It is quite clear that 'all four gospels ascribe to Jesus the consciousness of such a unique filial relationship to the Father'.[52] I suggest it is entirely appropriate to say of this knowledge, whatever else it may involve, that it is knowledge of the Father by acquaintance.

But do the disciples know God by acquaintance, that is, know God in some direct form of cognitive awareness? The New Testament shares with the Old Testament that proper caution about all such talk of directly seeing and knowing God. It is, after all, the *glory* of God that is seen in the face of Jesus Christ, 2 Corinthians 4: 6. Yet I think there is an important sense in which the disciples may be said to know God by acquaintance. It is in the way I indicated earlier with reference to John 14, although I think the point I am about to make applies to the New Testament as a whole.

The disciples live their lives 'in Christ'. They live out their lives *as* disciples in the conviction and hope that God was in Christ. They live in the new age begun by God in Christ and characterised by the gift of the Spirit. In and through the Church, its worship, teaching, obedience and fellowship they 'know the Father', they 'grow in the love and knowledge of God'. Their whole life is in this way related to God. They know the fear of the Lord, they experience God's grace, they live in hope.

It is in this 'total' sense of living in faith that we can say the disciples 'know' God. God is the foundation of their whole life as they have responded to Jesus Christ. Knowing God by acquaintance thus becomes not a matter of having a series of particular religious experiences, but of experiencing life as a whole in Christ. This understanding of acquaintance I shall substantiate and develop in the final Chapter.

KNOWING GOD BY DESCRIPTION IN THE NEW TESTAMENT

In Chapter 10 I argued that knowledge by description was an important feature of the Old Testament. This was evidenced in the stress placed upon teaching and instruction. The tradition of talk about God was passed on and become the possession of each new generation. Thus, although knowledge by description is indirect knowledge, it was by the direct method of teaching in the context of Israel's life that the knowledge of God was communicated.

Now I ask whether the New Testament has this concept of the knowledge of God by description? I believe it does. The New Testament writers certainly understood themselves to be in a position to say things about God, to affirm some descriptions as true, to deny others as false. I shall give evidence of this in a moment. But first, there are two qualifications to be made:

1   The making of these claims about God does not guarantee their truth. The New Testament writers, in saying what they do, reflect a tradition of speech about God. The tradition is largely Jewish, but is re-expressed in the light of their own experience of God in Christ. What we read are descriptive statements of God as the writers have come to understand and experience him. This does not guarantee that these claims are necessarily true or false. Any claim to knowledge can be challenged by the question 'How do you know about x?'. However, all I want to draw attention to is the fact that the New Testament writers understood that it was possible to say certain things about God, consciously or unconsciously, as description.

2   The second qualification to note is that the descriptions of God in the New Testament are not made using the words for 'know'. (there is a possible exception to this in the case of I Cor. 8: 4 discussed later). These words are used in a few cases where claims are made to know something about Jesus, e.g. The man with the unclean spirit knows who Jesus is, i.e. The Holy One of God, Mk. 1: 24. Nicodemas knows with others that Jesus is a teacher sent by God, John 3: 2 etc. But there are no direct references to descriptions of God using the words for 'know'.

This may be the case of a number of reasons. It may reflect an understanding of the meaning of the verbs to 'know' that restricted them to acquaintance and direct knowledge. Or it may be because God is so conceived in the New Testament that descriptions are impossible to 'know' but are expressed as matters of belief. Against this there is no evidence to suggest that the descriptions are related to the verb 'believe'. In fact, these descriptions appear to have the character of 'common' knowledge in the community of early Christians. Or again it may reflect a caution about saying anything descriptive of God lest this appear as 'idol-making'.

There may well be other explanations of the fact that the verbs for 'know' are not used with regard to the things the New Testament writers say about God. It is, however, my opinion that what is said about God 'defines' God within the New Testament. This way of speaking of God cannot be separated from its Old Testament inheritance. The affirmations are made, not just because they are the things believed about God, but because God is so conceived within the tradition. Thus, whether the verbs are used or not, these are the things 'known' about God, describing his character and enabling people to identify who it is that is being talked about.

The relationship of Old Testament and New Testament in this matter is illustrated in I Cor. 8: 4; here Paul's concern is the question of food offered to idols, 'of course, as you say, a false god has no existence in the real world. There is no god but one'. This latter conviction is already found in the Old Testament (e.g. Deut. 6: 4; Isa. 44: 8, etc). It is part of the 'tradition' which is the ground of the New Testament. We do not go too far if we suggest that 'in the New Testament there is not – nor in the nature of things can there be – any original doctrine of God' because the God of whom Jesus speaks is undoubtedly the God of Israel, 'known' to Israel. It is going too far, however, to deny that 'there is any new teaching about God in the New Testament'.[53] But the foundations of talk about God in the New Testament are laid in the Old Testament and this will become increasingly apparent as we look at what the New Testament says about God.

Elsewhere in the New Testament God is described as 'one'. Again with reference to the Old Testament, this is illustrated in Mark 12; 28–34. Jas 2: 19 refers to the faith that there is one God. He is the living God, I Tim. 3: 15, Heb. 9: 14; 10: 31. He is also God of the living, Mark 12: 26, where the reference is also to God of Abraham, Isaac and Jacob (see also Acts 3: 13). The reference to the 'fathers' reminds us that God is known as God of Israel, Matt. 15: 31.

God is good, Mark 10: 18. He is perfect (Matt. 5: 48) powerful (Mark 14: 62, 'the right hand of God', New English Bible), faithful (I Cor. 1: 9), wise (Rom. 16: 27), true (John 3: 33, Titus 1: 2), merciful (Rom. 2: 4), kind and severe (Rom. 11: 22). He is known as the God of peace (Rom. 15: 33; 16;20; I Thess. 5: 23, Phil. 4: 9; I Cor. 14: 33, Heb. 13: 20), the God of hope (Rom. 15: 13) and the God of love (2 Cor. 13: 11). He can also be described as eternal (Rom. 16: 26). Lord of heaven and earth (Matt. 11: 25) and one who is careful for his children (Matt. 6: 26–31; Luke 21: 30). He is both light (I John 1: 5) and spirit (John 4: 24) and love (I John 4: 9).

God is Father. This metaphorical description of God was not first introduced by Jesus, it was already part of the Old Testament concept of God, Deut. 14: 1, Ps. 89: 27 etc. Neither of these texts directly address God as Father, indeed nowhere in the Old Testament do we find God addressed in this way. There is a difference between Judaism and Jesus here, for he, unlike Judaism, addressed God as *Abba*.[54] This he does in Mark 14: 36. Other references to God as Father in the gospels include Matt. 7: 11; 6: 9 (Luke 11: 2), Matt. 23: 9, Mark 11: 25, Luke 6: 36; 12–30; 23: 34; 46. The thought of God as Father also appears in Rom. 8: 18 and Gal. 4: 6.

Particularly in the New Testament God is the God and Father of Jesus Christ, Rom. 15: 6, 2 Cor. 1: 3; 11: 21, Eph. 1: 3, Col. 1: 3, I Pet. 1: 3. He is the one who 'sent' Jesus his Son, John 3: 2: 17: 8. He is the one who raised Jesus from the dead, Heb. 13: 20. He is the one who was in Christ reconciling the world to himself, 2 Cor. 5: 19, Col. 2: 9. He is the God who was at work in Jesus, Acts 2: 32.

So the 'description' of God in the New Testament is inseparably related to Jesus the Christ. Paul can speak of Christ as the very image of God, 2 Cor. 4: 4, the image of the invisible God, Col. 1: 14–15. As such Christ is the revelation of the glory of God, 2 Cor. 4: 6. Peter speaks of Jesus as the Holy One of God, John 6: 69. No one has ever seen God, John 1: 18 and the New Testament is careful in its language about Christ, certainly careful about calling Christ 'God'. But the New Testament does assert that God's only son, he who is nearest to the Father's heart, he has made God 'known', John 1: 18. *Exēgēsato* used here means elsewhere in the New Testament 'to rehearse facts', 'to recount a narrative'.[55] In this sense it means 'knowledge about', indirect knowledge. It is Christ's knowledge of God that is direct. Yet, as I argued in the previous section the New Testament understands that to know Christ is in some important sense to know God.

All the above is, I believe, evidence for my claim that the New Testament conceives of knowledge of God by description. It is not, of course, description of God as a thing or material person. Since no one has 'seen' God this is impossible. It is quite noticeable that anthropomorphisms are not so prominent in the New Testament as the Old Testament and this may suggest change in the concept of God. Yet the New Testament description of God feeds upon the Old Testament, using the tradition but always in the light of what is believed to be God's richest act of revelation, the life, death and resurrection of Jesus Christ. The 'descriptions' of God we have given relate very much to his 'effects'. If for example the New Testament describes God as good (Mark 10: 18) his goodness is understood not primarily ontologically but in his relation to the world. To say this is not to set the ontological and the experiential in opposition. They are both present in the Old Testament and New Testament. But the experiential is predominant.

So the New Testament finds it possible to talk about God. It had an inheritance from the Old Testament and passed an inheritance on to later ages. Earlier in this study I drew attention to the concept of Objective Knowledge.[56] I suggested that Sir Karl Popper's concept of World 3, our common inheritance of objective knowledge, could

include the idea of 'The Faith' as something autonomous, something that could be called the deposit of the Faith, I Tim. 6: 20, 2
Tim. 1: 12; 14. These references in the New Testament suggest that
here the Faith is understood to have a content. It is not just the
'subjective' disposition of believing in God. It necessarily includes
believing certain things about God. Thus the New Testament speaks
of the 'faith which God entrusted to his people once and for all',
Jude 3, and there is good evidence of the New Testament containing
statements that are credal in nature, Acts 16: 13, Rom. 10: 9ff, I Cor.
12: 3, Heb. 4: 14, I John 4: 15. Other references indicate the importance of 'sound teaching', Rom. 6: 17, 2 Thess. 2: 15: 3: 6, 2 Tim. 1: 13.

These and other passages of liturgical, baptismal and pedagogical
interest I offer as further support of my contention that the New
Testament so conceives of God that certain things may be said about
him that are true descriptions.

KNOWLEDGE AND OBEDIENCE

In my comments upon the use of the word 'know' in the Old
Testament with reference to God, I drew attention to the relationship
between 'knowing God' and 'obeying God'. I indicated that the
knowledge of God in the Old Testament had a practical nature as
well as being a matter of intellect and experience. In fact any full
understanding of what 'knowing God' in the Old Testament means
would have to hold all these elements together because they are
inseparably related.

Thus far in any consideration of the New Testament material, I
have shown that again the knowledge of God relates both to experience and intellectual activity. Now I ask whether the same emphasis
on the 'practical', on the relation of 'knowing' and 'obeying', is a
feature of the New Testament understanding of the knowledge of
God. I shall argue that it is and that 'knowing God' is inseparably
related to participating in a particular form of life. I shall illustrate
this, first positively, then negatively, with reference to texts using
oida and *ginōskō*.

An important example of what I mean is given in the words of
Jesus to the Jews who asked him how he came by his teaching;
'Whoever has the will to do the will of God shall know whether
my teaching comes from him or is merely my own', John 7:17. C.
K. Barrett suggests that 'doing the will of God' does not refer to

some ethical obedience as a preliminary to dogmatic Christianity, but is a matter of believing in him whom God sent (6: 29).[57] The man who really 'knows' that Jesus has come from the Father is the man who seeks to do the Father's will as Jesus does the Father's will. There is this strong insistence on the ethical aspects of the Christian life in all of John's writings. It is imperative that people should choose to do the will of God, as Jesus himself does it (4: 34), because doing God's will is 'doing' the truth (3: 21) which involves believing in Jesus as the one whom God sent and also, in that act of belief, giving one's whole life in the community of obedience to God. It is only those who so believe and obey that will 'know' the source of the words of Jesus, that is, 'understanding and rightly valuing that which Jesus teaches'.[58] Knowledge and obedience are inseparably related.

This is again the case in John 8: 32, 'If you dwell within the revelation I have brought, you are indeed my disciples; you shall know the truth and the truth will set you free'. There is a holding together here of what we might call propositional and experiential knowledge. The 'truth' that liberates[59] is knowledge of what is truly real, the knowledge of divine reality given by the *logos* of Christ.[60] But as we have already seen such 'knowing' is not just an intellectual matter of entertaining a proposition in the mind. It involves the active relationship of man to God that expresses itself in obedience.

That the knowledge of God issues in the activity of love is spelt out by Paul; 'Of course, we all "have knowledge", as you say. This knowledge breeds concept; it is love that builds. If anyone fancies that he knows, he knows nothing yet, in the true sense of knowing. But if a man loves, he is acknowledged by God', I Cor. 8: 1–3. It is quite likely that Paul is here replying to a letter from the Corinthians that asserted their claim to 'knowledge'. This, Paul suggests, is something he shares with them. But it is quite clear that he does not conceive of belief in God as consisting in building up a number of propositions giving information about God, assuming such propositions to be true. It consists in being personally and rightly related to God.[61] This indeed involves propositions about God but Paul's stress is 'on the primacy of love over the possession of speculative knowledge'. Knowledge that breeds conceit and not love is not true Christian *gnōsis*.

That such knowledge may be the possession of his friends is the prayer of Paul. 'We ask God that you may receive from him all wisdom and spiritual understanding for full insight into his will, so that your manner of life may be worthy of the Lord and entirely pleasing to him. We pray that you may bear fruit in active goodness of every kind, and grow in the knowledge of God', Col. 1: 9–10. Once more knowledge is directly related to the doing of God's will. It is in this way sharply contrasted with gnostic speculation that need not have any practical repercussions. Thus the knowledge that is prayed for is not that of any 'higher worlds' but of the will of God, a concept of knowledge clearly determined by Jewish pre-suppositions.[62]

Later in the same epistle Paul argues, 'Stop lying to one another, now that you have discarded the old nature with its deeds and have put on the new nature, which is being constantly renewed in the image of its Creator and brought to know God', Col. 3: 10. The contrast between Old and New natures ought to find expression in the believer's behaviour. The new nature, the life in Christ, is being renewed in knowledge, that is, the ability to recognise God's will and commands and then to do it.[63] The new man in Christ, unlike the 'old man' who did not have this knowledge (Eph. 4: 17ff), now conducts his life in conformity to the Creator's will.

The same theme as is expressed positively in the above five references is made negatively in the following three. First in the discourse in which the disciples are warned against those who will persecute them it is said, 'They will do these things because they do not know either the Father or me', John 16: 3. The tragedy in the passage is that those who perform in this way against the disciples do so in the belief that they are following God's will. But this shows just how wrong they are and illustrates their complete failure to recognise in Christ the true nature and activity of God. They do not 'know' God and this finds expression in their reaction both to Christ and his disciples.

Paul often draws his letters to a close with some moral injunctions. This is the case in I Thessalonians as he calls the Christians to holiness, 'not giving way to lust like the pagans who are ignorant of God', 4: 5. The wrong attitude to God has 'natural' consequences for those whose lives express culpable ignorance. For Paul, Christian doctrine and Christian ethics are inseparable, for both express the life in Christ.

The third 'negative' reference is Titus 1: 16, a word against false teachers. 'They profess to acknowlege God, but they deny him by their actions'. It may be that there was an elite claiming to possess a privileged knowledge of God, either Jews or 'Gnostics'.[64] Whoever they were they seem to have lost the capacity to distinguish between good and evil both their reason and conscience being tainted. We do not know just what practices they indulged in, but whatever it is shows they do not 'know' God. 'Just as faith without works is dead, so the quality of man's life is the decisive test of his knowledge of God'.[65]

I conclude with one more reference that takes up this idea of a test directly. 'Here is the test by which we can make sure that we know him: do we keep his commands? The man who says, "I know him", while he disobeys his commands, is a liar and a stranger to the truth; but in the man who is obedient to his word, the divine love has indeed come to its perfection', I John 2: 3–5. It is quite probable that again we have a word directed against false 'gnostic' teaching. But the point is clear enough. The true knowledge of God is not a speculative matter but is a relationship with God finding expression in the whole of a Christian's life. The Christian obeys not in order to know God but because he knows God. As R. Bultmann puts it 'keeping the commandments is not the condition but the characteristic of the knowledge of God'.[66]

The above texts adequately supports my contention that the concept of the knowledge of God as *necessarily* involving obedience to God is a feature of the New Testament. As usual I have concentrated attention on instances where the verbs for 'knowing' are used. The case could be made even more complete if the basis of selection were broader, e.g. to include Jesus' warnings about hypocrisy, his own insistence upon love showing itself in action as revealed in many parables etc.

The Christian's knowledge of God, as expressed in the teaching of the New Testament, involves him in a particular form of life, at once ethical and religious. It is a form of life he shares with others, the new people of God in Christ. It includes both beliefs about Jesus and obedience to Jesus as the revelation of God.

CONCLUSION

In the preceding four sections I have shown that the various forms of knowledge claims I analysed earlier are present in the New Testament with reference to God. In this respect the New Testament is similar to the Old Testament. It follows from this variety of 'knowing' that the concept of the knowledge of God in the Bible is complex, too complex to admit of any single analysis.

As I have already said, it is not my purpose to give an account of *the* concept of the knowledge of God in the New Testament. However, there are three features of what 'knowing God' means to which I wish to draw attention. I do this because these features are related to what I said about knowing God in the Old Testament and will be seen to be significant in the argument of the final chapters.

1   As was the case with the New Testament, the concept of God in the New Testament is just 'given'. The understanding of 'God' in the New Testament directly relates to its Old Testament inheritance, although it is enlarged and sharpened by Jesus Christ. Within the New Testament there are no signs of disagreement about what knowing God entails, what God requires, what God is really like and how we come by our knowledge of God. But at no point is there any suggestion that there is no God. We might say that, as with the Old Testament, the New Testament tells a story in which the chief character is God. He may not always be obvious, but there is no doubt but that he is there.

2   Again, like the Old Testament, the knowledge of God in the New Testament is many faceted. It includes acknowledgement, recognition, obedience, etc. It is a practical, intellectual and experiential matter. In both Testaments it is understood that God must be loved by heart, soul, strength and mind. Since this is all there is to man it means 'knowing God' is something 'total' in life.

The 'form' of the knowledge of God is liturgical, social, pedagogic and ethical in character. The believers gather in community for worship. They collect the words of Jesus whom they call 'Lord'. They share their life together 'in Christ'. So again the concept of the knowledge of God is something that involves the whole of life. It is life 'in Christ'.

3   A feature of the life in Christ and the knowledge of God is the hope in which the believers live. The full knowledge of God is not the possession of anyone, not even the man in Christ. But he lives in hope that one day his knowledge will be whole, even if now it is only partial. This 'living in hope' is part of the knowledge of God in the New Testament.

12

God and Inferential Knowledge

In these final chapters of the study, my aim is to say as clearly as I can what the knowledge of God means in the light of the philosophical analysis and biblical exegesis undertaken in the previous Chapters.

First, I shall discuss the issues involved in making claims to know God inferentially, either from the world as a whole or from special events such as miracles. I shall look again at the question of evidence with regard to God and I shall also ask whether it makes any sense to speak of God acting in the world at all.

Then, in Chapter 13, I turn again to the question of knowing God by acquaintance and description. I shall be concerned with whether 'meeting God' is a logical possibility, with whether God can be described and with the context of religious experience.

Chapter 14, the final chapter, contains my concluding argument. It is that within Wittgenstein's concept of a form of life all the various knowledge claims I have analysed can be brought together. I shall argue that religious belief may be conceived of as a form of life and that what 'knowing God' means is to participate in this form of life; to be, in fact, a religious believer.

GOD AND INFERENTIAL KNOWLEDGE

So, in the light of my previous analysis of inferential knowledge claims, and of the expression of such claims to know God made in the Bible, I now ask in this Chapter whether God can conceivably be the object of inferential knowledge.

As I previously outlined,[1] inferential knowledge claims are of the form that someone knows that P. Three conditions have to be fulfilled if the claim is proper; viz (1) that P is true, (2) that P is believed to be true, and (3) that there are grounds or reasons for being sure that P which amount to more than just a matter of restating the belief that P. This third condition therefore concerns evidence, i.e. whatever it is that gives the claimant the right to be sure. Knowledge, by definition, cannot be erroneous. But knowledge claims can. Whenever there is a claim to know something by inference, this implies that the claimant is willing to give reasons for his claim. The claim fails if he is unwilling to give reasons or if the reasons he gives are logically inappropriate or can be shown to be factually inaccurate.

Now my question is, can God be known in these terms? Can he be inferred from something else? And if so, what? What would count as evidence for God? I have previously shown that in the Bible there are claims to know God that imply the possibility of knowing him by inference.[2] I shall now discuss the possibility of inferring the existence, nature or activity of God from such putative historic events as the Exodus from Egypt or the life, death and resurrection of Jesus.

The discussion will take the following form. First, I shall consider the general question of the possibility of making any inferences from the world to God. Second, I shall concern myself with issues that arise from asserting that an event, such as the resurrection of Jesus, is an act whereby God makes himself known. Third, I shall consider the possibility of ever having evidence for God. Fourth, I shall discuss the question of whether any assertions about God acting in the world are intelligible to us.

INFERRING GOD FROM THE WORLD

First then the question of inferring God from the world. The Cosmological Argument, for example, is an attempt to prove the existence of God from the world. The world is understood to provide empirical evidence from which it may logically be inferred that God exists. The Cosmological Argument is interesting in this connection because Aquinas, who propounded the argument in the first three of his famous *Five Ways*, appealed both to empirical evidence as his starting point and employed the notion of the causal agency of God. His intention was to show from the world that there is a Necessary Being who is the cause of the world. His argument is . . .

. . . Some things we encounter have the possibility of being and not being, since we find them being generated and corrupted, and accordingly with the possibility of being and not being. Now it is impossible for all that there is to be like that; because what has the possibility of not being, at sometime is not. If therefore everything has the possibility of not being, at one time there was nothing. But if this were the case, there would be nothing even now, because what is does not begin to be except through something which is; so if nothing was in being, it was impossible for anything to begin to be, and so there would still be nothing, which is obviously false. Not everything therefore has the possibility (of being and not being), but there must be something which is necessary. Now everything which is necessary has the cause of its necessity outside itself, or it does not. Now it is not possible to go on for ever in a series of necessary beings which have a cause of their own necessity, just as was shown in the case of efficient causes. So it is necessary to assume something which is necessary of itself, and has no cause of its necessity outside itself, but is rather the cause of necessity in other things, and this all men call God'.[3]

There are a number of important philosophical matters raised by such a statement, for example, that of the concept of 'necessary being'. But it is my intention to concentrate only on the emphasis of cause and effect.

Although the concept of cause and effect has two elements it is essentially a single concept. That is to say, the concept is of one whole which has at least two parts, i.e. one cause, the other effect or effects. It does not make sense just to speak of a cause by itself. It has to be a cause of something. In the same way an effect must be the effect of something, namely a cause. So the notion of cause makes sense in that given a cause there is an effect.

What follows from this is that the notion of cause only has application when in a whole consisting of parts, i.e. where there is a distinction between one thing and another within the whole. Suppose I am digging in my garden and uncover some broken pottery and small round metal objects. I am curious enough to ask what they are and how did they come to be in my garden. So I take them to the local museum where they are identified as Roman pots and coins. Further digging and discoveries lead to the inference that a large Roman community existed in these parts long ago. The evidence is good for such an assertion. I have an anwer to my question, how did these coins come to be in my garden? The answer is they are the 'effect' of Romans who once lived here. Thus, with reference to distinct factors within the world, the notion of cause and effect has application.

Problems arise when the question is asked 'what is the cause of everything?'. My illustration above about Romans and their coins made sense because the notion of cause and effect is applicable within the world, taking the world in the sense that Wittgenstein took it, namely 'all that is the case'.[4] Does it make sense to talk of the cause of all that is the case? I submit that it does not. The question of what is the cause of all that is the case does not make sense because the concept of cause is such that there must necessarily be a distinction between what is the case and what is the effect and if 'all there is' is understood to be one thing or the other, i.e. cause or effect, then there is no logical room left for this distinction. This is a strictly *logical* problem about asking what is the cause of 'all that is the case'.

The religious believer may well assert that this is not a problem for him because he denies the assertion that the world is all that is the case. He calls the world 'creation' and thereby logically implied that there is something other than the world which is the case, i.e. the Creator. With this distinction between God and the world he has the logical room necessary to employ the notion of cause and effect. The Creator is the cause, creation is the effect.

However, I suggest this only moves the religious believer on to another problem. If the Cosmological Argument is to work then 'all that is the case' must equal the world plus something. But the problem here is that the world is everything that is spatio-temporally identifiable. God, who is the 'something' proponents of the Cosmological Argument suggest is the cause of the world, is by definition distinct from the world. But if that is so then how do we identify God? If the religious believer wants to deny that the world is all that is the case, then he must give some indication of how whatever is other than the world is to be identified. How do you identify what is not, by definition, spatio-temporally identifiable but is said to be the cause of all that is spatio–temporally identifiable? I shall give attention to this problem later. I merely state it here. If the religious believer claims to have logical space in which to employ the notion of cause and effect to God and the World he must meet the challenge of how that which is more than the world is to be identified.

When I am told of the ancient Romans who left the coins long years ago in my garden it is at least possible that an account could be given of what these ancient Romans looked like. This would allow, if *per impossibile* I returned through the agency of a space time machine to my garden at the time of the ancient Romans, that

I should be able to identify an ancient Roman if they indeed existed. From the account I know how a Roman of those years ago could be identified. But the problem is – how do we identify God? As I say, I shall consider this problem below.

I have a further objection to the Cosmological Argument. I would maintain that what is happening in the Cosmological Argument is that ontological conclusions are being deduced from purely linguistic premises. The exponent of the argument uses the word 'cause' and argues that it is the logic of the word cause that causes must have effects. It is part of the 'grammar' of the word 'cause' that causes have effects and effects have causes. By definition 'effects' have 'causes'. This means that if there is anything to which the word 'effect' has application in its ordinary meaning then that thing will have a cause.

All this is true. But, of course, it is a quite separate question as to whether or not there is anything to which the word 'effect' applies. The exponent of the Cosmological Argument *chooses* to describe the world as an effect and then, relying purely on the definition of this word which he has applied to all that is the case, he infers that there is something which is the cause of all that is the case. This logical necessity, however, resides in the word 'effect' and there alone. Therefore, purely on the basis of a meaning of a word the exponent of the Cosmological Argument infers the existence of some entity, God, who is the cause of the world.

I am not saying that it does not make sense to say 'God created the universe'. Perhaps it is the case that God and the universe are related by reason of cause and effect. All I am now saying is that fact, if it is a fact, cannot be established simply by *speaking* of the universe *as* an 'effect' and thereby from the meaning of the word 'effect' alone deducing that the universe must have a cause.

Suppose for a moment that the exponent of the Cosmological Argument objects, asserting that he is not inferring an ontological conclusion from linguistic premises alone. He may argue that his argument is of a different character involving three features:

1   he observes certain phenomena in the world;
2   he invokes the relational idea of cause and effect, and treats what he has observed as an effect;
3   the phenomena and the relational notion when put together 'point him'[5] in a certain direction, namely the cause of these phenomena.

But this argument in no way turns aside the force of my previous objections. Of course one may take certain phenomena in the world, bring to them the notion of cause and effect and they will point in a certain direction. It might be argued that this is what the scientist is always doing. The scientist investigating certain phenomena will ask 'what is the cause of this?'. This relational idea does point him in a certain direction. He knows where to go looking for what would count as a cause. But this approach of the scientist only holds good if the scientist is pointed 'somewhere' to wherever *in principle* there could be a cause to be identified. But for the exponent of the Cosmological Argument the difficulty still remains of identifying that which is by definition not spatio-temporal, unlike all that the scientist *qua* scientist uses in his application of the cause–effect relation.

More than that the difference between the scientist and the metaphysician is that the scientist does not identify the causes of things purely on the basis of the language that he uses. He does say 'things must have causes' but not just because of the meaning of the words used but because he is committed to this way of organizing the phenomena which he observes. He uses the notion of cause and effect methodologically. As part of his method he goes looking for a cause of what he observes. But he does not affirm that there is a cause exclusively on the basis of language, which is what the exponent of the Cosmological Argument tried to do. And, most importantly, the scientist does not say he has found the cause until he can empirically *identify* it.

INFERENCES FROM PARTICULAR EVENTS

Now I come to my second consideration, the issues raised in asserting that certain particular events are acts of God in which God makes himself known. Both Old and New Testament pay special attention to particular events. In the Old Testament there is the Exodus from Egypt, with special reference to the Red (Reed) Sea Crossing. In the New Testament there is the whole event of Jesus, and in particular his resurrection from the dead. Both these particular events are understood within the biblical tradition to be acts by which God makes himself known, or at least actions in which God is the chief agent. It is asserted that these miraculous events take place because God caused them to take place.

It we are to infer the existence, nature or activity of God from these events two conditions must be fulfilled. First it would have to be established that the event in question actually did take place. This is a matter of historical scholarship. If it could be shown that the putative event was in fact only a legend, then the case would collapse. But second, there would have to be good reason to think that the event was caused by God and no one else. It would have to be shown that there was a direct inference from the event to God. Can either of these conditions be fulfilled in the case of, for example, the resurrection of Jesus?

I am asking whether the resurrection regarded simply and solely as an historic event comparable to any other historic event such as the execution of Charles the First in 1649 is logically credible. I stress *logically* possible. I am not asking whether people are able to believe in it a *psychological* sense. The answer to that would seem to me to be a clear 'yes'. But that only tells us about the 'credibility' (in a non prejorative sense) of some people. It is quite another question to ask whether the resurrection is *logically* credible. It is to ask about reasons for belief. Are there logically valid grounds for such a belief?

A penetrating argument against the logical credibility of the resurrection as an historic event was offered by David Hume. It is found in the now famous tenth chapter of his *An Enquiry concerning Human Understanding*.[6] I shall examine Hume's argument in order to see just what issues are involved.

Hume asserts that in our 'reasonings concerning matters of fact, there are all imaginable degrees of assurance from the highest certainty to the lowest species of moral evidence'.[7] If something has happened in history there are two possibilies. One, that what is said to have happened really did take place; and two, that those who say it did are lying, intentionally or not. When it comes to deciding between these two all we have to go on is experience. Experience includes memory, the testimony of witnesses, and our own experience of what generally happens. A wise man will ask whether there are other events similar to that which is said to have taken place. Has he experience of such events being accurately reported to have happened? A wise man, says Hume, proportions his belief to the evidence.[8] By 'wise' Hume here means rational. The more unusual the event, i.e. the stranger it is to our experience, then the heavier will be the evidence against it.

For Hume, a miracle is a violation of the laws of nature.[9] He does not conceive of these 'laws' in any metaphysical sense as being imposed upon nature, 'laws which never shall be broken'. These 'laws' are but expressions of our 'firm and unalterable experience' and that is all. They are not logically necessary. They may be denied without self contradiction. Exceptions may occur, falsifying what we experienced was the case. All this is logically possible. The question is 'is it probable?'.

A miracle therefore is conceived by Hume as an exceptional event. If we are faced with deciding whether or not the putative exception to the laws of nature did, as a matter of historical fact, occur we have as it were two sides of a balance before us. On the one hand there is our uniform experience that suggests that this sort of thing does not happen. But on the other hand there is the testimony of those who say the event did take place because they witnessed it. The occurrence of the event must be judged against the fact that 'there must be a uniform experience against every miraculous event, otherwise the event would not merit that application',[10] and the fact that some claim to have witnessed the miracle.

Now Hume argues that the balance tips in favour of the testimony of witnesses only if one condition is fulfilled. 'No testimony is suffcient to establish a miracle, unless the testimony be of such a kind, that its falsehood would be more miraculous, than the fact, which it endeavours to establish.'[11]

In the case of the resurrection we would have to put in the balance, on the one hand, that it is our uniform experience that when anyone is dead and buried they do not come back to life again, and on the other hand, the fact that the close friends of Jesus tell us this is in fact what has taken place. But what is the more miraculous, that Jesus rose from the dead or that the disciples who reported this event did not tell the truth? Hume puts it this way:

'When anyone tells me, that he saw a dead man restored to life, I immediately consider with myself, whether it be more probable, that this person should either deceive or be deceived, or that the fact, which he relates, should really have happened. I weigh the one miracle against the other; and according to the superiority, which I discover, I pronounce my decision, and always reject the greater miracle. If the falsehood of his testimony would be more miraculous than the event which he relates; then, and not till then, can he pretend to command my belief or opinion'.[12]

We can say that the putative miracle *probably* happened if, and only if, it would be an exception to our normal experience and a greater exception than the miracle itself to discover that those who reported it had lied. It is Hume's case against miracles that this condition is never fulfilled. He has four arguments in support of this contention, the first three being basically matters of historical consideration.[13] It is the fourth that is a philosophical issue. Hume's intention is to show that 'there never was a miraculous event established'. He claims that:

> in matters of religion, whatever is different is contrary; and that it is impossible the religions of ancient Rome or Turkey, of Siam, and of China should, all of them, be established on any solid foundation. Every miracle, therefore, pretended to have been wrought in any of these religions (and all of them abound in miracles), as its direct scope is to establish the particular system to which it is attributed; so has it the same force, though more indirectly, to overthrow every other system. In destroying a rival system, it likewise destroys the credit of those miracles, on which that system was established.[14]

Hume's argument is that whereas there is uniform experience that makes a miracle an exception, there is no uniform experience against false testimony. Indeed, one religion, on Hume's view, bears testimony against that of another, so that the miracles of one religion are evidence against another.[15] A believer who considers his own religion true but all others false must necessarily believe miracles connected with his own religion to have happened, but must necessarily believe those connected with other false religions, whatever the witnesses claim, have not done so. Therefore there is not a uniform experience against false testimony in the case of miracles.

So Hume sees the religious believer on the horns of a dilemma. On the one hand he is committed to the position that there is a uniform experience against the miraculous event taking place. On the other hand, there is no uniform experience against false testimony in regard to this kind of occurrence; indeed he might insist upon the false testimony of others. Therefore, on the basis of probabilities, it is logically impossible to conclude that it is more probable that a miracle, said in a religion to have occurred, really did so than those who said it did were lying, wittingly or unwittingly.

What then of the question of whether an extraordinary event like the resurrection of Jesus is sufficient reason for inferring the existence of God? There was a time when it was argued that miracles were evidence for the existence of God. Against this position Hume's reply is, in my judgement, conclusive. If there is a strong probability that a particular event has not occurred (and the resurrection of Jesus comes into that category) then a wise man who proportions his beliefs to the evidence will hardly feel that the God, who is said to have performed this doubtful feat, himself exists. It would not be rational to hold such a religious belief on the strength of any putative miracle.

On Hume's argument, if the miracle, exceptional as it is, is not in fact so exceptional as the fact that those who reported the miracle were not lying, then what is taken as evidence itself is very uncertain anyway, far too uncertain for any wise man to use in such an important argument as to the existence of God.

But suppose for one moment Hume were incorrect and that the veracity of the disciples could be demonstrated beyond reasonable doubt. Suppose that when they told the story of the empty tomb and the christophanies they were speaking the truth. What follows from this? It follows that an exceptional event has taken place. This is something outside our normal uniform experience. But what follows from this? Our curiosity follows for sure. How did this happen? We would feel compelled to enquire into this strange event. In this sense what follows is psychologically compelling. But does anything else follow? Since this is an empirically observable event we would look for its cause. Suppose we were unable to find any reason for the event's occurrence. Does this lead us to God? The answer is 'no, not necessarily'. If we were to posit 'God' as the answer to our question this would made 'God' logically equivalent to 'we don't know'. There is a logical gap between the historical statement 'Jesus rose from the dead' and the theological statement 'God raised Jesus from the dead.' If 'Jesus rose from the dead' is historically untrue then the statement 'God raised Jesus from the dead' is untrue also because the truth of the latter logically implies the truth of the former. But the statement 'Jesus rose from the dead' whether it be historically true or not, in no way necessarily implies that 'God raised Jesus from the dead.' This is because if we conceive of Jesus' resurrection as a spatio-temporal event then we cannot infer, simply from the proposition that this event has taken place, any proposition which refers to what is more, or quite other than a spatio-temporal event. God is not conceived of as a spatio-temporal event. It is therefore logically impossible to infer his existence from premises which have to do *solely* with spatio-temporal events. If it be a fact that Jesus rose from the dead, it cannot validly be concluded from that that God raised him.

This same argument applies to those who say that the existence of the church confirms or proves the resurrection of Jesus. The existence of the church does no such thing. It does reveal a continuity through the centuries of those that believed that Jesus rose from the dead, but that is all. It does not prove that the event happened. It certainly does not prove that God was the decisive agent in Jesus' resurrection.

To return to Hume for a moment, it is important to indicate just what it is, and what it is not, that he has shown. He has shown that the argument that a miracle demonstrated the existence of God is a poor one because of the high improbability of such an event ever having taken place. The event attributed to God, considered simply as a spatio-temporal historical event apart from the agency of God, would be highly improbable. With that I can think of no reason to disagree. But given that someone does believe in God, Hume has not shown that if that person were to say of the resurrection of Jesus that God did it that he is necessarily talking nonsense. That the event is improbable is one thing. That it is impossible is another. Hume does not argue that God's agency, raising someone from the dead, is logically impossible. He does say it is highly improbable, and he judges so improbable that wise men will not believe it. But a miraculous event is not self contradictory. It may cause us to reconsider what is and what is not to be understood concerning 'laws of nature'. Hume was at pains to show that these are simply a matter of what we call custom. That dead men have not risen in no sense means necessarily that no man should ever rise from the dead. Should such a resurrection be reported as having taken place we might count it incredible, improbable, but we are not entitled to say it could never have taken place. On the other hand, if we believed in God, the event might not be so incredible after all because the probability of its occurrence would then depend upon what we took the activity of God to be. Certainly we would not be indulging in any self-contradiction if we reported an event which was the very opposite of all we had ever experienced before.

WHAT COUNTS AS EVIDENCE OF GOD?

The heart of inferential knowledge is the making of inferences on the basis of what is taken to be good evidence. Would these miracles count as evidence for God? I have indicated that those who argued from the putative fact of a miracle to the existence of God were making an invalid inference. It is not logically possible to argue from an event in this world to the existence of something, or someone, who is outside or beyond this world altogether. Christians argue that God, by definition, is outside or beyond, or more than, this world. We could perhaps make inferences that concerned him validly if he were part of the world. But he is not, and so knowing God by inference is a logical impossibility.

This is not to say that God does not exist. It is only to say we cannot 'prove' his existence from the fact of the world or its history. Does this mean that it makes no sense to speak of evidence for God? It all depends upon what is meant by evidence, and what is taken to count as evidence.

Here I think an important distinction must be underlined. It is the distinction between what it is appropriate to ask *within* religious discourse and what it is appropriate to ask *outside* religious discourse. Essentially the distinction is between discourse where God is already the assumed basic concept, i.e. theological or religious language, and discourse where God is not so assumed. Both forms of discourse seem to me to be quite legitimate. But it is necessary to understand that both have their limitations and logic. That is to say, there are questions, assertions, etc. that are quite proper within and without religious discourse but which when misplaced become quite inappropriate. For example, the question 'What does the Lord require of you?' is a meaningful question *within* religious discourse to which there is an acceptable answer or answers. But *outside* religious discourse, i.e. in a situation where the concept of 'the Lord' is not given or is not understood, the question makes little sense. And alternatively the question, 'Is the concept of God one of which we can make sense?' is a proper one *outside* religious discourse and permits of its several answers. But conversely the question makes no sense *within* religious discourse. Of course the language used within religions is not entirely unrelated to that used without religion, an issue to which I have already drawn attention[16] and to which I shall give further attention later; yet I count the distinction valid and important.

The distinction I have drawn is not peculiar to religious language alone. It applies to all universes of discourse. As Wittgenstein amply showed, to answer a question in one language game with a concept from another is to end with nonsense and the confusion of category mistakes. This is illustrated simply by picturing a conversation between a road safety engineer and a strictly devout religious believer.

The road safety engineer says, 'You ought to readjust the brakes on your car', to which the other replies, 'No, I shouldn't, its Sunday.' Both statements are meaningful so long as they are properly 'placed'. But as they stand, the road engineer might well wonder what the fact that today is Sunday has got to do with the obligation all drivers have to keeping their brakes properly adjusted, while the religious believer might despair at this official who asks him to break one of God's commandments.

Now all this is to the point in considering the question of the demand for evidence and how far certain question can be pressed. Let us take the very basic question 'Does God exist?'. For the atheist nothing is evidence for God's existence. Indeed he will point to facts in the world that count against such a belief. Neither the universe as a whole, nor the particular events that religious believers deem most important, nor anything else will be such as to lead him to infer the existence of God. This will come as no surprise to us since we have seen that all attempts to infer the existence of God from the world as a whole or from special events in particular are invalid.

For the Christian theist, on the other hand, 'the world is charged with the grandeur of God'. The beauty of nature, the sense of moral obligation, the history of Israel, the life, death and resurrection of Jesus, the saints, his own religious awareness, all this and more is 'evidence' for God. Yet this is not 'evidence' used to convince him of the existence of God. The very thought of God is prior to these experiences so that he, like the atheist, is not inferring the existence of God at all.

It is not enough to say that one appeals to evidence and the other to counter evidence. It is not enough to say just that different people see different events in different ways. Rather is it that the theist and the atheist 'experience' the world differently, understand it differently, indeed understand themselves and their existence differently.

So the concept of God is one that is so basic as to have fundamental ontological significance for the religious believer and unbeliever. Settling the question of whether God exists or not is not a matter of appealing to evidence.

I have argued that neither from the universe, nor from special events like the resurrection of Jesus can God validly be inferred. This is not to say that God does not exist, or that the universe is not his creation, or that he has not acted in raising Jesus from the dead. It is simply to say we cannot infer from these events his existence. However, we must now move on to a fourth issue, the issue of whether or not it makes sense to talk of God acting in the world anyway.

THE CONCEPT OF GOD ACTING IN HISTORY

The issue I wish to discuss now is simply posed. For religious believers God is by definition a being who does not have a physical body. Does it make sense to speak of such a being *acting* in the world?

Let me underline that what I am discussing now is not whether in fact God does or does not act in the world but whether or not it makes sense to talk of God acting in the world. My concern is solely with language and logic. If I show that for God to act in the world is a logical impossibility then we must (logically) affirm that God does not act into the world whatever religious believers say about him. On the other hand, if I show that talk of God acting in the world is not logically self contradictory or unintelligible then that is *all* I have shown. I have not thereby shown that God has or does act in the world. But I am not intent on attempting to verify the claim theists make, I only wish to enquire whether the claim makes sense.

W. D. Hudson discusses this issue in his *A Philosophical Approach to Religion*.[17] He indicates that it is the claim of many philosophers,[18] that it is a necessary condition of an agent acting that he should have a physical body. Their view appeals to our normal experience and our ordinary use of words that arise from it. All actions which we have observed have been performed by an agent possessed of a physical body. If we were to observe an event caused by an agent we could not see, we would infer, on the basis of experience, that such an agent had a physical body, this being a necessary condition of acting. The argument is that having a physical body is a necessary even though it may not be a sufficient[19] condition of being an agent. So if God is a being who acts in the world, then it is logically necessary that he should have a physical body.

Having a body is not a sufficient condition of an agent's action because what is meant by an action cannot be fully explained in terms of bodily movements alone. The question 'what was x doing when he did y?', cannot be fully answered just by reference to the bodily actions involved. What x was *doing* might be any number of things in the action y. If y is swinging an arm then x might be throwing a ball, walking briskly, directing traffic, etc. etc. He might be doing any one of these things and in consequence merely describing the bodily movement involved would not serve as a sufficient condition for saying that a particular action had occurred.

We know what action has occurred when we know what the agent intended to do. An agent's action can sometimes be deduced or inferred from his bodily movements. But, as I have already indicated, his bodily movements may mislead us to what he is *doing*, that is what he intends his action to be. An agent's answer to the question, 'What are you doing?' has a final authority which nothing else can possess. Our inference from his bodily movements may be mistaken. But it is inconceivable that he should not know what he intends to do. His *intention* makes his action the action that it is. We cannot conceive of any action divorced from its intention. The consequences of an action like the bodily movements accompanying an action are something logically quite distinct from the agent's intention. But the action itself is not logically distinct from his intention.

What then is involved in saying that bodily movement is a necessary condition of any action? This is the question that is the one for the religious believer to face because no religious believer would want to affirm that bodily movement is a sufficient condition of God acting. The challenge of the philosophers to whom I have drawn attention is that bodily movement is a necessary condition of any action and that therefore, because God does not have a body, talk of God acting does not make sense. I shall argue, following Hudston, that it is an intelligible statement to say 'God acts in the world.'

There are two questions that have to be faced here. They are:

1   If God does not possess a body, can we conceive of him entering the flux of spatio-temporal events in the world in the way in which he must for us to say that he has acted, his action having made a difference in the world?

2   If God does not possess a body, how is he to be identified as an agent, a logical subject of the verb 'to act'? If these two questions can be answered positively then I believe I shall have shown that talk about God acting in the world is not unintelligible to us.

I shall take the two questions in order, taking as a paradigm of divine activity the Exodus from Egypt by the children of Israel.

1   *How Can God, if He Has No Body, Intervene in the Course of Spatio-Temporal Events as an agent?*

First, we must notice the distinction which can be drawn between an agent and his situation.[20] This is a logical gap illustrated in such questions as 'Are you going to take the new job offered you?' 'What are you going to do about your redundancy?' It makes sense to talk about someone 'standing back' and considering the situation in which they are set, but considering it as observers. To do this is often a wise approach to decision-making, appraising the situation before forming our intention.

This distinction is clear enough in the cases I have described. It applies to all situations in which people find themselves. But it can also be applied in the case of an agent and his own body. For example it makes sense to ask the question if you are a grown man, 'shall I grow a beard?' or 'what shall I do about my strained wrist?' It makes sense to conceive of an agent distinct from his situation and to conceive of his body as part of that situation. As an agent he is not being identified with his new job, his redundancy, his beard, his wrist or anything else which constitutes his situation. From all this he, as agent, is logically distinct. This is the case, so long as he remains an agent. It may perhaps not be the case in those situations of severe mental breakdown or inability. But then we could say that the person had ceased in some way to be an agent. But where the agent is capable of forming some intention there is a gap, a dualism between mind and body. The question 'what are you going to do about your body?' can always be put and it is never self answering. The distinction being drawn is important and it means that it is always difficult, if not impossible, to draw a line between those parts of any situation which are the agent's body and those parts which are something other than his body.

What then does an agent need to have in order to act? Does he need to have a body, which is logically different from the rest of his situation? I have shown that the concept of agency is logically distinct from that of bodily movement. Because an agent is distinct from his situation, which includes his body, it is possible to conceive of an agent without a body.

However, it may be objected that, valid though this distinction is, where action takes place it involves bodily movement. These two things cannot be equated but they do go together. My response to this would be to say that indeed, where action occurs, empirically observable changes occur. We cannot reduce the one to the other but they are related in that way and always occur together.

What conclusions can be drawn thus far with respect to God? First, that for God to act it is not logically necessary for him to have a body. But second, it is necessary when God acts for certain spatio-temporal events to have occurred in the world. This second assertion is no problem to the religious believer. The Bible never says that God acts in the world without some event taking place, indeed it would want to insist upon it. The Exodus event involves the waters being held back, an empirically observable event. These events can be described just as the bodily movements of a human agent can be described. I wish to throw a ball, and my arm moves. God wills to deliver his people from Egypt and the waters are held back for their escape. But in both cases the agent and his intentions are logically distinct from any bodily movements or spatio-temporal events open to observation.

Two conditions must be fulfilled for anyone to be an agent. They are that the agent has an intention to act and the means of fulfilling that intention. Having an intention cannot be equated with making certain bodily movements. But if the agent is to fulfil his action some spatio-temporal event or movement must take place. It is not logically necessary, for reasons I have given above, that the agent should have a body. It would still make sense to call him an agent if he intended something and was able to cause or able or prompt that intention's fulfilment.

Consider the statement, 'Cromwell suppressed the Levellers'. This is an intelligible statement to those who know the meaning of the words used. However, it does not require for its sense that Cromwell himself suppressed each individual Leveller. It does not require that he be physically able to suppress anyone. The statement might still be meaningful if Cromwell was completely physically incapacitated. So long as Cromwell had the intention of suppressing the Levellers and could find co-operative subjects to work out that policy then he would rightly be said to be the chief agent in the suppression of the Levellers.

I submit that it is intelligible to speak of God acting in the world if (a) he has the intention to do so and (b) he has the means to fulfil that intention. Neither point necessarily requires that God has a body. It does require his ability to use things and persons in the world as his willing subjects. This point would fit well with the 'tone' of many biblical statements. For example, the Exodus is the action of God, but Moses the servant of God leads the people out of slavery. The return from Exile is the act of God, but Cyprus of Persia is an instrument to fulfil God's intention. And in the New Testament there is the unique claim that the Word (intention?) of God became flesh in the Servant Messiah, the prophet from Nazareth. It might also be noted that if telekinesis is conceivable then the power to make spatio-temporally observable changes without bodily movement is not at all unintelligible.[21]

It is not my intention to say 'how' God acts in the world in the sense of describing the 'mechanics' involved. I am not sure whether this could ever be done. All I have argued thus far is that it is not a necessary condition of God being conceived of as an agent that he has a body. I move on to the question that has cropped up several times already and must now be faced, the question of identity.

2   *If God Does Not Possess a Body, How Is He To Be Identified as an Agent, a Logical Subject of the Verb 'To Act'?*
This is the problem of the identification of the agent. In the case of human beings we usually identify the agent by his body. 'Who scored the try?' asks the late-comer at the rugby match. 'Our new scrum-half', says the coach raising his arm and pointing, 'he's the one with the bald head and bushy beard'. The agent is identified with reference to his body. This mode of identification is not possible in the case of God.

However, as part of our normal experience, we do sometimes speak of an agent acting without reference to his body at all, yet identifying the action as his by reason of its effects. We say 'this must have been done by Smith, no one else would do it that way'. We deduce from what has happened that it must have been so and so. Or we attribute what has happened to his agency because we believe that it is the sort of thing he would have done.

Let us suppose that a house is burgled in a rather sophisticated manner. The experienced detective called to the scene of the crime observes what has happened, and immediately sends his assistant to check on the whereabouts of Ivan Jemmy, the notorious cat burglar. To the detective all the signs are there that this is Ivan's work. No one else acts in this way when it comes to house breaking. Of course, the detective may be wrong, but he may also be right and he would point to the 'effects' as justification of his claim that Ivan did it. The evidence is circumstantial and therefore not totally a matter of proof but, for the experienced detective, the identify of Ivan is inferred from what he has reason to believe is Ivan's work.

Now, if we have some such experience of identifying an agent by observing the effects of his activity, is it conceivable that we extend that notion to God? In the case of Ivan it is always logically possible that someone could have observed him in the act of burglary and thereby relate his identity to his bodily movements. It is also logically possible that Ivan can be identified without references to his actions as a burglar. Neither of these possibilities is open to us in the case of God. But let us further imagine that 'Ivan' is a fictitious name given by the police to a burglar they have reason to believe has committed a number of crimes all of a similar nature. It may or may not be the case that Ivan exists. It may or may not be the case that he has done all that the police believe he has done. But my point is, it makes sense for the police to talk about 'Ivan'. They know what they are talking about when they talk of 'Ivan', he is identified by his actions.

Now, since it is the question of identity only that we are concerned with here it seems to me quite conceivable that from observing certain events in the world, and bringing to them the question of who acted in this way, we could claim to have identified God. We have not tried to prove the existence of God from these events. We need not close our minds to the possibility of being mistaken. But there seem to me no reason why we should not speak of certain events in the world as being the means by which we identify God. The fact that God does not have a spatio-temporal location is nothing to the point. It is not necessary that Ivan should have a spatio-temporal location for us to say that this is his work. The question is only whether we can make sense of using certain spatio-temporal events as a means of identifying someone who is the cause of these events. This seems to me to be quite legitimate practice in the case both of Ivan and God. 'Proving' that it was Ivan or God is another matter and is not our concern here. But it does make sense to say that this is x's action although x has not been observed performing it, all the more since x and the bodily movements involved in the action are logically distinct. '*It would not be entirely unintelligible* to attribute something which goes on in the world to an agent even though one could not identify *anything in the world* as his hand. If this is intelligible then we *can* make sense of the notion of a bodiless agent and so of the belief that God acts in the world and meets with men.'[22]

This conclusion again fits well with the Biblical tradition which
asserts that God is known in some way by his actions in history.
It is a matter of fact that, in the biblical context, God was 'identified'
by the Israelites by reason of his encounters with special people
and his mighty acts. Thus if an Israelite was asked who God was
he might reply by talking about the One who called Moses, who
acted against Pharoah, who led his people out of Egypt, who gave
them the gift of the land etc. It is by constant reference back to the
Exodus that Israel was reminded of who God was. In the same
way in the New Testament a Christian might 'identify' God with
reference to the spatio-temporal event of Jesus the prophet from
Nazareth. God is the 'God and Father of our Lord Jesus Christ'.
Moreover, the theme is there in the Biblical thought of the God
who hides himself. He is not observed, but men may see his
shadow, his glory or his mighty acts.

Where there is in our experience something which happens which
is unusual to the point of uniqueness and consistently occurs, we
say the same person must be doing this. And it is this sort of
identification of God that the Bible points to.

Kai Neilsen,[23] commenting directly on Hudson's argument, does
not think that it has been shown that sense can be made of the
assertion that God acts in the world. He argues that whereas there
is a distinction between an agent and his bodily situation, these
are not totally separate. He finds the concept of 'disembodied
agency' unintelligible because the *meaning* of being an agent
includes that of possessing a body. This is but to repeat the initial
argument that having a body is a necessary condition of being an
agent. As Neilson argues . . .

> "Wherever there is a human agent there is a body" is not like
> "Wherever there is smoke there is a fire", but like "where there
> is a triangle there is a three sided figure". The agent or the "I"
> may be systematically illusive and not capable of being fully
> described in behavioural terms, but this does not at all show or
> even suggest what it could *mean* to speak of a bodiless person,
> self or agent.[24]

Of course, Neilsen was right in his assertion that 'wherever there
is a human agent there is a body' is like 'wherever there is a triangle
there is a three sided figure' because being human means possessing
a body. Being human indeed means more than that, but it at least

necessarily means just that. It makes no sense to say 'he is a human being but he has no body'. The analytic quality of the proposition lies in the necessary relation between persons and bodies. But this is no warrant to assert 'all agents must have bodies'. The 'must' does not have the force of logical necessity as Neilsen himself concedes in affirming that an agent is systematically illusive in terms of bodily descriptions. It may be difficult to say what being a bodiless agent means. But that is not the same as saying that it is logically inconceivable that a conscious being who has no body acts in the world and meets with men.

CONCLUSION

Can God be known inferentially? I have shown that this is a logical impossibility in the case of attempting to infer God's existence from the fact of the world or from special designated events within it. However, I have also shown that talk about God acting in the world, and therefore of certain events being the result of his activity, is not unintelligible to us. I have also argued that these 'acts of God' do not count as evidence for the unbeliever but neither are they used by the religious believer as evidence to demonstrate the existence of God. But, within religious discourse the possibility of inferring the characteristics of God, his will and his purposes, from these events is quite legitimate. My conclusion is that we cannot infer from anything the existence of God, establishing his existence, that is, as of some other 'thing'. But if we bring the concept of God to the world and its history, then inferences are possible and proper. The question now is whether this 'bringing of the concept of God to the world and its history' is in any way legitimate. But before answering that question in Chapter 14 I turn now to the possibility of God being known by acquaintance and description.

13

God and Knowledge by Acquaintance and Description

In an earlier Chapter I suggested that the distinction between knowledge by acquaintance and knowledge by description is that between direct and indirect knowledge.[1] Knowledge by acquaintance is a matter of the direct cognitive awareness of some one. Knowledge by description is a matter of indirect knowledge of some thing or person. I argued that direct knowledge was foundational of indirect knowledge. There were four features of knowing by acquaintance to which I drew particular attention, namely:

1 Knowing by acquaintance is personal. It has a first hand quality about it necessarily. This is not to say that it is private, for it must admit of some description. It is by making some such description that what we know by acquaintance passes out of private experience into the world of public truth.

2 Knowing by acquaintance is non-transferrable. This is but to say that I cannot have your experience and you cannot have mine. It does not mean that we cannot have similar experiences and describe them to one another.

3 Knowing by acquaintance admits of degree and development. This is illustrated in that it makes sense to speak of knowing something or some one better.

4 Knowing by acquaintance is always more than the sum total of knowledge by description. No amount of description can be the same as the experience of knowing by acquaintance. However, if there is said to be no possibility of giving a description of what is claimed to be known by acquaintance then the claim to knowledge by acquaintance makes no sense.

It is a matter of fact that a number of people claim to know God by acquaintance. They base their claim on an experience which they take to be direct cognitive awareness of God. Stories of direct cognitive awareness of God are recorded in the Bible; for example, Isaiah's experience in the Temple (Isa. 6).

It is my purpose in this chapter to examine the nature and logic of this sort of claim. I propose to do so in the following way. First, I will ask whether 'meeting God' is a logical possibility. Then, if the answer is affirmative, to ask whether God can be described. Thirdly, I shall consider what, if anything, follows from an assertion to know God by acquaintance. And fourthly, I shall draw attention to an important feature of the context of religious experience.

IS 'MEETING GOD' LOGICALLY POSSIBLE?

As I have already said, there can be no doubt that many religious believers talk of experiencing God, often with reference to particular incidents in their lives. I am not attempting here to say whether their claims are veridical or not. I am concerned only with the meaning and logic of such claims. If I can show that all talk of 'meeting God' involves logical impossibilities, then the conclusion must be that no one has ever 'met God' and religious believers are just deceiving themselves if they imagine they have 'encountered God' in a particular situation. If I show that 'meeting God' is a logical possibility I have not thereby established that anyone has in fact done so.

The main problem at issue is similar to that discussed in Chapter 12 concerning talk of God as a bodiless agent. Here the problem may be stated thus. When in ordinary discourse I say 'I met Jones' I imply, among other things, that I encountered his body. It is with reference to his body that I identify Jones and conclude that it is he and not Smith that I have met. Part of the meaning of 'meeting Jones' is 'encountering Jones's body'. However, when the religious believer claims to have met God he cannot logically imply that he has encountered a body. Traditional Christianity denies that God has a body. Can we make sense of this talk of meeting someone who, by definition, does not have a body?

I suggest that talk of meeting or encountering God does make sense for the reasons which I have earlier given. To meet Smith is not simply to come into sensory contact with Smith's body. This I think is clear from the logic of knowing by acquaintance. I have illustrated earlier that although there is a relationship between knowing by acquaintance and knowing by description, no amount of description can ever be the same as acquaintance. I may know everything there is to know *about* Smith, the colour of his eyes, the size of his body, the post he holds, where he lives, etc. etc. But all of this is logically distinct from being acquainted with Smith.

R. W. Hepburn discusses a scale of acquaintance where the physical body aspect becomes progressively less and less prominent.[2] His argument is, however, that if there is to be any sense in the notion of meeting Smith it is necessary that Smith should have a body. Even in the deepest experiences of acquaintance the features of Smith's body are necessarily presupposed. It is these that allow me to identify Smith with whom I am acquainted.

I shall come to the question of identification in a moment. For the present I reiterate my point that just as the concept of an agent is logically distinct from his body or situation, so the concept of acquaintance is logically distinct from the bodies involved in the situation. Hepburn suggests that the theologian speaks of meeting God on the analogy of meeting another man. But he complains that the theologian does not give directions as to how the experience of meeting a person is to be modified in the case of meeting God. This is the philosopher's challenge to the theologian to say how similar and how dissimilar the experience of meeting a person is in contrast with the case of the experience of meeting God. If the theologian's account of meeting God is so unlike the account of meeting a person then the analogy fails and we must say that with regard to the ordinary use of the word 'meet' religious believers do not 'meet God' and therefore they must mean something else by the assertion, or perhaps what they say means nothing at all. I believe this challenge can be met.

Let us first take the case of Smith meeting with Jones in such wise that Smith is able later to say that he knows Jones by acquaintance. What is involved here? It is necessary that there are two independent individuals, Smith and Jones. It is necessary that at some time at a spatio-temporal location they meet. It is necessary that their 'meeting' involves more than just observation of each other if they are to claim to be acquainted. It is true that it would be possible for Smith to say that he knows Jones by acquaintance because he saw him at a party. What this means is that Smith can identify Jones but all it amounts to is that Smith can give some kind of a description of Jones. For Smith to say he knows Jones by acquaintance, I submit, normally means that after the party, Smith might say, 'Jones and I talked a long time together, he told me his ideas, his interests etc. I really feel he gave something of himself to me.' Smith, being acquainted with Jones, *means* more than he is able to identify and describe Jones. Their relationship is personal and dynamic.

How does this apply in the case of, say, Smith meeting with God in such wise that Smith is able later to say that he knows God by acquaintance? First it is necessary that there are two independent individuals, Smith and God. It is necessary that at a spatio-temporal location they meet and relate to one another in the sense of 'giving' themselves to one another. It is necessary that they are able to identify one another. If these conditions can be met it makes sense to say Smith met God and knows him by acquaintance.

How like and unlike are these two cases? They are alike in that in both cases separate entities are involved. They are not alike in that in the case of Smith and Jones both have physical bodies, but in the case of Smith and God only Smith has a physical body. But the analogy holds so long as we can make sense of the notion of encountering someone who has not got a physcial body but can be identified.

As I have argued because of the distinction between acquaintance and description, I believe we can make sense of the notion of being acquainted with someone who does not have a body. But this is only the case if we can somehow identify who it is we have claimed to encounter. If this can be done then I have shown how like and unlike meeting God is compared with meeting Smith and also that meeting God is not so unlike meeting Smith as to make no sense. Much then hangs on the question of identification and to that I now turn.

CAN GOD BE DESCRIBED?

There are really two questions here. (1) Can God be described? (2) Can God be identified? The answer to the first is 'no' *if* description *means* bodily description. It is true that in the language and thought of the Old Testament reference can be made to God's face, hands, eyes, back, feet, etc. but the Christian tradition of talk about God has been that he has no physical body at all. In this sense there is nothing physcial about God to be described. Questions as to the colour of God's hair, the length of his legs, etc. make no sense in Christian theology because God is not conceived of in these terms at all.

However, it is with reference to their physical bodies that men identify one another. Hence the question, does the fact that God has no body mean that he cannot be identified? I earlier suggested that, after the manner of our experience of other people, it was possible to identify someone with reference to the effects of their actions. I wish now to suggest that it is possible to identify someone by reason of their effect upon us.

Suppose that one morning I meet two friends and tell them that last night I was at a party where I met a most objectionable man. I did not catch his name but he made everyone he met very cantankerous, argumentative and disagreeable. His presence seemed to throw a wet blanket over the whole evening, at least he had that effect upon me. One of my friends might reply that he was not at the party but my description of the effect of this man is very like that of someone he heard of recently who is said always to have that effect wherever he goes. My other friend may go further and say that it sounds like x whom he has met and who made the same impression on him.

From the information of the second friend I may have further information. I may now know that the name of the disagreeable man is x. It is, of course, possible that it is not x at all. It might be y, an equally disagreeable man as x, but unknown to my two friends. But my point is that it is conceivable that from my description of x's effect upon me, and from other people's knowledge of x, I can identify who it was with whom I was so unagreeably acquainted last night. That the identification may be mistaken is not to say that it necessarily is so.

Can this notion be extended to include God? I cannot see why not and indeed would suggest that the biblical material I have discussed fits well with it. For example in the case of Samuel hearing the voice and encountering someone he does not know, the identification is made for him by Eli (I Sam. 3).

It is logically possible that the identification may be mistaken. In the case of God there are no tests applicable as there are in the case of Smith meeting Jones. This is another feature of the unlikeness of the two cases. But the possibility of a mistake does not refute my argument that having an experience of God and being able to identify the experience as of God is not logically impossible. If this is so then I suggest the concept of encountering God is not unintelligible to us.

WHAT FOLLOWS FROM 'HAVING AN EXPERIENCE OF GOD?'

If we allow the logical possibility of encountering God in our experience does anything follow from that? It does not follow that anyone has in fact had an experience of God. It is a matter of empirical fact that many people claim to have or have had religious experiences, which I take to mean experiences of God. Does anything follow from this? It follows that all these people necessarily believe that God exists. It would make no sense to say 'I have had an experience of God but I don't believe that he exists.' However, although these people affirm that they have had an experience of God and that God exists, it does not follow that God does exist nor that their experience is indeed of 'God'.

It is necessary to see why this is so because it is not unknown for people to appeal to religious experience as a means to establishing the existence of God. This cannot be done because there is a logical gap between any account of religious experience and the belief that God exists. It is a similar logical gap to that which exists between any statement reporting an experience and any statement asserting the existence of what is claimed to have been experienced. That gap allows, for example, for the possibility of hallucination. It is always conceivable that what we claim to have experienced and what we may believe therefore exists is nothing but an hallucination.

Sometimes it is claimed that the experience of God which religious believers have is *sui generis*, immediate and self-authenticating.[3] It is not the case that having had the experience they then infer from it the existence of God. Rather, thought of God is inseparable from the experience; it is an experience of God and this is known immediately.

However, this claim hardly settles the question of the objectivity of God. Indeed I think it denies it. Earlier in my discussion of immediate knowledge,[4] I showed that immediate knowledge claims only relate to one's own mental state. The thought of God may come upon me with immediacy but what follows from this is only that I have the thought of God. It does not follow that God exists. I may have what I might call an experience of the peace of God, or the demand of God and no one is in a position to deny that I have had an experience such as I call the peace of God, but nothing follows from the experience as to whether or not God exists or whether there is anything other than my feelings to which 'the peace of God' or 'the demand of God' applies.

What of the claim that an experience of God is self-authenticating? It is not always clear just what this claim means. It may be straight forwardly psychological after the pattern 'This is an experience of the call of God, if you will answer and commit yourself to do God's will and you will find in your experience that it is of God'. Occasionally there are appeals to take the step of faith made just on this basis. 'Taste, then, and see that the Lord is good.'[5] Whether such an appeal is supportable would be discovered by empirical psychological surveys. However, I doubt whether this is what the claim to the self-authenticating nature of religious belief always is. I doubt whether the 'Do x and y will follow' approach allows for the unconditional nature of many religious statements, for example, the straight command 'follow me'.[6]

It may be that the claim to self-authentication is not a matter of psychology but of logic. If this is so I find it hard to see how the claim can stand. The claim would then be that our subjective experience has some infallible and self-authenticating 'mark' because it is an experience of God and therefore unique.[7] Suppose the claim is that I have experienced the peace of God. Now, in so far as 'the peace of God' refers to the characteristics of my subjective experience, then its assertions makes no references to the world about me. It is a description of the state I am in and there is nothing external to myself to show whether the claim be true or false. But if 'the peace of God' were taken to be that infallible mark of the presence of something other than myself, then its absence would be sufficient to deny the experience really was of something objective. But then what was taken to be infallible is not so. For if we are to preserve its infallibility we only do so by making it a matter of definition and that will require that we can only determine whether the experience was real by referring to something other than the experience itself. Therefore it is not self-authenticating.

In the end we cannot get behind the experience to know whether the experience is genuine or illusory as to its subject matter. We can describe the experience, compare our descriptions with those of others. We may even feel able to talk of probabilities other than possibilities. But we shall always run short of certitude in any argument from religious experience to the objective existence of God; and the reason will not just be psychological, it will be a matter of logic.

THE CONTEXT OF RELIGIOUS EXPERIENCE

We never do just have an 'experience'. It is always an experience of something; pain, colour, God etc. We may misinterpret or misunderstand our experience, but they are always experiences of something.

Now, supposing someone asks me whether I have had the pleasure of experiencing 'schumpf'. My answer would be 'no' because I have no idea of what 'schumpf' is. Can you eat it? Is it alive? Is it a place, or a mineral, or what? Whatever it is, I have no concept of schumpf and so, as far as I am concerned, I have had no experience of 'schumpf'. Suppose then that my questioner tells me that 'schumpf' comes from a long lost Devon dialect and means 'being out of breath'; I understand the concept of being out of breath and can tell my questioner now that I have experienced 'schumpf' but it was not a pleasure.

All of this but illustrates the point made by Popper to which I have already drawn attention,[8] that all our experiences are context dependent and conceptually loaded. It is logically necessary therefore that someone should have the concept of God prior to having an experience of God.

My purpose in making this point again is to draw attention to an important aspect in answering the question 'can God be known by acquaintance and by description?' The reference to the matter of the 'context' of our experience is not just a social observation, although of course the social context cannot be ignored. It is also a reference to the logical context, the place where talk of knowing God by acquaintance and description is logically 'at home'.

I have argued that we can make sense of talk about experience of God although clearly God is not conceived of as a physical object among many others of which we may have experience. What I am suggesting is that the distinction between language within religious discourse and language outside religious discourse is again important. The concept of knowing God by acquaintance is 'at home' in religious discourse. Experiences of God are 'at home' in religious belief. It is time to look more closely at this distinction and what it means for our understanding of the concept of the knowledge of God. I shall come to it now in Chapter 14, the final chapter.

14
The Knowledge of God as a Form of Life

INTRODUCTION

The purpose of this study has been to examine, both by way of philosophical analysis and biblical exegesis, the concept of the knowledge of God. I have argued that there are different forms of knowledge claims expressed in the various uses of the word 'know'. Each of these uses allowed for particular knowledge claims to be made, although each had its proper use and logical limitations. I also argued that such was the varied nature of these claims that they could not be reduced to a unified homogeneous account of what knowledge is. I claimed that in the case of the words 'know' and 'knowledge' what we had after analysis was not a definition but a number of proper uses of the words showing 'family resemblances'.

Further, I have showed that these forms of knowledge claims are present in the both Old and New Testaments with respect to God. I made no attempt to unify these claims in order to propound, as it were, what the knowledge of God in the Bible is for that would have been to have gone beyond my purpose. What I have shown is that the concept of the knowledge of God in the Bible is many faceted.

Now I wish to suggest that Wittgenstein's notion of a 'form of life' is a concept within which these claims can meaningfully be drawn together. More than that, I propose to explore, so far as I am able, the idea that religious belief may be one such form of life and to suggest the thesis that it is possible to elucidate the concept of the knowledge of God by showing that we can bring the various notions of knowledge together within the concept of a form of life. I shall do this systematically examining the various claims in the light of this possibility. But I begin by saying what I understand forms of life to be.

150

FORMS OF LIFE

Just what Wittgenstein meant by the phrase 'form of life' is a complicated and controversial matter. He uses the phrase five times in *Philosophical Investigations*, once in *On Certainty* and once in *Lectures and Conversations on Aesthetics, Psychology and Religious Belief*.[1] I shall quote these in full.

> . . . to imagine a language means to imagine a form of life. (*Investigations*, 19)

> 'Here the term "language-game" is meant to bring into prominence the fact that the *speaking* of a language is part of an activity, or of a form of life',   *Investigations* 23.

> It is what human beings *say* that is true and false; and they agree in the *language* they use. That is not agreement in opinions but in form of life', *Investigations* 241.

> 'Can only those hope who can talk? Only those who have mastered the use of a language. That is to say, the phenomena of hope are modes of this complicated form of life'.   (*Investigations*, p.174)

> It is no doubt true that you could not calculate with certain sort of paper and ink, if, that is, they were subject to certain queer changes – but still the fact that they changed could in turn only be got from memory and comparison with other means of calculation. And how are these tested in their turn?
>   What has to be accepted, the given, is – so one could say – *forms of life*.   (*Investigations*, p.226).

> Now I would like to regard this certainty, not as something akin to hastiness or superficiality, but as a form of life. (That is very badly expressed and probably badly thought as well). (*O.C.*, p.358).

> 'Why shouldn't one form of life culminate in an utterance of belief in a Last Judgement?   (*Lectures*, p.58).

These references contain a number of different emphases. Sometimes forms of life and language-games seem to be almost identical in the sense that each language-game has its own related form of life. Sometimes the concept of a form of life appears to be wider than that, reflecting Wittgenstein's interest not just in language but in the relationship of language and reality, thought and being.

J. F. N. Hunter has offered a classification of interpretations of 'forms of life', three from other philosophers and the fourth his own.[2] These four interpretations are as follows:

1   *The Language-Game Account*
On this view a form of life is virtually the same thing as a language-game. To those who look it will be clear enough what the 'game' is. There are therefore as many forms of life as there are language-games.

2   *The Behaviour-Package Account*
Like the first account this one also says that if anything is a form of life there is something formal about it. On this view a form of life is a package of language and behaviour. Language-games and behaviour are conceived to be logically distinct. Not all language-games are forms of life. The illustration of behaviour-package Hunter gives is 'pity'. If we pity someone we shall perform certain gestures and actions, as well as verbalising our pity. If we are performing these actions we shall be likely to express our pity, but only 'likely to', there is no logical necessity about it. Hunter suggests 'we are jointly inclined to engage in the behaviour and . . . to say the words'. Both the above interpretations of forms of life envisage something standardized and communal.

3   *The 'way of life' account*
Here the form of life is the whole way of life followed by some community. Thus monks have a way of life and politicians likewise. It makes sense to contrast nineteenth and twentieth century ways of life.

4   *The 'organic' account*
This is Hunter's own interpretation where he argues that speaking a language is a form of life in the sense that it is 'something typical of a living being'. Speaking a language is understood to be a biological or organic phenomenon of living beings in the same sense as the growth and development of living organisms is typical of them. This interpretation of a form of life has therefore an individual non-standardized reference, unlike interpretations 1 and 2.

How do these interpretations relate to the quotations given above where Wittgenstein used the phrase 'form of life'? I shall examine each in turn, beginning with the references in the *Philosophical Investigations*.

. . . to imagine a language-game means to imagine a form of life.
(*Investigations*, p.19).

If by 'means' Wittgenstein means 'involve', 'implies', or 'signifies' then Interpretations 1 and 2 are immediately brought to mind. Certainly Wittgenstein thought that a language cannot be described without describing the circumstances of its use which includes the related actions. On the other hand Hunter suggests that 'means' can be read 'as about equal to "is a case of"'.[3] If this is so then his own interpretation (Interpretation 4) is possible, understanding 'speaking' as part of the way a living being functions.

Hunter also suggests there is a comparable option about the interpretation of *Investigations* 23, 'Here the term "Language-game" is meant to bring into prominence the fact that the *speaking* of language is part of an activity, or of a form of life'. The options relate to the meaning of 'part of an activity'. If it means that speaking in conjunction with other things forms an activity as a whole, as it were, then again this echos Interpretations 1 and 2. But if it means 'any given utterance is part of a general competence in using the expression it contains', then Hunter argues this 'competence' would be what is meant by a 'form of life'. Since Wittgenstein italicised 'speaking' Hunter suggests that this later understanding fits well with his interpretation.

Hunter finds further support for his understanding of 'form of life' in *Investigations* 241, 'It is what human beings *say* that is true or false; and they agree in the *language* they use. That is not agreement in opinions but in form of life'. He understands 'agree in the language they use' to mean 'agree in the way they speak' which fits his interpretation. On the other hand if the phrase 'agree in the language they use' means 'agree in the language-game' then Interpretations 1 and 2 are possible.

The case of *Investigations*, p.174 is also complex in the sense that different understandings are possible without being contradictory. 'Can only those hope who can talk? Only those who have mastered the use of language? That is to say the phenomena of hope are modes of this complicated form of life'.

If hope or hoping were the form of life referred to here then it would fit the behaviour-package account (Interpretation 20). Hunter, having distinguished the 'phenomena of hope' from hope or hoping itself, suggest that 'this complicated form of life' refers to the use of language or the mastery of the use of language, but not to hope or hoping. By the 'phenomena of hope' Hunter means facial expressions, certain feelings and thoughts etc. So what does it mean to say that the 'phenomena of hope' are modes of the use of language? Hunter argues that the 'phenomena of hope', being distinct from hope, have 'a sort of secondary status as hope'. When anyone says they hope, they do not report on their feelings or features, they *express* hope. This expression is a 'primary' thing that is shown in the secondary phenomena, but it is the saying we hope that makes the feeling and features the 'phenomena of hope'. Thus Hunter still stresses the use of the language. But 'we could, even if we don't often, use the word "hope" without any of the phenomena of hope occurring'.[4] Thus Hunter's interpretation is that using the word 'hope' is the form of life.

It is interesting here to call the mind the reference in *Lectures*, p.58, 'Why shouldn't one form of life culminate in an utterance of belief in a Last Judgement?' Of this Hunter very briefly in a footnote says that the 'way of life' account of forms of life is the only plausible one in this case.[5] But he clearly does not conceive of 'hoping' as a 'way of life' similarity. It is not easy to see why.

The fifth reference from *Investigations* is from page 226:

> It is no doubt true that you could not calculate with certain sorts of paper and ink, if, that is, they were subject to certain queer changes – but still the fact that they changed could in turn only be got from memory and comparison with other means of calculation. And how are these listed in their turn? What has to be accepted, the given is – so one could say – *forms of life*.

Here the interest centres on what is meant by 'the given'. Hunter admits that in the 'ordinary philosophical sense' it means that forms of life are public, ultimate, common ways of doing things. But in an 'odd' sense[6] Hunter suggests it could mean that a form of life is an 'inarticulate certainty . . . ' that I know something even if what I know keeps appearing to be not so'. Hunter's example of such a state of affairs is my writing '4' and it changing to '5' yet my being inarticulately certain that '5' is not what four is. So the 'form of life' on this view is simply my functioning in that way as the person I am and it does not make sense to speak of it as constituting a standard. This understanding of forms of life makes them individual. Against this interpretation one might claim that the ordinary philosophical understanding of 'given' makes more sense and in the light of another statement of Wittgenstein's, 'What we have rather to do is to *accept* the everyday language-game . . . ' *Investigations* p.200, Interpretations 1 and 2 are more plausible.

Hunter concentrated his attention on *Philosophical Investigations*. For this reason he does not comment on *OC* (p.358), 'Now I would like to regard this certainty, not as something akin to hastiness or superficiality, but as a form of life. (That is very badly expressed and probably badly thought as well)'. In the next paragraph Wittgenstein asserts, 'But that means I want to conceive it as something that lies beyond being justified or unjustified; as it were, as something animal.'

That last phrase would obviously attract the attention of Hunter as supporting his 'organic' account of forms of life. It might be suggesting that the 'certainty' referred to is a form of life in the sense of a natural function of the living being. Living beings have a capacity to be certain as they have capacities for others functions.

But it is at this point that Hunter's interpretation seems most inappropriate because, so it seems to me, the certainty of which Wittgenstein speaks here is far from being a biological function. Remembering that *On Certainty* is something in the nature of a debate with G. E. Moore, consider the following:

> But why *am* I so certain that this is my hand? Doesn't the whole language-game rest on this kind of certainty? Or: isn't this "certainty" (already) presupposed in the language-game? Namely by virtue of the fact that one is not playing the game, or is playing it wrong, if one does not recognize with certainty'. (*OC*, p.446)

What is the nature of 'this certainty' presupposed in the language-game?' It may be one of two things according to our understanding of 'presupposing'. A presupposition may be an empirical precondition, or a logical implication. For example, a game of water polo presupposes both physical fitness and team membership, in that it is empirically impossible to play if physically unfit and logically impossible to play if not a member of a team.

The 'certainty' of the above quotation may therefore be *either* of the nature of an empirical precondition of participation in a language-game that the participator be certain of its fundamental propositions *or* of the nature of a logical implication of anything said within a language in that its fundamental proposition is taken for certain. The first view understands the capacity to be certain as an empirical precondition in language-games. Certainty is an organic function, as Hunter would say. The second view is that fundamental propositions are presupposed as logical implications in language-games.

It seems to me that in *OC* (p.446) 'presupposed' means logically implicit. The 'certainty' referred to is not a biological or psychological function or capacity. And this is the case, I submit, in *OC* (p.358).

Hunter's interpretation of 'forms of life' is therefore unacceptable here. But that does not mean it is wholly wrong or worthless. There is clearly a relationship between language-games and forms of life. But the two are not always spoken of in the same way by Wittgenstein. For example, when he speaks of language-games he is often concerned with rules whereas 'forms of life' have a different emphasis because rules come to an end somewhere. Hunter draws attention to an important point in emphasizing the active, functional feature of forms of life and the 'biological' nature of many of Wittgenstein's phrases bears this out, cf. *OC* (pp. 204, 287, 359 and 559).

Yet I do not think Hunter's account does full justice to the relationship of language-games and form of life. Wittgenstein argued that we cannot understand language except as part of an activity which is more than just speaking. It is in this respect that language-games and forms of life are related. In examining forms of life we inevitably come up against a certain kind of ultimacy. This I have indicated in the phrase 'fundamental proposition' in regard to language and Wittgenstein indicated in such phrases as 'I have reached bedrock, my spake is turned, this is simply what I do' (*Investigations*, p.217). It is also in this sense that I believe we must understand his comment about forms of life being given (*Investigations*, p.226).

A language-game without a form of life would be a meaningless concept for Wittgenstein. We too must think of them together, for together both come down to some concept, some fundamental propositions that constitute the language-game and have an ultimacy of justification and experience in forms of life.[7] These issues will be drawn out further as I now turn to the various forms of knowledge claims I have analysed to see whether they can be held together within this concept of a form of life. I begin with inferential knowledge and falsification.

INFERENTIAL KNOWLEDGE AND FALSIFICATION

I have brought inferential knowledge and falsification together because in both cases the key issue is the appeal to evidence. In the case of inferential knowledge claims it is always legitimate to ask the claimant what reasons or grounds he has for the assertion he makes. What, in fact, is his evidence. In the case of falsification I argued that a necessary condition of a knowledge claim is that not only does it have to have truth conditions but also verification conditions.[8] These verification conditions relate to the question of evidence by which we know or have reason to believe that the asserted proposition is true.

Now my question is, given the concept of a form of life what is the application and what the limitations of evidence?

Let us begin by noticing an assertion of Wittgenstein's. 'Why shouldn't one form of life culminate in an utterance of belief in a Last Judgement?'[9] This is an important quotation for my purpose because it brings together the concept of a form of life and an expression of religious belief. What is of immediate interest are two things Wittgenstein said with respect to evidence for such a belief. In discussing the nature of belief in a Last Judgement he asserts . . .

The point is that if there were evidence, this would in fact destroy the whole business.[10]

Later he raises the question of a man who had dreamed about the Last Judgement.[11] Would this count as evidence? Wittgenstein says . . .

If a man said to me after a dream that he believed in the Last Judgement, I'd try to find out what sort of impression it gave him.[12]

Wittgenstein seems to be saying two things here about evidence and religious belief:

1   That if there were evidence and appeals made to evidence then this would destroy the belief as religious belief. You do not need evidence in the case of religious belief and indeed, if you had it, it could cause the whole case to collapse.

2   But, dreams can be significant as evidence in religious belief.

These two references to evidence are not contradictory. They serve to indicate an important distinction relating to forms of life and language-games. The distinction is this. On the one hand there are some propositions for which the appeal to evidence is inappropriate. These are fundamental propositions. On the other hand, these fundamental propositions determine what counts as evidence within the language-game.

What is the fundamental proposition? The nature of a fundamental proposition is perhaps best made clear by calling attention to how pointedly Wittgenstein differentiated a fundamental proposition from a hypothesis. The essential point is that, in the nature of the case, hypotheses are things which you have evidence for, whereas it does not make sense to say you have evidence for fundamental propositions. Fundamental propositions are of such character that, unlike hypotheses, it does not make sense to doubt them. As Wittgenstein said of fundamental propositions, 'They do not serve as foundations in the same way as hypotheses which, if they turn out to be false, are replaced by others' (*OC*, p.402). Hypotheses may be true or false (*OC*, p.153). They may have evidence for or against them and may be tested for truth or falsity (*OC*, p.163). They need grounds (*OC*, p.110) and, most importantly, they can be doubted (*OC*, p.337).

Fundamental propositions are not true or false in the ordinary meaning of those terms, says Wittgenstein. They are true in the peculiar sense of being the unmoving foundation of language games (*OC*, p.403). Unlike hypotheses they are not open to testing (*OC*, p.119). The thought that we can doubt fundamental propositions Wittgenstein describes as a hollow notion and illustrates this with reference to a school boy who keeps asking whether the world existed one hundred years ago (*OC*, p.310). Elsewhere he said, 'If someone doubted whether the earth had existed a hundred years ago, I should not understand, for *this* reason: I would not know what such person would still allow to be counted as evidence and what not' (*OC*, p.231). Fundamental propositions therefore, in contrast with hypotheses, are incontrovertible.

Fundamental propositions are beyond evidence. But within a form of life or language-game they determine what counts as evidence. The essential distinction is between propositions which are *within* the game and propositions which *constitute* the game. These latter are what I mean by fundamental propositions.

Thus, in regard to my question about the limitations and application of evidence we can say the following. The notion of evidence has application within a language-game or form of life. Given the fundamental propositions, inferences can be made, arguments offered, which legitimately appeal to evidence. But, of course, it must be appropriate evidence. The question of 'appropriateness' is the issue of the limitation of the notion of evidence. It's limitation is within the language-game or form of life. The fundamental propositions as I have shown above, are not founded on appeals to evidence. In their case the notion of evidence does not apply. But these fundamental propositions determine both the nature of the application and the limitation of whatever is appealed to as evidence within a language-game.

Thus to come back to the case of dreams as evidence for the Last Judgement. What would it be to have evidence for belief in a Last Judgement? And would a dream of the Last Judgement count as such? On this Wittgenstein says:

> Suppose somebody made this guidance for this life: believing in the Last Judgement. Wherever he does anything, this is before his mind. In a way, how are we to know whether to say he believes this will happen or not?
> Asking him is not enough. He will probably say he has proof. But he has what you might call an unshakeable belief. It will show, not by reasoning or by appeal to ordinary grounds for belief, but rather by regulating for all in his life'.[13]

I do not propose to embark upon a detailed analysis of the nature of religious belief, but it seems to me that here Wittgenstein is drawing attention to an important feature of it. It is the case that a religious belief is not, and does not purport to be, a statement of objective fact alone. It may be such a statement, but to understand its meaning in those terms only is to misunderstand it. An expression of religious belief is not simply an assertion that something or other is, or will be, the case. Wittgenstein indicates here, what others have shown elsewhere,[14] that account must be taken of the 'force' in the religious believer's life of the assertion he makes because this too is part of its meaning. The religious believer holds his belief 'before his mind'. It is there in his thoughts, it 'regulates for all in his life' and this is shown by the way he leads his life.

Now, what could count as evidence for such a belief? Supposing someone were to assert that he knew that the number of bricks in his new house was 5059. Suppose further you asked how he knew this and he answered, 'I dreamed it is so', we would not count that as in any way evidence for an assertion of that character. It would be ludicrous to count on dreams as providing information in the business of quantity surveying.

But suppose that we are familiar with a man whom we notice that he is always respectful and deferential towards Mr x. We ask him why this is. He replies by saying that he had a dream of the Final Judgement and in this dream Mr x, for whom he had earlier had no great regard, was approved and welcomed. He goes on to say that upon waking from the dream he saw, not only Mr x, but his whole life in a new light. He saw that the way to live his life was the way Mr x lives. Ever since the dream, whenever he has thought of Judgement, he has thought of Mr x and the image of that man's life. So he speaks of and treats Mr x with respect because he has become a pattern to follow and because of the meaning given to his religious belief in a Last Judgement. This all results from the dream.

Someone may object at this point and suggest that a dream is very poor evidence for something upon which to base your life in a regulative explanatory sense. But what is the force of such an objection? Why shouldn't a dream he understood as evidence in these terms? The history of religious belief is replete with examples. St Paul's reason for going to Macedonia will suffice as illustration (Acts 16: 9–10). Builder's files may give evidence as to the number of bricks in a particular house and would be acceptable as such. Why should not dreams count as evidence in the case of religious belief?

Again the objector may say that this doesn't make sense to him, he does not play that game. To him it is irrational to take dreams as evidence. But two things may be said in reply. First, the fact that he does not play the game and counts it irrational says nothing about the game, its meaning, its rationality, or what may or may not be acceptable as evidence within it. Second, it may further be worth enquiring what it is that regulates the objector's life and what reasons he can give for holding whatever it is he does hold before his mind. Can that be shown to be 'rational' either in its own terms, or in the terms of another game?

It is in terms such as these I have outlined above that a religious believer may speak of evidence *within* the language-game of religious belief. The fundamental propositions of the language-game and form of life of religious belief are not, for reasons I have given, things which anyone has evidence for. It is these propositions that determine what counts as evidence within the game.

What I have been saying thus far raises a number of important philosophical questions. For example, if in the case of religious belief there are certain fundamental propositions in the sense that I have defined them, can we speak of the knowledge of God as the knowledge of these fundamental propositions? But this question presupposes the more basic question of whether or not it makes sense to speak of knowing fundamental propositions at all. This is a subject about which there has been a great deal of discussion of late arising out of the work of G. E. Moore.

Moore was the champion of 'common sense'.[15] He argued that in the universe there are an enormous number of material objects e.g. human bodies, chairs, stones, railway engines etc. He argued that human beings have minds, that is, they perform acts of consciousness. This marks them off from the vast majority of material objects to which no acts of consciousness can be attached. He further argues that 'we believe that we *know* an immense number of details about particular material objects and acts of consciousness, past, present and future'.[16]

It is this claim to knowledge that interests us. Moore's case was that all the complexity concerning what constitutes 'knowledge' is really about what we mean by 'knowing'. When we say we know things we say there are certain things which, as it were, fit in with what we mean so completely that if we cannot be said to know these things then we cannot be said to know anything. Moore is making here not a psychological but a logical point about what he understands the meaning of the word 'know' to be. He argued that if we do not know that here is one hand on my left wrist and here is another on my right, then we do not know anything at all. This is common sense for Moore and he is more sure that this is indeed his hand before his face than all the questions of scepticism.

The sort of assertions of common sense Moore made, e.g. 'The earth has existed for many years past', are assertions that we can all understand. Not to know the truth of such a statement would be to live in a world of *un*common sense. For the sort of propositions

Moore claimed to know, we all know. Should anyone ask for proof that these propositions are true then they make a demand that cannot be met because, for anyone who knows the langauge, they are matters of common sense. So according to Moore, a proposition such as 'Here are two hands' is not susceptible to proof, but the inability to prove the proposition to be true in no way disqualifies us from claiming that we know it and that it is true. What Moore suggested is that there are some propositions that cannot be proved, that is, are not matters for which we have or need evidence, but nevertheless are known to all who share the common sense view of the world. These we might call Moore's fundamental propositions.

So it is clear that Moore thought it made perfectly good sense to speak of knowing fundamental propositions. Wittgenstein was not so sure. He thought Moore's use of the word 'know' in these contexts rather odd. Wittgenstein's point about fundamental proposition was that they could not be doubted as is the case with hypotheses. He says:

> To say of a man, in Moore's sense, that he *knows* something; that what he says is therefore unconditionally the truth, seems wrong to me – it is the truth only inasmuch as it is an unmoving foundation of his language-game. (*OC*, p.403)

This states quite clearly Wittgenstein's position. It makes sense to speak of 'knowing' a hypothesis, where there is evidence to back up the claim. (*OC*, p.504). But the sort of propositions Moore claims to know are not in the nature of hypotheses. The unmoving foundations of language-games are therefore inappropriately named if we refer to them as knowledge. Later Wittgenstein draws this out further:

> I really want to say that a language-game is only possible if one trusts something (I did not say "can trust something"). If I say "Of course I know that that's a towel" I am making an *utterance*. I have no thought of a verification. For me it is an immediate utterance. I don't think of past or future (and of course it's the same for Moore, too). It is just like directly taking hold of something, as I take hold of my towel without having doubts.
> And yet this direct taking hold corresponds to a *sureness*, not to a knowing. (*OC*, p.509–11)

It is in terms such as these that Wittgenstein does not deny the truth of the propositions Moore claims to know. He says that if Moore knows them then we all know them. But this, according to Wittgenstein is a misuse of the word 'know'. What he does say of Moore's propositions, as I have indicated above, is that to doubt their truth would be non-sensical in normal situations. It is in this sense that Wittgenstein gives the same 'status' to these propositions as Moore. It is just that he does not understand them as cases of knowledge. For example, he argues that the normal use of words like 'hand' where there is no doubt of their meaning, 'shows that absence of doubt belongs to the essence of the language-game, that the question 'How do I know?' drags out the language-game, or else does away with it' (*OC*, p.370). To seek to apply tests for proof etc. is not to play the game. And nothing useful is achieved by claiming to know the fundamental propositions of the game.

What Moore is disclosing in his assertion 'I know that here is my hand' according to Wittgenstein, is not new information hitherto unknown but 'a proposition of grammar' (*OC*, p.57). The proposition Moore 'knows' embody rules of meaning in the sense that to deny such a proposition would be but to show oneself ignorant of the meaning of the words used. Thus Wittgenstein argues:

'If "I know etc." is conceived as a grammatical proposition, of course the "I" cannot be important. And it properly means "There is no such thing as a doubt in this case" or "The expression 'I do not know' makes no sense in this case'. And of course it follows from this that "I *know*" makes no sense either'.

(*OC*, p.58)

But as A. J. Ayer has suggested 'if this proposition (i.e. I am seeing red) is true does it make no sense to say that I do know that it is true?'[17] It would certainly be odd to say that within a form of life and language-game grounded in fundamental propositions it was quite proper to make knowledge claims but that the fundamental propositions on which the whole rested we do not know. That would be tantamount to saying that what we know rests on what we do not know. Can this dilemma be resolved?

I think that a former pupil of Wittgenstein's, Norman Malcolm, has gone a long way to showing that it can in his much debated essay 'Knowledge and Belief'.[18] In this essay Malcolm draws a distinction between what he calls the 'strong' and the 'weak' sense of 'know'. The distinction shows itself between cases of knowledge claims where we recognize the possibility of being wrong and those where we recognize no such possibility. When anyone makes a claim to know in the weak sense it implies that 'he did not absolutely exclude the possibility that something could prove it to be false'.[19] 'Know' is used in the strong sense 'when a person's statement "I know that P is true" implies that the person who makes the statement would look upon nothing whatever as evidence that P is false'.[20] In the strong sense of know therefore no possibility of refutation is admitted.

Malcolm, like Moore, does not restrict this distinction to analytically true propositions. He extends the strong sense of 'know' to certain propositions about the external world. These are propositions for which the 'knower' requires no further evidence other than what he directly perceives, e.g. 'Here is an ink bottle'. The point about such a proposition for Malcolm is not just that it would not make sense to say that he did not know that here is an ink bottle but that he could not possibly say what he would take as a ground for doubting that here is an ink bottle. It is in this sense that Malcolm's point is not a psychological but logical one.[21] The point about the strong cases of 'know' is not that there is evidence for or against anyone holding the propositions to be true but that there is no possible doubt that the propositions could turn out to be false. In this way the question of evidence for strong cases of know does not arise. Indeed Malcolm goes on to argue that before anyone gets to the point of talking about evidence, proof, disproof, etc. we must notice that 'in order for it to be possible that any statements about physical things should *turn out to be false* it is necessary that some statements about physical things *cannot* turn out to be false.'[22]

This seems to me a strong argument. If I claim to know something is the case, e.g. that at this moment of writing I have a pen in my hand, I cannot think what, in this instance, I could possibly take as grounds for doubting the fact. It is true that I have a pen in my hand. And if it is true, I see no logical reason why I may not say I know I have a pen in my hand. It is not just a matter of my being sure that this is the cae. It would not make sense for me to doubt that it is the case, to say that I did not know I had a pen in my hand. What possible ground could I have for doubting it? In the end all I could say is 'I know this is my hand, I know this is a pen and I know this pen is in my hand.' Anyone who agreed with me on the meaning of these words but still denied my knowledge claim I would not be able to understand.

The two questions above that indicated Malcolm's understanding of strong and weak sense of 'know' illustrate again this point about propositions that are 'beyond' evidence and propositions for which evidence is applicable. In the weak sense of 'know' the possibility of being wrong means that new evidence may be forthcoming. The notion of evidence has application here. But it is also limited here because there could not possibly be forthcoming any evidence to show the strong use of 'know' to be incorrect. Malcolm's strong sense of 'know' has the characteristic therefore of what earlier I called fundamental propositions. Malcolm therefore would say that it does make sense to say we 'know' fundamental propositions but not in the same way as the weak sense of 'know'.

One further question arises at this point in the light of what I have said about fundamental propositions. Given that there are such propositions, which are not themselves propositions for which we have evidence but rather determine what the nature of evidence shall be in any context, are there some fundamental propositions that are *the* fundamental propositions in the sense that everything, if it is going to make sense, must fit in with these?

For example, A. J. Ayer is critical of Moore's argument on the ground that he treated metaphysical questions as 'internal' to common sense.[23] He suggests that Moore implied that there is just the game of common sense as he illustrated it in his various propositions which he claimed to know and that all meaningful 'knowledgeable' propositions must fit in with that. Moore seemed to imply there are some fundamental propositions that are *the* fundamental propositions for everything. In his criticisms of Moore, Ayer refers to a distinction drawn by Rudolph Carnap.

The distinction Carnap drew was between what he called internal and external questions.[24] Internal questions are those that arise within the framework of a conceptual system. These questions are settled by applying the criteria the system supplies. External questions are those relating to the existence or reality of the framework itself.

The distinction concerns the way existential questions may or may not be answered. Internal questions can find answers from within the conceptual framework in which they are set, from within the system operating in that particular discourse. In this sense the notion of evidence is applicable. But external questions cannot be settled in this fashion for external questions are about the framework itself. The distinction is well illustrated thus. The question 'do material objects exist?' considered as an external question is not one that can be straightforwardly answered by reference to evidence but is a question of whether there is to be a system of rules or conceptual framework concerning the concept of 'material object'. But the question 'does my pen exist?' considered as an internal question, is answerable in terms of the system rules governing the use of material–object questions.[25]

Carnap was not arguing that the 'existence' of any framework thereby established the reality of what the framework involved. Indeed, on the contrary he argued that although 'the introduction of the new ways of speaking does not need any theoretical justification, all we are accepting in using the 'new way of speaking' is 'new linguistic forms'. One does not imply the ontological reality of the entities in question. In fact, Carnap offered a quite different approach to those who suggested that the ontological status of an entity must be settled before we can talk about it meaningfully. Carnap's argument is that we can talk about such an entity if we choose to adopt the linguistic form but this is a practical, not theoretical question as far as he is concerned. Commenting upon whether or not we choose to accept a particular linguistic form he says . . . .

> The acceptance cannot be judged as being either true or false because it is not an assertion; it can only be judged as being more or less expedient, fruitful, conducive to the aim for which the language is intended. Judgements of this kind supply the motivation for the decision of accepting or rejecting the framework.
>
> Thus it is clear that the acceptance of a framework must not be regarded as implying a metaphysical doctrine concerning the reality of the entities in question.[26]

It is in the light of all this that the question of evidence is discussed by Carnap. He is quite clear that anyone who makes what we might call an 'internal assertion' is obliged to justify it by providing evidence. What would be appropriate evidence would be determined by the linguistic form being used, the framework in operation. But to ask for evidence for the framework, to ask for justification of the use of a particular linguistic form, is to ask an impossible question. It is impossible because where could you possibly go for an answer? How would you answer a question like 'do material objects exist?' Carnap calls such 'pseudo-questions'.[27]

Such questions, of course, are asked. They are pseudo-questions not in the sense that they cannot be expressed in grammatically well formed sentences but in the sense that there is no conceivable way of answering them. Either the questioner chooses to entertain the proposition fundamental to the system or he does not. But the justification of the choice, according to Carnap, is practical not theoretical. And being practical inevitably means is 'justification' is within its own terms.

This distinction of Carnap seems to me to be very important. It has similarities with Wittgenstein's understanding of the varieties of language-games. Carnap speaks of conceptual frameworks and by this I take him to understand that 'linguistic forms' in the last analysis relate to certain concepts that are just fundamental. In the same way I suggest that Wittgenstein conceived of forms of life or language-games that go down in the last analysis to fundamental propositions.

I began this consideration of inferential knowledge and falsification within the concept of a form of life by asking what is the application and what the limitation of evidence. The answer is that within a form of life and language-game the notion of evidence readily applies. Both inferential knowledge and falsification makes sense in this way within the form of life where the notion of evidence has application. But forms of life and language-games are logically constituted by fundamental propositions, or tacit presuppositions,[28] that are 'beyond' evidence but determine what counts as evidence within the game.

How does all this relate to the concept of the knowledge of God? I wish to suggest tentatively that the concept of God is the fundamental proposition of the form of life or language-game of religious belief. As such the existence of God is not a matter of evidence at all. As such God can only be known in the sense that all fundamental propositions can be known, in Malcolm's strong undoubtable sense. But within religious belief the notion of evidence has application, so that it makes sense to speak of inferential knowledge and falsification.

This suggestion I submit is quite in keeping with what came to light in the survey of knowledge claims of an inferential form in the Bible. There I found that no attempt is made to prove the existence of God. Such is the nature of biblical belief that God is the fundamental presupposition of the whole. Indeed to ask for proof of God is to ask, as far as religion is conceived, a pseudo-question. It is to ask a question belonging to another language-game, metaphysics perhaps. It is not a religious question. Religious questions, like the Bible, take the concept of God as 'given'.

But we also saw that within the Bible story it is understood that appeals to evidence can quite legitimately be made. Thus there is the concept of the acts of God, for that he is active is part of the concept of God in the Bible. The exodus from Egypt, the defeat of enemies, the success of crops, the resurrection of Jesus, dreams, visions, unusual events, all of these and other things can be appealed to as evidence of God within the Bible.

I move on now to consider whether knowledge by acquaintance and immediate knowledge can also be brought within the concept of a form of life.

KNOWLEDGE BY ACQUAINTANCE AND IMMEDIATE KNOWLEDGE

I am putting together immediate knowledge and knowledge by acquaintance because they have a certain important feature in common. This feature is that they eliminate a move which needs to be made in the kinds of knowledge claims with which generally they are contrasted. Immediate knowledge is contrasted with inferential knowledge. If anything is known by inference an answer must be found to the question, 'How do you know this?', which is logically distinct from the conviction that one does know it. Immediate knowledge eliminates this move or necessity.

Knowledge by acquaintance is contrasted with knowledge by description. Where knowledge by description is concerned the question always arises 'Does this description have any application?' There is no such question where acquaintance is concerned. 'Does the description that I have in my mind of the man John Smith apply to a man John Smith who actually exists?' is one question that makes sense. 'Does my acquaintance with John Smith apply to any man who actually exists?' is a question that makes no sense.

From my enquiry into the various forms of knowledge claims made with respect to God in the Bible, I was able to show that both Old and New Testaments speak of knowing God by acquaintance. I have already discussed in the previous Chapter whether such claims are intelligible to us or not, concluding that they are. The question which I now wish to consider is, 'Given the concept of a form of life can the notions of knowledge by acquaintance and immediate knowledge be brought within it?'

Of all the questions about knowledge claims and their possible incorporation within the concept of a form of life, I find this question about knowledge by acquaintance and immediate knowledge the most difficult to deal with briefly and clearly. However, I propose to make the following points that seem to me to be important.

What I wish to do is, using Malcolm's notion of knowing[29] and Wittgenstein's notion of fundamental proposition,[30] to relate both to the concept of a form of life and more particularly to religious belief as a form of life. In so doing I shall try to give some illumination to the notion of knowing God by acquaintance, and knowing God immediately.

The reason why I chose to work with Malcolm and Wittgenstein's notions is that both bypass, as it were, moves in knowledge claims which correspond to the kind of move which, as I said a moment ago, is a feature of knowing by acquaintance and knowing immediately.

It will be recalled that Malcolm drew a distinction between two senses of know; the strong sense where nothing could conceivably count as evidence against the proposition and the weak sense where the possibility of new evidence leading to the revision or rejection of the proposition was recognized. In so far as a man knows something in a strong sense, at that time, the question 'how do you know this?' does not arise for him because it is unintelligible to him that he should be wrong about what he knows.[31] This is not because he has some reason for knowing what he knows that is a good reason. He would be in that condition if he were using know in the weak sense. Rather it is that he is not available, in a logical and not merely psychological sense, to the idea that he should have reasons for or against his assertion. In making the assertion in the strong sense he has come to something ultimate for him, a kind of end point.

This I suggest illuminates the notion of what it is to know immediately in terms of a language-game. Anyone who plays the language-game knows the fundamental conceptions which make the game the game it is in this strong sense of Malcolm's. From within the game at least it is unintelligible to the participator to consider what it would be to have reasons for the fundamental propositions. The question 'how do you know?' does not arise in the game. The participant 'just knows'. The question of reason or grounds is bypassed.

In the case of Wittgenstein's notion of fundamental propositions, a contrast can be drawn between these and ordinary empirical propositions. All empirical propositions which are treated as hypotheses may relevantly be questioned as to whether what they assert really is the case. But Wittgenstein called fundamental propositions 'grammatical propositions' in the sense that 'there is no such thing as doubt in this case'. These are propositions that constitute language games and the question 'does this accurately describe some given state of affairs?' is a question that does not arise. This is because nothing counts or would count as 'a state of affairs' unless it somehow was related to these fundamental propositions.

This I suggested illuminates the notion of knowledge by acquaintance with reference to language-games and forms of life. It makes sense to ask whether what is known by description has application; it does with all empirical propositions as hypotheses. But it does not make sense to ask whether what we know by acquaintance really exists. Again it is a case of something we 'just know'. The question of application is bypassed.

Turning now to the concept of a form of life, in a previous section I argued that Wittgenstein understood forms of life to be something natural. Forms of life are not something to do with our life, they *are* our life. Participating in a form of life, constituted by its fundamental propositions, is responding to things just as they are because 'things just as they are' is inseparably related to the fundamental propositions of the forms of life. So we might say that a form of life is what we do and in the last analysis, what we know is what we do. As Wittgenstein says:

"I know all that". And that will come out in the way I act and in the way I speak about things in question.   (*OC*, p.395).
    You must bear in mind that the language-game is so to say something unpredictable. I mean: it is not based on grounds. It is not reasonable (or unreasonable). It is there – like our life.
                                                            (*OC*, p.559)

So now I ask, can the notion of knowing God by acquaintance and knowing God immediately, in philosophical terms, be equated with knowing certain fundamental propositions or knowing in the strong sense? And can these two be brought together within the notion of a form of life?

An important feature of Malcolm's strong sense of know is its emphasis on the personal. In the case of the strong sense of know Malcolm argues that the person who made the statement would not look upon anything whatever as evidence of its falsity. He could not conceive of any possible grounds for the statement's refutation. However, it does make sense that anyone other than the claimant should doubt the statement. Malcolm considers it perfectly conceivable that 'I *could* think both that he is using 'know' in the strong sense and that nonetheless what he claims he knows to be so might turn out not to be so'.[32] Knowing in the strong sense therefore relates to 'what *I* say', '*my own case*' and to what is intelligible or unintelligible 'to *me*'. Knowing in these terms has the quality of personal commitment about it.

Wittgenstein's notion of a form of life, I have argued, is something natural. It is what we do. His notion of fundamental propositions is inseparably related to the notion that what we know in the last analysis is what we do.

I suggest that these two notions from Malcolm and Wittgenstein come together in this sense. For the man who claims to know God by acquaintance or know God immediately there is a personal commitment to a way of acting. It may be that a religious believer would claim more than this in knowing God by acquaintance but, philosophically speaking, this I suggest is at least part of what his assertion must mean. This logically connects with the notion of a form of life because the notion of a form of life is 'this is how I live and I find my identity in living in this way.'

Thus, for example, for the man who claims to know God by acquaintance, it is not an open question as to whether he wills to do the will of God or not. There may be a decision as to whether he will be a religious man or not but, on this view of a form of life, whether he will be religious or not is not some kind of a conclusion at which anyone arrives, it is something that either you decide to do or not to do. At *OC* (p.362) Wittgenstein says 'But doesn't it come out here that knowledge is related to a decision?' The previous paragraph (p.361), is not about religious belief but it does include one of the very rare references to God in *On Certainty*. I suggest that in a context where he refers to revelation and God it is significant that Wittgenstein goes on to speak of 'knowing' as a form of decision. Being religious, as he says, is there – like our life.

So I suggest that, in the last analysis, the notion of knowing God by acquaintance is commiting oneself personally to ways of acting

which are what it means to know God. For example, if a religious
believer claims to be acquainted with God the judge what this
means for him is doing certain things e.g. obeying God's laws,
doing justice, loving mercy etc. Or as John says, 'Here is the test
by which we can make sure that we know him: do we keep his
commands? The man who says "I know him", while he disobeys
his commands, is a liar and a stranger to the truth: but in the man
who is obedient to his word, the divine love has indeed come to
its perfection', I John 2: 3–5.

KNOWLEDGE BY DESCRIPTION AND 'OBJECTIVE KNOWLEDGE'

It has been possible, thus far, to draw the various forms of 'knowing'
or knowledge together within the concept of a form of life. I have
also been able to show that, if religious belief is conceived of as a
form of life, then the knowledge of God with regard to evidence,
acquaintance and immediacy is a meaningful concept, all the more
since it can be illustrated at all points with reference to what is said
about knowing God in the Bible. I come now to examine the notion
of knowledge by description and objective knowledge to see
whether they too relate to this concept of a form of life.

A feature that knowledge by description and 'objective knowledge' have in common is that in both cases something is received
or inherited. Popper's notion of 'objective knowledge' included the
thought that knowledge was independent of every human being.
It is the product of human minds yet is autonomous. As such it is
every person's inheritance. Knowledge by description is indirect
knowledge. It is dependent upon someone's knowledge by acquaintance but as they tell us what they know, and so inform us, their
knowledge becomes public. So teaching and instruction becomes
possible. We can be taught what is the case even though we have
not necessarily ourselves experienced what is the case. This is knowledge by description.

Can the notions of 'objective knowledge' and knowledge by
description be brought within the concept of a form of life?

Popper's criticism of so much talk about knowledge is that it
assumed it was something that was located in men's minds. A
knowledgeable person was someone whose mind had been 'filled
up', as an empty bucket might be filled up, by the pouring in of

facts.[33] Popper thought this most misleading and, as I outlined earlier, he developed his notion of World 3 and 'objective knowledge'. World 3 is the world of ideas, art, ethics, religion etc. But these are not imprisoned in World 2, the world of our own minds. They are preserved and to be found in World 1 objects such as books, libraries, galleries etc. World 3 is the objective content of thought. In World 3 there are the hitherto unfalsified hypotheses with which and upon which scientists work. Here also are the myths and stories men have told as they have tried to express their experience of life in words. Science and non-science both inhabit World 3.

Can this notion in any way be related to Wittgenstein's concept of a form of life? I believe it can and in this way. Wittgenstein continually concerned himself with the relationship of language, thought and reality to each other. For a child to learn a language means more than just being able to mouth the words. Along with the words come whole systems of fundamental propositions into which, in a way, we are born. That language learning is more than speech is implied in *Investigations* 23, 'Here the term "language-game" is meant to bring into prominence the fact that the *speaking* of language is part of an activity or a form of life.'

In my earlier discussion of forms of life I indicated that on Hunter's 'biological' account a form of life is functioning in a certain way as an individual and is not necessarily communal. This seems to me to be wrong because it overlooks the relation between language and life. Learning a language may be personal but cannot be a private exercise because language must be communal. And the 'reality' the use of language expresses is also communal. It is just there.

Wittgenstein understood that there were some things that were 'given', that had to be accepted.

What we have rather to do is to *accept* the everyday language-game, and to note *false* accounts of the matter *as* false'.[34]

It is no doubt true that you could not calculate with certain sorts of paper and ink, if, that is, they were subject to certain queer changes – but still the fact that they changed could in turn only be got from memory and comparison with other means of calculation. And how are these listed in their turn? What has to be accepted, the given is – so one could say – *forms of life*'.[35]

Wittgenstein argues that forms of life are common, public, ulti-mate, correct ways of doing something. For example, in the business of being taught to make calculations, explanation must come to an end; it ends in trust or acceptance (*OC*, p.34). The interesting thing, claimed Wittgenstein (and here there is another echo of Popper) is not what goes on in the 'inner process' but how mathematical propositions are used (*OC*, p.38). They are used in a system which is just there, independent of every user of mathematical proposi-tions. Wittgenstein argues that 'knowing' is not a matter of subjec-tive certainty. The certainty may be subjective but not the knowledge (*OC*, p.245). That I know I have two hands is not a matter of belief, even of well founded belief. It is that 'any "reasonable" person behaves like *this*' (*OC*, p.254).

It was also part of Popper's concept of objective knowledge that criticism should have a full part. A consequence of this is that even our most basic assumptions we treat as neither fixed nor final. It is by the exercise of criticism that knowledge grows by way of question proving and answering.

Can this notion of 'evolutionary' objective knowledge be related to Wittgenstein's thought? It can in the sense that Wittgenstein understands that it is possible for our fundamental propositions to be modified, reappraised, even to fall into disuse when a particular language-game becomes obsolete and forgotten. Wittgenstein speaks of the river-bed of thought shifting, 'but I distinguish bet-ween the movement of the waters on the river bed and the shift of the bed itself' (*OC*, p.97). Our picture or understanding of the world can and does change. Yet initially our understanding of the world is an inheritance and it is with this that we live and work. 'But I did not get my picture of the world by satisfying myself of its correctness; nor do I have it because I am satisfied of its correct-ness. No: it is the inherited background against which I distinguish between true and false' (*OC*, p.94).

Therefore, in so far as the notion of a form of life has the emphasis of just being given, Popper's concept of objective knowledge can be brought within it both with regard to the emphasis on the autonomy of the inheritance and with regard to its development and change.

What is the situation with knowledge by description? Knowledge by description is indirect knowledge; it is what we are taught and told. It comes to us from someone else. It is what we can pass on to another. Does this knowledge relate to the concept of a form of life?

One question that can always be asked of a claim to knowledge by description is, does what you claim to be the case correspond to what actually is the case? In other words, does what you claim to know by description have application? This is but to ask for reasons or grounds as to why the claim is made. It is to ask about the truth of the claim. All assertions of knowledge by description can be challenged in this way. It may be that the first way the challenge is met is by reporting that you know x because y told you that x and you have no reason to doubt y because he has always spoken the truth before. This would be to begin to justify your claim that you know x.

By contrast, as I have shown above, fundamental propositions, as conceived by Wittgenstein and as they relate to forms of life, are beyond 'justification'. They are not propositions of which you have grounds or reasons. They are just there – like our life. I have also argued, following Wittgenstein, that in the last analysis fundamental propositions come down to a particular way of action. They are what we do. Yet it is also the case that Wittgenstein understood fundamental propositions as defining concepts.

A set of propositions may well define a particular concept. They are the things that can be said about the concept and make it the concept it is. Wittgenstein's illustration concerns the problem of formulating the proposition, 'There are physical objects'. What does this proposition mean? We can instruct someone who does not know what a chair is or what 'physical object' means by saying 'a chair is a physical object'. This is instruction about the use of words and about the concept of a 'physical object', which is a logical concept (*OC*, p.36). It is knowledge by description in that the proposition goes some way to defining the concept of 'physical object'. In the same way, I suggest, a set of fundamental propositions about God define the concept of God. They tell us what God is. What they do not tell us is whether there is anything to which this concept applies. I shall return to this point in a moment.

It is, of course, part of what knowing the concept of God means that we know how to speak about God. This is a matter of knowing what is proper and what improper in talk about God, what is part and what is not part of the 'picture' the religious believer uses.

Wittgenstein spoke of religious belief as using a picture, a mental picture.[36] The use could be both psychological or logical. By using a picture in the psychological sense he meant holding something before one's mind, for example, the picture of the Last Judgement. Using a picture in the logical sense concerned using a 'technique' that consisted in learning specific 'connections'.[37] The technique in using the picture relates to understanding the logic of these connections. It is concerned with what is or is not said. Wittgenstein illustrated this by referring to the religious believer's picture of God's eye.[38] But, as he says, it would not make sense for a religious believer to ask about God's eyebrows. In the normal use of language eyes normally imply eyebrows. But this is not so in the case of God. So learning to use the picture is learning what conclusions to draw and what not to draw from the words used to express the picture.

Thus within the language-game there is a logic of what can and what cannot be said. This is in some way learnt from others as they describe the concept of God by saying the logically appropriate things about him. Again Popper's conception of knowledge as some kind of deposit has application here for in the two biblical chapters of this work I drew attention there to the theme of 'the deposit of the faith', of the possibility of true and false teaching about God.

But to return to the question of whether all these descriptions have application. I suggest that within a language-game there would be ways of examining whether what is said has application, in the sense of being proper, with regard to the particular concept. But to verify or falsify the existence of such fundamental propositions as 'There is a God', 'There are physical objects', 'There is moral obligation', is logically impossible. Thus, although the question may be asked, it is difficult, if not impossible to say where anyone could go for an answer. If there were reasons available as an answer then clearly the propositions would have lost their fundamental status. I believe I have shown that the notion that knowledge is something received, that can be taught, that we are born into and inherit is something that can be brought within Wittgenstein's concept of a form of life. And again, the emphases of teaching, receiving, learning are all part of the concept of what it is to know God in both Old and New Testaments.

KNOWING HOW AND KNOWING THAT

In Chapter 7 I drew attention to the distinction drawn by Gilbert Ryle between knowing how and knowing that. 'Knowing how' Ryle argued is essentially an activity, logically prior to 'knowing that'. His argument was directed particularly against those who suggested that to do one thing well required two elements, thought *and* action. According to Ryle, there is no gap between intelligence and practice corresponding to the familiar gap between theory and practice. To do one thing well is to 'know how'. It is not a matter of doing two things at all.

The point I wish to make here is that knowledge, in the last analysis, is a kind of activity. We shall see that there are parallels between what Ryle says in this connection and what Wittgenstein had to say in *On Certainty* about the ultimate grounding of knowledge.

Wittgenstein said, 'It is our *acting* which lies at the bottom of the language-game.'[39] Fundamental propositions, according to Wittgenstein, are neither propositions, in the ordinary sense, nor rules. For the person who is committed to them, they cannot, like propositions, be either true or false because that person cannot logically doubt them so long as he plays the language-game which they constitute. But again, they are not like rules in the sense that nobody invented them, nor laid it down that they should be observed. They are like rules in that they can be extrapolated from the way we speak and think about the world. But their ultimate grounding is not like either (1) Hypotheses or (2) the rules of an axiomatic system. Hypotheses may be true or false. The rules of an axiomatic system might be invented. But according to Wittgenstein, such fundamental propositions as 'The world existed some time before our birth', 'Nature is uniform', etc. are things that we know in the sense that this is how we act. In the last analysis, to know these fundamental propositions is to behave in a certain way.

How does this apply in the case of religious belief? Wittgenstein, it will be remembered, said he could conceive of a form of life culminating in an utterance of belief in a Last Judgement.[40] This fundamental proposition then, 'There will be a Last Judgement', must be a case in point. According to Wittgenstein, to know – in the particular sense in which to know this is to know a grammatical proposition – that there will be a Last Judgement therefore must be to behave in certain way.

In what Wittgenstein says of the notion of the Last Judgement he fills out the idea of it as a fundamental proposition by saying that this is something which is held in the foreground of a man's mind and regulates for all his life. This suggests that the man who believes in a Last Judgement is a man who acts in a certain way. It is not the case that he is a man who knows something and

therefore acts upon what he knows. *To know* the fundamental proposition *is to act* in a certain way. Wittgenstein is not saying that
there are certain things that are known to be true because they
authenticate themselves in action. Nor is he saying that there are
certain actions which we can perform only because we already
know certain things. It is not that knowledge is authenticated as
knowledge by action. Neither is it that action is authenticated as
reasonable by knowledge. It is not this kind of dichotomy at all in
Wittgenstein's thought. The point is that, in the last analysis, to
know is to act.

This, I submit, is the case in religious belief. What I have already
said concerning what knowing God in the Bible means suggests
that an analysis of the concept of the knowledge of God as a matter
of action is by no means inappropriate. Three illustratiions can
suffice here.

That knowing God in the Old Testament is understood as not
simply believing that certain things are the case, but means to act
in a particular way, is indicated in Jer. 22; 16. The prophet describes
a good King of Israel who dispensed justice to the lowly and poor
– is this not to know God?

In the New Testament the words of Jesus in John 7: 17 bring
together doctrine and obedience. 'Whoever has the will to do the
will of God shall know whether my teaching comes from him or
is merely my own.' It is not that the disciples, or anyone else,
should do something in order to know, or that they must know
something, or believe it, as a necessary prelude to action. It is that
the 'knowing' and 'doing' are inseparable.

The third illustration is to recall the apparent contradiction
between Paul and James on the relationship of faith and works,
e.g. in Rom. 3; 28 and Jas. 2: 17, 25. I say the contradiction is only
apparent because both Paul and James are placing different emphases on the word 'faith'. For Paul 'faith' means belief and trust,
whereas James seems to use 'faith' as meaning acceptance of particular propositions such as even the demons share, 2: 19. Both Paul
and James would agree that living the life of faith is a matter not
just of intellectual acceptance of certain propositions, nor of just
doing certain things, but is a total response in life, a knowing how
and a knowing that.

Of course, there is scope for interpretation in these passages and
much more could be said, but I submit that they do suggest that
this idea, that knowledge is ultimately action, is not at all alien to

the Biblical way of looking at things. If we conceive of the knowledge of God as action this, I suggest, is quite in line with the biblical thought.

One further point. It would appear that there is the closest connection between the idea of knowing God and the idea of personal commitment. This connection illuminates just what is meant by personal commitment. Ian Ramsey spoke helpfully of discernment/commitment situations.[41] These situations have a characteristically personal quality about them. Something is both seen and done. But discernment/commitment are not two separate actions. They are rather the two sides of *one* coin. It will not do to say that the person who commits himself perceives or intuits in any way that something is the case, i.e. knowing that. Neither will it do to say that he sets himself to act in a certain way, knowing how to live. These two things are one in the notion of commitment. It is both a case of knowing that and knowing how in a discernment/commitment situation, in the sense of assenting to a fundamental proposition but also in the sense of acting in a way which is a natural response to the stimuli encountered. Thus light is shed on the notion of commitment with reference to knowing how and knowing that.

There is, in the end, a mystery here and I have not solved it. The mystery is that the notion of knowledge, apart from religion, seems to run out into this question of how 'knowing how' and 'knowing that' are held together, that is, how the fundamental propositions we believe in and the rules that we live by relate. The mystery is that in some way the one is the other. But it is impossible to illuminate this further and, indeed, all that Wittgenstein could say about it is 'This is how we live'.

But I suggest, this philosophical mystery seems astonishingly congenial to religious belief because, in the case of religious belief, that these things are held together is what the exponents of religious belief have always said. That you cannot analyse religious belief into knowing something and doing something, as though these were two separate independent elements in the same thing, is evidenced in the Bible. The knowledge of God, in the last analysis, the religious believer can say, is, 'That is how I live my life'.

Consider these two propositions. (1) The population of Exeter is 94 000 people. (2) There will be a Last Judgement. Now take the question, 'What are you going to do about it?'. To pose this question after the first proposition makes little sense in that it does not arise with any naturalness. But it does arise naturally following the second proposition. This is the case with all assertions in religious belief and the naturalness of the question 'What are you going to do about it?' reveals something of their logic. Propositions of religious belief cannot be treated like other propositions in the sense that there is little point in just assenting to them. To know these propositions, to know God, in the last analysis, is something you do.

CONCLUSION

What I claim to have shown in this chapter is that all the various uses and meanings of the words 'know' and 'knowledge' I analysed earlier can be drawn together in the concept of a form of life. In Chapter 9 I gave particular attention to Wittgenstein's *On Certainty* and it must be quite apparent that *On Certainty* has been a dominant influence in this concluding chapter. These last notes of Wittgenstein have been particularly helpful in illuminating the meaning of doubt, the understanding of the relation of language-games, the importance of fundamental propositions and the reason why some questions just come to an end.

Wittgenstein is notoriously hard to understand. This is because all the time he was asking questions and then questioning the answers which occurred to him. In his case this process had no end so that his writings read like perpetual and unending dialogues with himself. The effect which this sometimes produces is the impression of an argument that is circular and constantly turns back upon itself.

However, in so far as I have been able to understand Wittgenstein, I have found his philosophy stimulating. In particular, his concept of a form of life seems to me to be one which helps to elucidate both the concept of knowledge and the concept of religious belief. I think it can be seen that what he says in *On Certainty* fills out this notion of a form of life and, in an exploratory spirit, I have tried to bring religious belief under review with tools he has suggested. My conclusion is this.

I argue (1) that a form of life is a concept within which the various knowledge claims can be drawn together and (2) that these various forms of knowledge claims have application in the case of God.

I propose, therefore, that religious belief may be considered as a form of life. This implies that religious belief goes down, in the last analysis, to fundamental propositions in Wittgenstein's sense and to particular ways of speaking and acting. I suggest that to conceive of religious belief in this manner is philosophically and biblically acceptable. What is involved is the following:

1   Religious belief is constituted by the concept of God. Within this general concept of God certain definitions constitute the various forms of religious belief. But either way, the concept of God is defined by fundamental propositions in Wittgenstein's sense, i.e. propositions concerning God that cannot be doubted logically either in religious belief as a whole or in one particular form of religious belief.

2   As such, the existence of God is beyond doubt by those who share the particular form of life and language-game constituted by this concept. The concept of God is not one for which there is any evidence available for those who do not share the form of life. However, the concept does determine what counts as evidence within the form of life. So the religious believer can understand talk about God acting in the world, etc.

3   Since the religious believer holds the concept of God before his mind both his experience of life and his explanations of the world will be determined by the concept of God. Within a form of life it makes sense to speak of experience of God, both personally and corporately.

4   For the religious believer, what he knows is what he does. To be a religious believer is something total. It is a person's life. As such it involves a quality of personal application and dedication.

5   Religious belief is something that can be taught. Within the language-game there are things that can be said and things that cannot be said. As such, within the form of life there is an inherited tradition of speech governed by the fundamental concept. But this is not to say that the fundamental propositions may not be moulded and changed.

All of this fits well with what we found in the examination of the Biblical claims to know God.

    (a)   The Bible, as a whole, simply accepts the concept of God as given. It does not set out to establish that there is a God. It simply speaks about him.

(b) Therefore within the Bible certain events may be understood as evidence of God's activity. They tell us more
about one already known.

(c) Because the religious believer responds practically and
intellectually in terms of God, religious experiences are
open to him. Of this the Bible gives good evidence.

(d) To know God in the Bible is a practical matter. Again this
is well evidenced in both Testaments.

(e) The Bible clearly understands that teaching and instruction in the ways and will of God is not only possible but
necessary.

In summary, therefore, I suggest that the concept of religious
belief goes down in the last analysis to the concept of God and it
is this concept that makes religious belief what it is. Knowledge of
God means participating in religious belief. It is to be a religious
believer. Religion is not the means of coming to the knowledge of
God. It *is* the knowledge of God because it is logically constituted
by the concept of God and what is constituted by this concept can
be described as knowledge, in all its various forms, as the argument
of this final chapter has sought to show.

Notes

CHAPTER 1: PURPOSE AND METHOD

1. H. P. Owen, *The Christian Knowledge of God* (London: The Athlone Press 1969) p.1.
2. This work was published first in 1921 in a German edition. The English translation appeared in 1922. Quotations come from a new edition of the translation by D. F. Pears and B. F. McGuiness (London: Routledge & Kegan Paul, 1972).
3. *Tractatus*, 3.203.
4. Ibid., 4.221.
5. Ibid., 4.22.
6. Ibid., 3.25.
7. Ibid., 2.021.
8. For fuller treatment of Wittgenstein's philosophical pilgrimage see G. Pitcher, *The Philosophy of Wittgenstein* (Englewood Cliffs, N.J.: Prentice–Hall, 1964) and A. Kenny, *Wittgenstein* (London: Allen Lane, 1973). For the relationship of Wittgenstein's work to religious belief see W. D. Hudson, *Ludwig Wittgenstein: the Bearing of his Philosophy upon Religious Belief* (London: Lutterworth Press 1968); 'Some Remarks on Wittgenstein's Account of Religious Belief' in *Talk of God*, Royal Institute of Philosophy Lectures, vol. 2 edited by G. N. A. Vesey (London: Macmillan, 1969); *A Philosophical Approach to Religion* (London: Macmillan, 1974) pp. 3–25; and *Wittgenstein and Religious Belief* (London: Macmillan, 1975).
9. This work was first published posthumously in 1963. Quotations come from the translation by G. E. M. Anscombe (Oxford: Basil Blackwell 1972).
10. *Investigations*, p.421.
11. Ibid., p.23.
12. Cf. *Philosophical Papers*, edited by J.O. Urmson and G.J. Warnock (Oxford University Press 1961) and *How to do things with Words*, edited by J.O. Urmson (Oxford University Press 1962).
13. W.D. Hudson, *A Philosophical Approach to Religion* (London: Macmillan, 1974) p.7.
14. I. T. Ramsey, *Religious Language* (London: SCM Press, 1969) pp.49ff.
15. Ibid., p.66.
16. Ibid., p.68.
17. Cf. W. D. Hudson, *A Philosophical Approach to Religion* (London: Macmillan, 1974) p.163.
18. J. Macquarrie, *Principles of Christian Theology* (London: SCM Press, 1966) p.129.
19. Cf. D. D. Evans, *The Logic of Self-Involvement* (London: SCM Press, 1963) pp.15ff.

20. Cf. 'Biblical Theology' in *A Dictionary of Christian Theology*, edited by Alan Richardson (London: SCM Press, 1969) p.36.
21. A good example, using the concept of covenant is W. Eichrodt: *Theology of the Old Testament*, vol. 1 and 2 (London: SCM Press, 1961 and 1967).
22. This work is now in English translation, *Theological Dictionary of the New Testament* (London: W.B. Eerdmans Publishing Co., 1964).
23. Cf. J. Barr, *The Semantics of Biblical Language* (London: Oxford University Press 1961), *Old and New In Interpretation* (London: SCM Press, 1966) and *Biblical Words for Time* (London: SCM Press, 2nd rev. edn., 1961). See also 'Trends and Prospects in Biblical Theology', *The Journal of Theological Studies* (New Series, Oct. 1974) for a more recent survey.
24. For an autobiographical description of the movement into biblical theology see H. H. Rowley, *The Unity of the Bible* (London: The Carey Kingsgate Press, 1955) pp.1–29.
25. It is part of Barr's criticism to question the supposed correlation between patterns of thought and forms of language. Cf. *The Semantics of Biblical Language*, pp.1–20.
26. J. Barr, *J.T.S.*, Oct 1974, p.270.
27. As is implied, with respect of the Old Testament, by Th. C. Vriezen, *An Outline of Old Testament Theology* (Oxford: Basil Blackwell 1958) p.128.
28. *Biblical Works for Time*, p.11.
29. *The Semantics of Biblical Language*, p.270.

CHAPTER 2: TOWARDS A DEFINITION OF KNOWLEDGE

1. *Philosophical Investigations*, 1: 340.
2. *Tractatus*, 3: 25.
3. *Philosophical Investigations*, 1: 23.
4. Ibid., 1:11–12.
5. *The Blue and Brown Books* (Oxford: Basil Blackwell 1960) p.18.
6. *Philosophical Investigations*, 1:65.
7. Ibid., 1:66.
8. Ibid., 1:67.
9. H. Khatchadourian, 'Common Names and "Family Resemblances"' in *Wittgenstein: the Philosophical Investigations*, edited by G. Pitcher (London: Macmillan, 1970) p.207.
10. G. Pitcher, *The Philosophy of Wittgenstein* (Englewood Cliffs, N.J.: Prentice-Hall, 1964) p.215.
11. Ibid., p.219.
12. Cf. E. K. Specht, *The Foundations of Wittgenstein's Later Philosophy* (London: Manchester University Press 1960) p.130.
13. *Philosophical Investigations*, 1:67.
14. Op. cit., p.226.
15. See for example R. Bambrough, 'Universals and Family Resemblances' and H. Khatchadourian, 'Common names and "Fam-

ily Resemblances"' reprinted in *Wittgenstein*, edited G. Pitcher. Comments on Bambough's article and its implications are made by L. Pompa, 'Family Resemblances' in *The Philosophical Quarterley*, vol. 17, 1967, pp. 63–9 with replies by P. M. Huby and J. E. Llewellyn and a further note by Pompa in vol. 18. See also J. W. Thorp 'Whether the Theory of Family Resemblances Solves the Problem of Universals', *Mind*, 1972 pp. 567–70 and J. Nammour, 'Resemblances and Universals', *Mind*, 1973 p. 516–24.

16. *Philosophical Investigations*, 1:69.
17. R. Bambrough, 'Universals and Family Resemblances', *Wittgenstein* p.197.
18. Cf. J. Nammour, 'Resemblances and Universals', *Mind* vol. LXXXII, 1973, p.524.

CHAPTER 3: INFERENTIAL KNOWLEDGE

1. A. J. Ayer, *The Problem of Knowledge* (London: Penguin Books 1972) p.35.
2. For example, E. L. Gettier, 'Is justified True Belief Knowledge?' in *Knowledge and Belief*, edited by A.P. Griffiths (London: Oxford University Press 1968) pp.144–6.
3. J. Hick, *Faith and Knowledge* (London: Macmillan, 1967) p.208.
4. Op. cit., p.35.
5. This argument is fully developed by Karl Popper. His work will be considered in greater detail in Chapter 8.
6. Op. cit., pp.145ff.
7. For a full discussion of Gettier's note and the discussion it has provoked see R. K. Shope, *The Analysis of Knowing* (Princeton University Press, 1983).

CHAPTER 4: IMMEDIATE KNOWLEDGE

1. H.H. Price, *Belief* (London: Allen & Unwin, 1969) p.87.
2. Ibid., p.90.
3. Ibid., p.88.
4. Cf. H. H. Farmer, *The World and God* (London: Nesbit, 1955) pp.24–5.

CHAPTER 5: KNOWLEDGE BY ACQUAINTANCE AND DESCRIPTION

1. The distinction in use is illustrated in some languages by different words to express different sense of know, e.g. in German, *wissen* and *kennen*.

2. B. Russell, 'Knowledge by Acquaintance and Knowledge by Description' in *Mysticism and Logic* (London: Longmans, Green, 1919) pp. 209–32 and *The Problems of Philosophy* (London: Oxford University Press 1973) ch. 5.

3. *Mysticism and Logic*, p.209.

4. *The Problem of Philosophy*, p.25.

5. Ibid., p.28.

6. We follow Russell's terminology here. He indicates that knowledge by description may be of 'a so and so', thus being an 'ambiguous' description. In his writings on this theme he concentrated on definite description. By 'ambiguous' Russell did not mean ambiguous in meaning but in reference.

7. H. H. Price, *Belief* (London: Allen & Unwin, 1969) p.69.

8. *Mysticism and Logic*, p.219.

9. As it is for example by D. W. Hamlyn, *The Theory of Knowledge* (London: Macmillan, 1973) p.105.

10. Cf. P. Helm, *The Varieties of Belief* (London: Allen & Unwin, 1973) p.80.

11. Ibid., p.81.

CHAPTER 6: FALSIFICATION

1. In *New Essays in Philosophical Theology* edited by A. Flew and A. MacIntyre (London: SCM Press, 1969) pp.96–9.

2. Ibid., p.98.

3. Cf. R. S. Heimbeck, *Theology and Meaning* (London: Allen & Unwin, 1969) p.88. Most of Chapter 3 of this book is a discussion of Flew's paper and its implications.

4. *New Essays in Philosophical Theology*, pp.103–5.

5. Ibid., p.103.

6. On this see the writings of John Hick, especially *Faith and Knowledge* (London: Cornell University Press 1970) pp.169–99.

7. Op. cit. pp.47ff.

8. 'Theology and Falsification is Retrospect' in *The Logic of God*, edited by M. L. Diamond and T. V. Litzenberg (Indianapolis: The Bobbs-Merrill Company 1975).

CHAPTER 7: KNOWING HOW AND KNOWING THAT

1. G. Ryle, 'Knowing How and Knowing That' in *Proceedings of the Aristotelian Society*, vol. XLVI, 1946 pp.1–16 and *The Concept of Mind* (London: Hutchinson's University Library, 1949) ch. 2.

2. *The Concept of Mind*, p.32.

3. *PAS* p.7.

4. *PAS* p.8.

5. *PAS* p.9.

6. *PAS* p.11.

7.   R. J. Ackerman sees the analysis of knowing how as useful for devising teaching methods but as having little other philosophical interest. Apart from teaching methods 'only trivialities seem forthcoming'. *Belief and Knowledge* (London: Macmillan, 1973) p.61.
8.   *PAS* p.14.
9.   *The Concept of Mind*, p.43.
10.   Cf. D.W. Hamlyn, *The Theory of Knowledge* (London: Macmillan, 1970) pp.103ff.
11.   *The Concept of Mind*, p.54.
12.   *PAS* p.15.

CHAPTER 8: OBJECTIVE KNOWLEDGE

1.   K. R. Popper, *Objective Knowledge* (London: Oxford University Press 1974) p.1.
2.   Ibid., p.9.
3.   Popper insists that no hypothesis should be given up easily. Without resorting to dogmatism it should be defended as best it can and only abandoned when clearly refuted, ibid., p.30.
4.   He is a self-declared admirer of common sense and argues for 'common sense realism' concerning the external world. It is the common sense, or popular view, of epistemology that he attacks, ibid., pp.32–105.
5.   Ibid., pp.60ff where the illustration of the mind as a clean slate ready to be written on by the sense is used. See also, 'The Bucket and the Searchlight', pp.341–61.
6.   Ibid., p.66.
7.   *The Logic of Scientific Discovery* (London: Hutchinson, 1959) p.280.
8.   *Objective Knowledge*, p.121.
9.   Ibid., pp.115ff.
10.   B. Magee, *Popper* (London: Fontana 1973) p.71.
11.   *Objective Knowledge* p.193.
12.   Ibid., p.108.
13.   *Popper*, p.11.
14   K. Popper, *Conjectures and Refutations* (London: Routledge & Kegan Paul 1969) p.38.
15.   *Objective Knowledge* p.25.
16.   Ibid., p.25.
17.   J. Hick, *God and the Universe of Faiths* (London: Macmillan, 1973) ch2.
18.   J. Hick, *Faith and Knowledge*, 2nd edn (London: Cornell University Press 1966) pp.169ff. The parable of the two travellers referred to later is on pp.177ff.
19.   See the sympathetic discussion of this view by T. Penelhum, *Problems of Religious Knowledge* (London: Macmillan, 1971) pp.68ff.
20.   W. W. Bartley, *The Retreat to Commitment* (London: Chatto & Windus, 1964).
21.   Ibid., p.146.

22. Ibid., p.150.
23. Cf. M. Wiles, *The Remaking of Christian Doctrine* (London: SCM Press, 1974) ch. 1. The same point is made in *Christian Believing*, the report of the Doctrine Commission of the Church of England (London: SPCK, 1976) pp.3ff.
24. See W. D. Hudson, *A Philosophical Approach to Religion* (London: Macmillan, 1974) pp.184ff.

CHAPTER 9: ON CERTAINTY

1. L. Wittgenstein, *On Certainty* (Oxford: Basil Blackwell 1974) p.534.
2. These are 'A Defence of Common Sense' and 'Proof of an External World'. Both papers appear in G. E. Moore, *Philosophical Papers* (London: Allen & Unwin, 1959).
3. The references are to the number paragraphs of *On Certainty*. A. Kenny imagines the whole as a discussion between Moore, Wittgenstein and Descartes. Cf. A. Kenny, *Wittgenstein* (London: Allen Lane, 1973) pp.203ff.
4. This is to understand the nature of language—games as being constituted by a certain tacit presupposition; in the case of religious belief, the tacit presupposition is the concept of God. Cf. W. D. Hudson, *A Philosophical Approach to Religion* (London: Macmillan 1974) pp.8ff. I shall discuss the question of fundamental propositions and the possibility of doubt in the final chapter.
5. But see the discussion in the final chapter for a qualification on this remark.

CHAPTER 10: THE KNOWLEDGE OF GOD
IN THE OLD TESTAMENT

1. Cf. F. Brown, S.R. Driver, C.A. Briggs, *A Hebrew and English Lexicon of the Old Testament* (London: Oxford University Press 1952).
2. Cf. R. Bultmann, *ginōskō* in *Theological Dictionary of the New Testament*, edited by G. Kittel (Michigan: W. B. Eerdman's Publishing Company 1965) vol. 1, p.697.
3. These studies by Winton Thomas cover a number of years of work. The initial discussion is in 'The Root *yada*' in Hebrew' in *The Journal of Theological Studies*, 1934, pp.298–306. Further articles in the same journal appear in 1935, pp. 409–12, 1936, pp.59ff, 1937, pp.404–5, 1938, pp.273–4, 1940, pp.43–4, 1941, pp.64–5, 1948, pp.143–4, 1953, pp.23ff, 1954, pp.56–7, 1955, pp.226, 1956, pp.69–70, 1960, p.52, 1963, pp.93–4, 1964, pp.54–7. Further articles on the same theme are found in *The Jewish Quarterly Review*, 1946, pp.177–8 and in *Journal of Jewish Studies*, 1955, pp.50–2.

4. Cf. J. Barr, *Comparative Philology and the Text of the Old Testament* (London: Oxford University Press 1968) pp.1–13.

5. Cf. the discussion of this issue by P.R. Ackroyd, 'Meaning and Exegesis' in *Words and Meanings*, edited by P. R. Ackroyd and B. Lindars (London: Cambridge University Press 1968) pp.1–14.

6. Cf. D. F. Payne, 'Old Testament Exegesis and the problem of ambiguity', in *The Annual of the Swedish Theological Institute in Jerusalem*, vol. 67, 1967, pp.48ff.

7. For example, Payne, in the article cited above, questions whether the Arabic root *wada'a* does have the meaning Winton Thomas and G. R. Driver claim for it. It is far from clear whether 'Humiliation' is denoted by the verb. He is also critical of the discussion of the meaning of *yada'* by Winton Thomas because a number of the passages on which the theory is based have 'suspect' texts and, further, no account is taken of the possibility of ambiguity.

8. All Biblical quotations in the thesis will be made from the *New English Bible*. It will also be my practice to speak of Yahweh rather than follow the NEB's practice of referring to 'the Lord'.

9. Cf. G. Von Rad, *Deuteronomy* (OTL), p.51.

10. Cf. S. R. Driver, *Deuteronomy* (ICC), p.77 where the translation of *yada'* is 'call to mind, reflect, consider'.

11. Among numerous references Exod. 15:11 and Ps. 135:5 may be cited. Cf. R. E. Clements, *Exod. (CBC)*, p.108.

12. Cf. J. P. Hyatt, *Exod.* (NCB), p.189.

13. Cf. E. W. Nicholson, *Exodus and Sinai in History and Tradition* (Oxford: Basil Blackwell 1973) p.69; G. H. Davies, *Exodus* (Torch) p.149.

14. This is to recognize the force of the 'Kenite hypothesis'. As H. H. Rowley argues, this hypothesis does not mean that Moses simply 'mediated' the religion of the Kenites to the Israelites. It is just to acknowledge a possible contact and reference between Moses and the Kenites in Midian. cf. H. H. Rowley, 'Moses and Monotheism' in *From Moses to Qumran* (London: Lutterworth Press 1963) pp.35–63.

15. Cf. *The Psalms* (OTL), p.637.

16. A. A. Anderson commenting on this psalm draws attention to the experiences of the Egyptians decribed in Exod. 7:5, 14:4, 18, etc. cf. *The Psalms* (NCB), vol. 1, p.112.

17. Both S. R. Driver, *Deuteronomy* (ICC) p.101 and G. A. F. Knight, *A Christian Theology of the Old Testament* (London: SCM Press, 1959) p.227 stress the importance of the covenant in this passage. See also N. Snaith, *Distinctive Ideas of the Old Testament* (London: Epworth Press 1944) p.100.

18. NEB reads 'be reminded'.

19. Cf. M. Noth, *Leviticus* (OTL), p.176.

20. Cf. J. Gray, *Joshua* (NCB), p.67; J. A. Soggin, *Joshua* (OTL), pp.66ff.

21. Cf. J. R. Porter, 'The Background of Joshua III–V', *Svensk Exegetisk Arsbok*, XXXVI, 1971.

22. The whole text must be treated with some caution. Both J. W. Wevers, *Ezekiel* (NCB), p.156 and G. A. Cooke *Ezekiel* (ICC), p.219 suggest

190 *Notes to pp.66–9*

that the text is a later gloss. The phrase is not found in the Septuagint. In any event the NEB translation must be judged to be very 'interpretive' in its reference to idols which does not appear in the hebrew text.

23.   Cf. Th. C. Vriezen, *An Outline of Old Testament Theology* (Oxford: Basil Blackwell 1958) p.158. See also his comments on p.238.

24.   Cf. K. W. Carley, *Ezekiel among the Prophets* (London: SCM Press, 1975) p.73.

25.   The Deuteronomist's emphasis on God's election can be detected here although it is not so explicit in the rest of Ezekiel. Cf. K. W. Carley, *Ezekiel* (CBC), p.127.

26.   Ezekiel dates the election of Israel from Moses and not from the patriachs whom he ignores.

27.   J. W. Wevers, *Ezekiel* (NCB), p.152 understands the phrase to relate to Yahweh's reputation which is inextricably bound up with the fortunes of Israel. R. C. Dentan, *The Knowledge of God in Ancient Israel* (New York: The Seabury Press 1968) p.188 argues that where God's action is declared to be for his name's sake this is not so much to defend his reputation as to demonstrate his power and show what kind of a God he is.

28.   For different opinions as to whom are being addressed see A. Weiser, *The Psalms* (OTL), p.366 and A. A. Anderson, *The Psalms* (NCB), p.360.

29.   Because of the 'freely formulated phrase', K. W. Carley suggests the passage has a late origin, cf. *Ezekiel Among the Prophets* (London: SCM Press, 1975) p.93.

30.   The passage is missing from the account in 2 Kgs. 21:1–10.

31.   This may be because it is distinct in being the successful plague, or because the account has been 'worked over' including Passover Law, The Feast of Unleaven Bread and the Law of Firstlings Cf. J. P. Hyatt, *Exodus* (NCB), pp.128ff.

32.   Cf. M. Noth, *Exodus* (OTL), p.92, who considers 11:7ff 'an ill considered addition made without any regard to the narrative context'.

33.   The passage is difficult to analyse. J. P. Hyatt, *Exodus* (NCB), p.173 suggests that vv. 6–8 are out of place and represent the work of the Priestly redactor. They would be better placed after vv.9–12. The language and later references, cf. vv.32ff suggest the incident follows rather than preceeds Sinai.

34.   Cf. J. A. Soggin, *Joshua* (OTL), p.57.

35.   The passage falls into two parts; vv. 11–17 is a theophany, part of the hero-saga of Gideon while vv.19–24 is an aetiological legend concerned with Ophrah.

36.   Cf. J. Gray, *Judges* (NCB), p.302.

37.   Cf. G. F. Moore, *Judges*, p.198.

38.   'The OT, with delightful impartiality, is quite confident that the soothsayers of the Philistines are capable of supplying correct information!' W. Eichrodt, *Theology of the Old Testament* (London: SCM Press, 1961) vol. 1, p.297.

39.   Cf. H. W. Hertzberg, *I and 2 Samuel* (OTL), p.59.

40. Cf. J. Mauchline, *1 and 2 Samuel* (NCB), pp.78ff where Exod.8: 23; Deut. 13:1; Judg. 6:17; I Sam. 2:34; 14:10; Isa. 7:10–17 are also cited as similar cases.
41. Cf. M. Noth, *Numbers* (OTL), p.128. The particular exegesis offered here is dependent upon the source criticism, as described by Noth, that argues that the Dathan and Abiran story is a unit independent of the surrounding Korah stories.
42. Cf. W. Zimmerli, *Erkenntnis Gottes nach dem Buche Ezechiel* (Zurich: *Abhandlugen zur Theologie des alten und neuen Testaments*, XXVII, 1954), 'Ich bin Jahwe', in *Geschichte und Altes Tesament, Festschrift Alt*, (Beiträge zur Historischen Theologie, Tubingen 1953) pp.179–209. The translation 'formula of self-representation' is that of D. Granskou, Cf. *Revelation as History*, edited by C. Pannenberg (London: Macmillan, 1969) p.38. I am indebted to the article 'The Concept of Revelation in Ancient Israel' by Rolf Rendtorff in this collection, pp.25–53.
43. This is again the translation of Granskou. R. E. Clements (see note 45) speaks of the 'recognition formula'.
44. Cf. R. Rendtorff, op. cit., p.41.
45. Cf. R. E. Clements, *Exodus* (CBC), p.38.
46. Cf. J. P. Hyatt, *Exodus* (NCB), p.103.
47. Cf. R. E. Clements, *Exodus* (CBC), p.43.
48. It is not easy to distinguish the sources here. J. P. Hyatt, *Exodus* (NCB), p.105 suggests the text is from J but the later verses where all the waters are turned to blood are from the P narrative, cf. M. Noth, *Exodus* (OTL) p.67ff.
49. Verse 17 has a transition from speech by Yahweh to speech by Moses. This may indicate an imperfect text or may be evidence of A. R. Johnson's argument for the 'extension of personality' in the Hebrew concept of God. *The One and the Many in the Israelite concept of God* (Cardiff: University of Wales Press, 1961).
50. Cf. K. W. Carley, *Ezekiel among the Prophets* (London: SCM Press, 1975) pp.37ff. R. Rendtorff, op. cit., p.43.
51. Cf. R. Rendtorff, op. cit., p.44.
52. Cf. Th. C. Vriezen, *The Religion of Ancient Israel* (London: Lutteerworth Press 1969) p.249. Cf. also the parallels in 'The Cyrus Cylinder' in *Documents from Old Testament Times*, edited D.W. Thomas (London: Thomas Nelson, 1958) p.92 C. Westermann argues that Deutero-Isaiah could not have been dependent on the cylinder, *Isaiah, 40–66* (OTL), p.158.
53. Cf. C Westermann, *Isaiah 40–66* (OTL), p.161.
54. Clearly something has happened to the Hebrew text here since vv. 3–6 is a prose passage surrounded by poetry. Are vv. 4–6 a gloss on v. 3? Or is the whole passage a marginal gloss? For a discussion of these issues see J. L. McKenzie *Deutero-Isaiah* (Anchor), p.127 and C. Westermann, *Isaiah 40–66* (OTL), p.248.
55. Cf. W. Eichrodt, *Ezekiel* (OTL), p.15.
56. Ibid., p.95.
57. Cf. K. W. Carley, *Ezekiel* (CBC), p.149; W. Eichrodt, *Ezekiel* (OTL), pp.311ff.

58.   J. W. Wevers argues that it is the people who are profaned by reason of their forced absence from their country, *Ezekiel* (NCB), p.174.

59.   J. Gray, *I and 2 Kings* (OTL, 2nd edn.) p.231 suggest that 'Yahweh is God' reflects a regular audible response in the cult. H. H. Rowley understands the passage as coming from the Deuteronomic editor, dated near Deutero-Isaiah when there is expressive monotheism, *The Faith of Israel* (London: SCM Press, 1961) p.72.

60.   Cf. W. Eichrodt, *Theology of the Old Testament* (London: SCM Press, 1961) v.I, p.225.

61.   Cf. J. Gray, *I and 2 Kings* (OTL), 2nd edn, p.401 where he argues that the reference to Abraham may indicate the typical interest of the Elohist narrative source.

62.   Interestingly the second half of v.37 suggests, after the pattern of the Deuteronomist, that Yahweh has caused the backsliding of his people, although this is not the only possible reading of the text. It may mean that Yahweh has turned their hearts back to himself.

63.   Cf. H. H. Rowley, *The Faith of Israel* (London: SCM Press, 1961) pp.25ff.

64.   E. Cohen, *The Psalms* (Soncino Press) p.53.

65.   G. Von Rad, *Wisdom in Israel* (London: SCM Press, 1972) p.162.

66.   H. H. Rowley, *The Faith of Israel* (London: SCM Press, 1961) p.24.

67.   Dreams are understood by the OT to be potentially a medium of revelation although this is more a feature of the old traditions cf. Th. C. Vreizen, *OT Theology* (Oxford: Basil Blackwell 1958) pp.243ff; H. H. Rowley, *The Faith of Israel* (London: SCM Press, 1961) pp.31ff.

68.   'According to Israelite conception Yahweh, despite his transcendental character, had a close connection with the Holy Place where he was worshipped', J. Lindblom 'Theophanies in Holy Places in Hebrew Religion', *Hebrew Union College Annual*, 32, (1961) p.92.

69.   J. Barr suggests that this is an important feature of OT Theophanies Cf. 'Theophany and Anthropomorphism in the OT' in Supplement to *Vetus Testamentum*, VII (Leiden 1960).

70.   H. W. Robinson, *Inspiration and Revelation in the Old Testament* (London: Oxford Univesity Press 1946) p.38.

71.   J. N. Schofield, 'Angel' in *A Theological Word Book of the Bible*, edited A. Richardson (London: SCM Press, 1957) p.18. Barr's article cited above indicates the fact that the God whom Israel worships appears in living human likeness although it is not the form of the appearance that is the crucial factor in Theophanies.

72.   A. R. Johnson 'Angel of the Lord' in *Dictionary of the Bible* Revised Edition edited by F. C. Grant and H. H. Rowley (Edinburgh: T. and T. Clark 1963) p.31.

73.   *The One and the Many* (Cardiff: University of Wales Press 1961) p.29.

74.   J. Barr, op. cit., p.34.

75.   J. Barr, op. cit., p.38.

76.   Cf. P. R. Ackroyd, *I Samuel* (CBC) p.43, W. McKane, *I and 2 Samuel* (Torch) p.42.

77.   The significance of the story is broader. Because of the faithfulness of Samuel, the importance of Shiloh as a place where Yahweh would appear is confirmed. H. W. Hertzberg, *I and 2 Samuel* (OTL), p.41.

78. Cf. Von Rad, *Deuteronomy* (OTL), p.85, S. R. Driver, *Deuteronomy* (ICC) p.127.

79. J. H. Eaton, *The Psalms* (Torch), p.220.

80. Cf. A. A. Anderson, *Psalms* (NCB), p.638.

81. Cf. Westermann, *Isaiah 40–66* (OTL), p.120. See references in the earlier section to the work of Zimmerli on the phrase 'I am He'.

82. Ibid., pp.121. cf. the reference to Zimmerli in the previous section.

83. Th. C. Vreizen, *The Religion of Ancient Israel* (Lutterworth Press, 1969) pp.237, F. G. Downing goes too far when he suggests that Jeremiah promises that God will completely control his people, that he will set in men an automatic programme device, an internal control which they will not be able to escape. *Has Christianity a Revelation?* (London: SCM Press, 1964) p.39.

84. Cf. W. A. L. Elmslie, *How Came our Faith* (London: Cambridge University Press 1958) p.306.

85. Cf. B. W. Anderson, 'The New Covenant and the Old' in *The Old Testament and Christian Faith*, edited B. W. Anderson (London: SCM Press, 1964) p.235.

86. Cf. R. C. Dentan, *The Knowledge of God in Ancient Israel* (New York: The Seabury Press 1968) p.223.

87. H. W. Wolff, *Hosea* (Hermenia), p.53.

88. J. L. Mays, *Hosea*, (OYL), p.174.

89. J. Muilenburg, 'The Intercession of the covenant Mediator (Exod. 33: l, 12–17)' in *Words and Meanings* edited by P. R. Ackroyd and B. Lindars (London: Cambridge University Press 1968) pp.159–81.

90. Cf. J. P. Hyatt, *Exodus* (NCB), p.316.

91. Cf. J. Barr, 'Theophany and Anthropomorphism in the Old Testament', supplement to *Vetus Testamentun VII* (Leiden, 1960) pp.31–8.

92. Cf. Th. C. Vriezen, *An Outline of Old Testament Theology* (London: Basil Blackwell 1958) pp.171ff.

93. Ibid., p.148.

94. Cf. M. Noth, *Exodus* (OTL), p.60.

95. Perhaps little or nothing of consequence should properly be drawn from this uncertain text which in fact many editors omit. Cf. C Westermann, *Isaiah 40–66* (OTL), p.166.

96. R. de Vaux, *Ancient Israel* (London: Darton, Longman & Todd 1961) p.272.

97. See Chapter 8.

98. R. C. Dentan, *The Knowledge of God in Ancient Israel* (New York: The Seabury Press 1968) p.40.

99. Cf. A. A. Anderson, *The Psalms* (NCB), p.291; A. Weiser, *The Psalms* (OTL), p.311. M. Dahood, *The Psalms* (Anchor) suggests that 'those who know you' means 'those who have received your revelation'. Thus after the manner of Amos 3:2. Israel knows Yahweh in the covenant relationship, p.224.

100. H. B. Huffmon, 'The Treaty Background of Hebrew *yada*' in *Bulletin of the American School of Oriental Research*, 1966 no.181, p.31ff.

101. F. G. Downing, *Has Christianity a Revelation?* (London: SCM Press, 1964).

102. Cf. O. Kaiser, *Isaiah 1–12* (OTL), p.158.

103.   G. Von Rad, *Wisdom in Israel* (London: SCM Press, 1972) p.66.
104.   G. Von Rad, *Wisdom in Israel* (London: SCM Press, 1972) p.68.
105.   Ibid., p.63.
106.   J. L. Mays suggests 6:1–3 may be a liturgical expression of the demanded penitence, *Hosea* (OTL), p. 87. So also H. W. Wolff, *Hosea* (Hermeneia), p.117 who suggests it should be understood in terms of the popular piety influenced by the canaanization of the Yahweh cult.
107.   This is not necessarily a total rejection of sacrificial worship. It probably means more a statement of priorities. Loyalty in covenant obedience is more important to Yahweh than sacrifice. Cf. H. McKeating, *Amos, Hosea and Micah* (CBC), p.111.
108.   Cf. J. L. Mays, *Hosea* (OTL), p.98.
109.   H. W. Wolff, *Hosea* (Hermeneia), p.138.
110.   H. McKeating, *Amos, Hosea and Micah* (CBC) p.95.

CHAPTER 11: THE KNOWLEDGE OF GOD IN
THE NEW TESTAMENT

1.   Cf. P. Thomson, '"know" in the New Testament', *The Expositor* 1926, pp.379–82. He cites the judgement of J. B. Lightfoot, Westcott and Souter in support of his argument.
2.   J. H. Moulton and G. Milligan, *The Vocabulary of the Greek Testament* (London: Hodder & Stoughton, 1930) p.439. In agreement with this view is H. Seesemann, *'oida'*, *Theological Dictionary of the New Testament*, vol.5 (Grand Rapids, Michigan: W. B. Eerdmans, 1967) vol.116. W. F. Arndt and F. W. Gringrich, *A Greek-English Lexicon of the New Testament* (London: Univeristy of Chicago Press, 1957) give the same range of meaning for both words, cf. p.150–61, 558–9.
3.   V. Taylor believes there is a distinction between the two words in the NT and cites Mark 4:13 as evidence. *The Gospel According to St Mark* (London: Macmillan, 1959) p.258.
4.   Cf. W. F. Albright and C. S. Mann, *St Matthew* (Anchor) p.103: F. V. Filson, *St Matthew* (Black) p.118.
5.   V. Taylor, *The Gospel According to St Mark* (London: Macmillan, 1959) pp.199ff. A fuller discussion is given by F. G. Borsch, *The Christian and Gnostic Son of Man* (London: SCM Press, 1970) and B. Lindars, *Jesus, Son of Man* (London: SPCK, 1983).
6.   Cf. F. V. Filson, *St Matthew* (Black) p.118. Cf. M. D. Hooker, *The Son of Man in Mark* (London: SPCK, 1967) pp.81–92.
7.   Cf. E. Haenchen, *The Acts of the Apostles* (London: Basil Blackwell 1971) p.390.
8.   *Kai yinwskēte* is omitted in some manuscripts.
9.   Cf. B. Lindars, *St John* (NCB), p.376.
10.   C. H. Dodd, *The Interpretation of the Fourth Gospel* (London: Cambridge University Press 1953) p.257.
11.   Cf. B. Lindars, *St John* (NCB) p.485.

12. Cf. R. Bultmann, *The Gospel of John* (London: Basil Blackwell 1971) p.631.

13. Cf. C. K. Barrett, *The Gospel According to St John* (London: SPCK, 1958) p.284.

14. Cf. C.H. Dodd, *The Interpretation of the Fourth Gospel* (London: Cambridge University Press 1953) p.377.

15. Cf. J. N. Saunders, *St John* (Black) p.331; R. Bultmann, *The Gospel of John* (London: Basil Blackwell 1971) p.620.

16. Cf. B. Lindars, *St John* (NCB), p.481.

17. Cf. C. H. Dodd, *The Interpretation of the Fourth Gospel* (London: Cambridge University Press 1953) p.169.

18. *pas oikos Israël* is the only occurrence of a phrase common in Jewish prayers, cf. F. F. Bruce *The Acts of the Apostles* (London: Tyndale Press 1962) p.96.

19. Cf. E. Haenchen, *The Acts of the Apostles* (London: Basil Blackwell 1971) p.183.

20. Cf. C. S. C. Williams, *The Acts of the Apostles* (Black) pp.66ff.

21. See the discussion by G. R. Beasley-Murray, *Baptism in the New Testament* (London: Macmillan, 1963) pp.126ff.

22. Cf. C. H. Dodd, *Romans* (Moffatt), p.87.

23. Cf. G. Bornkamm, *Early Christian Experience* (London: SCM Press, 1969) p.81.

24. Cf. F. F. Bruce, *I and 2 Corinthians* (NCB), p.198.

25. Cf. R. McL. Wilson, *Gnosis and the New Testament* (London: Basil Blackwell 1968) p.40.

26. Cf. C. H. Dodd, *The Johannine Epistles* (Moffatt) p.115.

27. Cf. G. Bornkamm, *Early Christian Experience* (London: SCM Press, 1969) pp.50ff.

28. B. Gärtner draws attention, however, to a number of instances of preaching to the Gentiles where reference is made to the natural world as a medium of God's revelation. These references are from Paul's sermons in The Acts of the Apostles, e.g. 14:15–17; 17–24ff. *The Areopagus Speech and Natural Revelation* (Uppsala: Acta Seminarii Neotestamentici Uppsaliensis 1955) p.81.

29. For a discussion of the textual details see C. K. Barrett, *Romans* (Black), p.16.

30. Cf. C. H. Dodd, *Romans* (Moffatt) p.138.

31. Cf. G. Bornkamm, *Paul* (London: Hodder & Stoughton 1975) p.152.

32. The phrase 'saviour of the world' appears in the NT in works of a later date. There is little ground for supposing that the primitive tradition gave the title to Christ. Here, the evangelist may even have been conscious of a certain dramatic propriety in putting it in the mouth of the Samaritans, who in this gospel represents in some sort the Gentile world over the Jews. Cf. C. H. Dodd, *The Interpretation of the Fourth Gospel* (London: Cambridge University Press Ltd, 1953) p.239. See also J. Marsh, *St John* (Pelican) p.227.

33. Cf. B. Lindars, *St John* (NCB), p.198.

34. Cf. R. Bultmann, *'gnosis'* in *Theological Dictionary of the New Testament* Vol. 1 (Grand Rapids, Michigan: W. B. Eerdmans, 1967) p.713. H.

Conzelmann, *An Outline of the Theology of the New Testament* (London: SCM Press, 1969) pp.103, 127. G. Bornkamm, *Jesus of Nazareth* (London: Hodder & Stoughton, 1963) p.227. F. G. Downing, *Has Christianity a Revelation?* (London: SCM Press, 1964) pp.87ff.

35.   Cf. A. Richardson, *An Introduction to the Theology of the New Testament* (London: SCM Press, 1961) p.43. R. G. Fuller *The Mission and Achievement of Jesus* (London: SCM Press, 1963) pp.89ff. J. Jeremias, *New Testament Theology,* vol.1 (London: SCM Press, 1971) pp.56ff. A. R. C. Leaney, *St Luke* (Black) p.179. R. McL. Wilson points out that in the *Gospel of Thomas,* Matt. 11:27 is not cited although the preceding verses are quoted. *Gnosis and the New Testament* (London: Basil Blackwell 1968) p.44.

36.   Cf. J. Jeremias, *The Prayers of Jesus* (London: SCM Press, 1967) p.49. T. W. Manson, *The Mission and Message of Jesus* London: Ivor Nicholson & Watson, 1937) p.371. A. H. McNeile understands *paradothē* as having the sense of 'entrusted', as does the NEB. *The Gospel according to St Matthew* (London: Macmillan, 1961) p.162.

37.   Cf. Amos 3:2. See the discussion by G. B. Caird, *St Luke* (Pelican) pp.145ff.

38.   R. G. Fuller, op. cit. p.85.

39.   Cf. A. R. C. Leaney, *St Luke* (Black) p.179. C. H. Dodd also suggests that John's theology goes further than this statement, *The Interpretation of the Fourth Gospel* (London: Cambridge University Press 1953) p.166.

40.   J. A. T. Robinson, *The Human Face of God* (London: SCM Press, 1972) p.186.

41.   J. M. Creed suggests Luke's change is only stylistic, *The Gospel According to St Luke* (London: Macmillan, 1930).

42.   Jeremais argues that these terms, The Father, The Son, express the intimate knowledge that a father and son alone have of each other. The titles came to stand absolutely as proper names for God and Christ. Cf. *New Testament Theology* vol.1 (London: SCM Press, 1971) pp.56ff.

43.   Cf. J. Marsh, *St John* (Pelican), p,370.

44.   Cf. B Lindars, *St John* (NCB), p.473, who argues for this translation. This is followed in NEB margin. Lindars claims this reading is adopted by Hoskyns, Bultmann, Barrett, Sanders, Marsh and Schackenburg. For further discussion see C. H. Dodd, op. cit., p.164 and C.K. Barrett, op. cit., pp.283ff.

45.   R. E. Brown, *St John* (Anchor), p.631. Brown stresses the covenant theme in this passage, and understands 'knowing' basically as acknowledgement. To 'know' Jesus is to acknowledge who he is.

46.   Cf. B. Lindars, *St John* (NCB), p.480.

47.   Cf. C. H. Dodd, op. cit., p.165.

48.   R. E. Brown, *St John* (Anchor) pp.752–3. Substantially the same points are made by C. K. Barrett, op. cit., pp419–20.

49.   C. K. Barrett, op. cit., p.383.

50.   Cf. F. W. Beare, *Philippians* (Black), p.114.

51.   A. E. Harvey, *Companion to the New Testament* (Oxford and Cambridge University Press 1971) p.637.

52. F. V. Filson, St Matthew (Black), p.141.
53. Cf. 'God', in *Vocabulary of the Bible*, edited by J. J. Von Allmen (London: Lutterworth Press, 1964) pp.146ff.
54. For a discussion of the concept of God as Father and Jesus' use of *Abba*, see J. Jeremias, *New Testament Theology*, vol.1 (London: SCM Press, 1971) pp.61–8; W. G. Kümmel, *The Theology of the New Testament* (London: SCM Press, 1974) pp.40ff and H. Conzelmann, *An Outline of the Theology of the New Testament* (London: SCM Press, 1969) pp.99ff.
55. Luke 24:35, Acts 10:8; 15:12, etc. Cf. C. K. Barrett, *The Gospel According to St John* (London: SPCK, 1960) p.141.
56. See Chapter 8.
57. C. K. Barrett, *The Gospel According to St John* (London: SPCK, 1960) p.262. He indicates that this is the interpretation of Bultmann.
58. C. H. Dodd, *The Interpretation of the Fourth Gospel* (London: Cambridge University Press 1953) p.158.
59. The word 'free' occurs only here and in 8:33 and 36 in the Fourth Gospel.
60. Cf. C. H. Dodd, op. cit., p.177.
61. C. K. Barrett, *I Corinthians* (Black), pp.189ff.
62. Cf. E. Lohse, *Colossians* (Hermeneia), p.25.
63. Cf. R. P. Martin, Colossians (NCB), p.107. See also E. Lohse, *Colossians* (Hermeneia), p.43.
64. Cf. J. N. D. Kelly, *The Pastoral Epistle* (Black), p.237.
65. Ibid., p.237.
66. R. Bultmann, *The Johannine Epistles* (Hermeneia), p.25.

CHAPTER 12: GOD AND INFERENTIAL KNOWLEDGE

1. See Chapter 3.
2. In indicating that there are claims to know God that imply the possibility of inference, it must be remembered that I also asserted that there was much more involved in such claims than just that of making an inference.
3. This is the translation of A. Kenny, *The Five Ways* (London: Routledge & Kegan Paul, 1969) p.46.
4. *Tractatus*, 1.
5. Cf. W. A. Christian, *Meaning and Truth in Religion* (Princeton University Press, 1964) pp.28–30.
6. I shall quote from the edition edited by L. A. Selby-Bigge (London: Oxford University Press, 1902).
7. Ibid., p.110.
8. Ibid., p.110.
9. Ibid., p.114.
10. Ibid., p.115.
11. Ibid., p.116.
12. Ibid., p.116.
13. Cf. R. Swinburne, *The Concept of Miracle* (London: Macmillan, 1970) pp.15ff.

14. Op. cit., p.121.
15. There seem to me to be a number of questionable features in this particular argument from Hume. Does difference in religion mean contrary? Are different miracles in different religions contradictory of each other? They might be if related to the same event, but there does not appear to be any such pair of alleged miracles.
16. See Chapter 1.
17. (London: Macmillan, 1974) pp.165ff. An earlier discussion of this problem by Hudson is in *Ludwig Wittgenstein* (London: Lutterworth Press, 1968) pp.46ff. I am much indebted to Hudson's argument in the paragraphs that follow.
18. See for example P. Edwards, 'Some Notes on Anthropomorphic Theology' in *Religious Experience and Truth: Symposium*, edited by S. Hook (London: Oxford University Press 1961) pp.242–3. The sense of talk of meeting God is discussed by R. W. Hepburn, *Christianity and Paradox* (London: Watts, 1966) pp.24–48. More recent discussions are found in T. F. Tracy, *God, Action and Embodiment* (Grand Rapids, Michigan: W.B. Eerdmans, 1984); G. M. Jantzen, *God's World, God's Body* (London: Darton, Longman & Todd 1984); and V. White, *The Fall of a Sparrow* (Exeter: The Paternoster Press, 1985).
19. For a discussion of such matters see D. F. Pears, *Freedom and the Will* (London: Macmillan, 1964).
20. Cf. The argument of S. N. Hampshire in *Freedom and the Will*, pp.80ff where he comments on this distinction previously described in *Thought and Action* (London: Chatto & Windus 1960) ch.1.
21. Both R. Swinburne, *The Concept of Miracle* (London: Macmillan, 1970) p.56 and B. Mitchell, *The Justification of Religious Belief* (London: Macmillan, 1973) p.8 refer to telekinesis.
22. Hudson, W.D., op. cit., p.176.
23. Cf. *Contemporary Critiques of Religion* (London: Macmillan, 1971) pp.120ff.
24. Ibid., p.124.

CHAPTER 13: GOD & KNOWLEDGE BY ACQUAINTANCE & DESCRIPTION

1. See Chapter 5.
2. R. W. Hepburn, *Christianity and Paradox* (London: Watts 1966) pp.32ff.
3. Cf. H. H. Farmer, *The World and God* (London: Nisbet, 1955) pp.14ff.
4. See Chapter 4.
5. Psalm 34: 8.
6. For a discussion of these matters see T. R. Miles, *Religious Experience* (London: Macmillan, 1972) pp.55ff.
7. I am following closely here an argument by A. Flew, *God and Philosophy* (London: Hutchinson, 1968) p.132.
8. See Chapter 8.

CHAPTER 14: THE KNOWLEDGE OF GOD AS A
FORM OF LIFE

1. *Lectures and Conversations on Aesthetics, Psychology and Religious Belief,* edited by C. Barrett, (Oxford: Basil Blackwell, 1970). Hereafter this work, which is a compilation of notes taken by students of some lectures Wittgenstein gave in Cambridge will be referred to as *Lectures*.
2. J. F. M. Hunter, '"Forms of Life" in Wittgenstein's *Philosophical Investigations*', *American Philosophical Quarterly*, Oct. 1968, vol.5, pp.233–43.
3. Ibid., p.239.
4. Ibid., p.241.
5. Ibid., p.235.
6. Hunter draws attention to Wittgenstein's phrase 'so one could say . . .' in support of this 'oddness', Ibid., p.241.
For a discussion of Wittgenstein's work in this respect see Patrick Sherry *Religion, Truth and Language Games* (London: Macmillan, 1977).
7. This distinction between truth conditions and verification conditions I discussed on pp.32–5.
8. *Lectures*, p.58.
9. Ibid., p.56.
10. Ibid., p.61.
11. Ibid., p.62.
12. Ibid., pp.54–5.
13. Ibid., pp.54–5.
14. Cf. D. D. Evans, *The Logic of Self Involvement* (London: Student Christian Movement Press, 1963). Evans spends the first part of this book in analysing the nature of statements of religious belief. He draws heavily on the work of J. L. Austin.
15. I have already drawn attention to his two most celebrated essays on this theme in Chapter 9.
16. *Some main problems of Philosophy,* quoted by A. J. Ayer in *Russell and Moore* (London: Macmillan, 1971) p.163.
17. A. J. Ayer, 'Wittgenstein on Certainty' in *Understanding Wittgenstein*, edited G. Vesey (London: Macmillan, 1974) p.229.
18. The essay first appeared in *Mind*, vol. 51 (1952). It is reprinted in *Knowledge and Belief*, edited by A. P. Griffiths (London: Oxford University Press 1967) pp.69–81. It is to this edition that the following references are made.
19. Ibid., p.73.
20. Ibid., p.72.
21. Ibid., p.81.
22. Ibid., p.78.
23. Cf. A. J. Ayer, *Russell and Moore* (London: Macmillan, 1971) pp.182ff.
24. R. Carnap, 'Empiricism, Semantics and Ontology' in *Revue Internationale de Philosophie* (Bruxelles, 1950) pp.20–40.
25. Cf. P. Helm, *The Varieties of Belief* (London: Allen & Unwin, 1973) p.29.

26. Op. cit., pp.31–2.
27. Op. cit., p.37.
28. *Investigations*, p.179.
29. See above p.163ff.
30. See above p.158ff.
31. Cf. 'Knowledge and Belief', in *Knowledge and Belief*, edited A. P. Griffiths, (London: Oxford University Press, 1968) p.81.
32. Op. cit., p.81.
33. See above p.45.
34. *Investigations*, p.226.
35. *Investigations*, p.226.
36. *Lectures*, pp.54ff.
37. Ibid., pp.70ff.
38. Ibid., p.71.
39. *OC* p.204.
40. *Lectures*, p.58.
41. Cf. *Religious Language* (London: SCM Press, 1969) pp.11ff.

Index